Resisting the Holocaust

Resisting the Holocaust

Edited by
Ruby Rohrlich

Oxford • New York

First published in 1998 by
Berg
Editorial offices:
150 Cowley Road, Oxford, OX4 1JJ, UK
70 Washington Square South, New York, NY 10012, USA

Berg is the imprint of Oxford International Publishers Ltd.

Library of Congress Cataloging-in-Publication Data

A catalogue record for this book is available from the Library of Congress

British Library Cataloguing-in-Publication Data

A catalogue record for this book is available from the British Library

ISBN 1 85973 211 9 (Cloth)
1 85973 216 X (Paper)

Typeset by JS Typesetting, Wellingborough, Northants.
Printed in the United Kingdom by WBC Book Manufacturers, Bridgend,
Mid Glamorgan.

Dedication

This book is dedicated to my sons, Matthew Rohrlich Leavitt and Michael Rohrlich Leavitt. Both, computer mavens, have helped me with problems I've experienced in working with the computer. Matthew lives in Maine, Michael in Virginia. After I retired, as Professor Emerita in anthropology, from the City University of New York, I accepted Michael's invitation to move near him, and his life and mine became intertwined once again, especially by our mutual interest in Jewish history, above all, in the Holocaust. I am very grateful to Michael for the tremendous help he has given me in compiling this anthology. He has also made it possible for me to accept living in Washington D.C., after my good life in New York City.

Contents

Contents

Introduction
Ruby Rohrlich

The key word, the key concept of this book is "resistance," the resistance of Jews and non-Jews, women and men, to the Holocaust. What constitutes resistance? The definition is far from simple; the term embraces a variety of operations, actions and movements performed by individuals, groups and nations. Sociologist Nechama Tec, herself a survivor, and the author of numerous books and articles about the Holocaust, defines acts of resistance as "motivated by the intention to thwart, limit or end the exercise of power by the oppressor over the oppressed" (Tec 1997: 4). For Jews during the Holocaust, simply surviving can be considered a form of resistance to the German goal of Jewish extermination. For non-Jews, behaving humanely toward victims was a form of resistance, considering the propaganda to which they were exposed, together with the threat of dire punishment.

Survivors of the Holocaust know best from personal experience what resistance means, but their ideas about the nature of resistance, as about everything else, are various and differ greatly. To some, resistance is active; it means fighting, using a stick, a gun, taking your chances, knowing the odds are against you. For active resistance to take place with any degree of success what is required are intelligence, logistics, communication among the various units, leadership, support by the non-fighting environment, and perhaps, above all, luck. It means inflicting as many casualties as you can, knowing that in the end you will most likely not come out of it. The idea is to thwart the German's will, to make the sacrifice of one's life mean something. This view of resistance assumes death for the resister.

In his article "Resistance and Choices" Steve Paulsson (1997) maintains that the most common of the active Jewish responses to the Holocaust was not resistance but evasion, that is, running like hell.

300,000 Polish Jews fled to the Soviet sector in 1939–40; 25,000 Warsaw Jews fled from the ghetto and hid "on the Aryan side." And even in Berlin, under Himmler's nose, 5,000 Jews managed to find hiding places. Philip Friedman estimated that 200,000 Jews survived by going into hiding, and when we take into account cases like that of Anne Frank, the number who tried it was much higher, probably over 300,000. Many more tried to flee to neutral countries. All told, nearly a million Jews took the path of evasion, and most of these survived.

Survival in this way was not a cowardly, passive act, nor was it a matter of being "rescued." The initiative nearly always came from the Jewish side; all sorts of practical and psychological barriers had to be overcome, and life in hiding (the journey to the "green frontier") was constantly beset with difficulties and dangers. On the other hand, it would be stretching the definition of resistance a bit thin to describe evasion as a form of resistance. It is an authentic, normal human response to danger, and absolutely the most sensible thing for unarmed civilians to do under these circumstances, if there was any glimmer of hope."

According to Alexander Kimmel, another Holocaust survivor, passive resistance among the Jews flourished, and in many forms. When the Germans tried to starve the Jews to death, they responded with massive smuggling. After the Jews learned that deportation meant torture and death, they jumped from the moving trains; they built hiding places, the so-called bunkers; they printed underground newspapers (polemic resistance). Since the Germans wanted to destroy Jewish culture as well as Jewish lives, resistance could include gathering for religious services when this was forbidden, recording events for posterity, organizing educational classes. Staying with one's family as long as possible was resistance to the German objective to dehumanize the Jews, although this form of behavior decreased the possibility of fighting actively.

Tec (1997:1) points out that although favorable conditions for Jewish resistance to the Germans were virtually non-existent, yet the Jews resisted to a significant degree. Jewish underground organizations were set up in seven major ghettos (Bialystok, Cracow, Czestochowa, Kovno, Minsk, Vilna, Warsaw) and in forty-five minor ghettos. Jewish armed uprisings took place in five concentration camps and in eighteen forced-labor camps. Yuri Suhl in *They Fought Back* (1967:1) maintains "that in practically every ghetto and in every labor and concentration camp there existed a Jewish underground organization that kept up the prisoners' morale, reduced physical suffering, committed acts of sabotage, organized escapes, collected arms, planned revolts and, in many instances, carried them out."

An essential requirement for organized, prolonged, armed resistance was the support of one of the Allied powers – the UK, the USA, the Soviet Union. The armed resistance groups that made any impact had such support, but the Jews were consistently denied it by the UK and the USA.

In most resistance groups Jews were prevented from organizing into separate units. An exception was the French Maquis, where the Jews formed their own underground sections. Although they made up less than 1 percent of the French population, an estimated 15 to 20 percent of the Maquis was Jewish. The main Polish resistance movement, the *Armja Krajowa* (AK) or Home Army, had many subgroups, some of which were antisemitic, while others supported Jews. According to Tec, an unspecified number of Jews participated in the smaller Polish underground, the Polish Communist organization (PPR). "By mid-1943, when the Soviet Union exercised control over most of the partisans in the forests, the Jews were officially shielded from antisemitic excesses" (Tec 1997:3).

In June 1941 Auschwitz was "upgraded" from a labor camp to an extermination camp, especially for Jews at Birkenau. Primo Levi, chronicler of Auschwitz, who was himself incarcerated in this camp, emphasized "that the concentration camp system . . . had as its primary purpose shattering the adversaries' capacity to resist" (Levi 1989:38). By punishing the whole community for the actions of one individual, resistance – of Poles as well as of Jews – to oppression and terror was stifled.

Another means of destroying resistance was to privilege some of the prisoners. In both the ghettos and the lagers death by hunger, or by diseases induced by hunger, was the prisoner's usual destiny; obtaining extra nourishment required a privilege which the prisoner might obtain by the willingness to collaborate with the Nazis in their gruesome involvement of the Jews in their own extermination. In the lager the privileged prisoner, the prisoner-functionary, the "*kapo*," became the chief of the labor squad and the barracks, and had absolute power over the non-privileged prisoners.

The extreme case of collaboration, the *Sonderkommandos*, (called Special Squads by the SS) were the only prisoners who had enough to eat for a few months. They maintained order among the new arrivals who were to be sent into the gas chambers, extracted the corpses from the chambers, pulled gold teeth from jaws, cut women's hair, sorted and classified the contents of the luggage, transported the bodies to the crematoria and oversaw the operation of the ovens, extracting and eliminating the ashes. These prisoners numbered from 700 to 1000 members in Auschwitz. Since, beginning in 1941, the population of

Auschwitz was almost 95 percent Jews, the Special Squads were made up largely of Jews, who did the most heinous of the jobs connected with the killing of the prisoners, their fellow Jews.

Why did the Special Squads accept the tasks imposed on them? Why didn't they prefer death? To these primal questions Primo Levi's answers are factual (Levi 1989:58):

> Not all did accept; some did rebel, knowing they would die. Concerning at least one case we have precise information. A group of four hundred Jews from Corfu who in July 1944 had been included in the squad, refused without exception to do the work and were immediately gassed to death.
>
> Filip Muller, one of the squads' very few survivors, tells of a companion whom the SS pushed into the oven alive.

And there were many cases of suicide at the moment of recruitment or immediately after.

Some of the prisoners who performed diverse duties in the camps' administrative office had access to the most secret information of the lagers and later became their historians.

> One does not know whether to admire more their personal courage or their cunning, which enabled them to . . . help their companions in many concrete ways, by attentively studying the individual SS officers with whom they had contact and sensing who among them might be corrupted, who dissuaded from the crueler decisions, who blackmailed, who deceived, who frightened by the prospect of a *redde rationem* at the war's end. (ibid., 45)

Some members of the Special Squads were also members of secret defense organizations within the lager, and the power they wielded was counterbalanced by the extreme risks they ran; they were both "resisters" and the repositories of secrets.

"Finally," Levi (ibid., 58) points out,

> it was the Special Squad which in October 1944 organized the only desperate attempt at revolt in the history of the Auschwitz Lager.
>
> The personnel of two of the five Auschwitz-Birkenau crematoria, poorly armed, and without contacts with the Polish Partisans outside the Lager or the clandestine defense organization inside the Lager, blew up Crematorium No. 3 and engaged the SS in battle. The battle was soon over. A number of the insurgents who managed to cut the barbed wire and escape to the outside were captured soon afterward. Not one of them survived, approximately four hundred and fifty were immediately killed by the SS, among whom three were killed and twelve wounded.

It is not true that no rebellion ever took place in a lager. The rebellions of Treblinka, Sobibor and Birkenau have been described many times, with abundant details. Other forms of resistance took place in minor camps.

> These were exploits of extreme audacity worthy of the deepest respect, but not one of them ended in victory, if by victory is meant the liberation of the camp. The excessive power of the guarding troops was such as to cause its failure within minutes, since the insurgents were practically unarmed. Their actual aim was to damage or destroy the death installations, and permit the escape of the small nucleus of insurgents, something which at times (for example, in Treblinka, even though only in part) succeeded. The Birkenau revolt was unleashed by the special *Kommandos* attached to the crematoria: these were desperate, exasperated men but well fed, clothed and shod. (ibid., 158)

The great majority of Germans, young people in particular, considered Jews their enemies. The rest, with very few heroic exceptions, abstained from any form of help out of fear of the Gestapo; whoever sheltered or even simply assisted a Jew risked terrifying punishment. Nevertheless, "a few thousand Jews survived through the entire Hitlerian period, hidden in Germany and Poland in convents, cellars and attics by citizens who were courageous, compassionate and, above all, sufficiently intelligent to observe for years the strictest discretion" (ibid.).

Perhaps the least-known chapter in the story of Jewish resistance is the one dealing with Jewish resistance in Nazi Germany. It has only recently come to light that in the very heart of the Nazi fortress, Berlin, there operated from 1937 to 1942 a Jewish underground group, the *Baum-Gruppe* (Baum Group), consisting of young Jewish men and women of varied political persuasions, who found a common bond in their implacable hatred of the Nazi regime and in their dedication to combat it by whatever means were available. The story of the group's underground activities lay buried for a long time in the secret archives of the Gestapo. Professor Ber Mark, leading Holocaust historian and director of the Jewish Historical Institute of Warsaw, a pioneer in the study of Jewish resistance in Nazi Germany, examined the original Gestapo files and other material, and published his findings in a monograph that appeared in the quarterly *Bleter Far Geszichte,* Warsaw, Vol. XIV (Warsaw) 1961.

The Jewish community of Germany from 1934 to 1943 did not develop a large-scale resistance movement. After nearly a century of emancipation and equality, the German Jews were suddenly struck by terror and discriminatory laws. They could not count on the German population for any significant support, and the German resistance movement as a whole was too weak to come to their aid. Also, the German Jews lacked both a tradition of struggle and proper leadership. The *Reichsvereinigung vom Deutschen Judentum* played the role of a Judenrat and thwarted the development of a resistance movement. For these reasons, according to Ber Mark, "the Jewish population of Germany, even before November, 1938 (prior to the Crystal Night) was politically and morally disarmed, economically crippled, psychically broken, and in a state of resignation" (Mark, 1967:55).

But side by side with the ever-spreading mood of resignation, a resistance movement emerged within the ranks of the thinking youth which, under the circumstances, carried considerable weight. Even before the war a number of illegal Jewish resistance groups existed in Germany which organized active political resistance and sabotage. They maintained contact with other German and international resistance groups, but were isolated from the rest of the population, which branded them as traitors. They were Communists and left-wing Zionists, and after the outbreak of the German–Soviet war they were convinced that "the mighty coalition of the Soviet Union, England and the United States will fully destroy the eternal aggressor" (ibid., 61).

Of special importance are the memoirs of two active members of the Baum Group, Charlotte and Richard Holtzer, who survived the war. After June 22, 1941 the Baum Group organized resistance among the foreign slave laborers in the Siemens electrical motor plant in which a number of Baum Group members were employed. At the beginning of May 1942 Goebbels organized in Berlin an anti-Soviet exhibit which the leaders of the Baum Group partially destroyed. They were arrested, their leaders were tortured, and the members were executed or sent to concentration camps.

In Lodz, as in other ghettos, as well as in the lagers, there were nuclei of bold political resistance, with Zionist, Bundist or Communist roots.

> There were insurrections that cost a frightful price in human lives and the collective sufferings inflicted in reprisal, but they proved that it is false to say that the prisoners of the German Lagers never tried to rebel. The insurgents intended to bring the secret of the massacre to the attention of the free world. Indeed, and those few who . . . had access to the organs of information spoke. But they were almost never listened to or believed. (Levi 1989:159)

It is taken for granted that resisters to the Holocaust were male and little has been written about the fact that many women, both Jewish and non-Jewish were outstandingly heroic.

The women couriers of the Warsaw ghetto underground "knew no fear and knew no rest," according to Emanuel Ringelblum, archivist of the Warsaw ghetto. One courier was Wanda, hero of the story "Little Wanda with the Braids" by Yuri Suhl (1967:51–54). Slight of figure, with long blonde braids, she wore a flowered kerchief on her head, on which there was also a price of 150,000 zlotys. Smiling shyly, with lowered eyes, she shot to death about thirty German officers. Born of a Hassidic family, Wanda was a very active member of the left-wing student movement. When the Wehrmacht marched into Poland, she became deputy commander of an underground task force, which blew up the railway lines at several points in Warsaw, paralyzing for many hours vital communications to the front. They also blew up the meeting place of the Wehrmacht and German elites, and bombed the editorial offices of a collaborationist newspaper. Wanda was arrested in July 1943, and taken to the torture cellars of the Gestapo, but she did not betray her comrades. In the spring of 1945, the Polish government posthumously awarded Niuta Teitelboim, "little Wanda" as she was called in the underground, the Grunwald Cross, the highest battle decoration in the Polish army.

Mala Zimetbaum was caught in a German round-up of Antwerp Jews and transported to Auschwitz, as told in "The Escape and Death of the 'Runner,' Mala Zimetbaum," by Giza Weisblum (1967:182–181). Since she spoke several languages the SS made Mala an interpreter and a runner, so she could move freely from one part of the camp to another. One of her functions was to assign the sick released from the hospital to various work details. She saved the lives of many women by urging them to leave the hospital as soon as possible because of impending selections. Mala's barracks was located very close to the barbed wire fence near the path that led to the crematoria. Through the walls she could hear the wailing of the children, the shouting of the SS, the barking of their dogs, the screams of the beaten, and the shooting. She and a fellow prisoner, the mechanic Edek Galinski, planned to escape together to tell the world what was happening, but they were caught, and although tortured by Berger, "the devil of Auschwitz," they did not speak. When brought to the place of execution by the camp commander, Mala tried to cut her wrist with a razor, but was stopped and taken to the crematorium. The Antwerp city government put a plaque on the house where Mala had lived: "To Mala Zimetbaum, Symbol of Solidarity, murdered by the Nazis in Auschwitz, August 22, 1944."

For Germaine Ribière, as for other members of the *Amitié Chrétienne,* the rescue of Jews was a top priority, a patriotic duty, part of their resistance to Nazism. Germaine constantly criss-crossed France to bring together the underground, visit camp internees, find or distribute information or funds, "figure out ways to hide Jews and get them into Switzerland" (Ribière, 1997:79). In her journal, Germaine wrote:

> It was August, 1942. I went to see Rabbi Deutsch. He had just learned that the arrests of foreign Jews were about to take place. They were going to put social workers into the camps intended for foreign Jews, to organize efforts to help. In reality, all they cared about was to keep up appearances so that they could say that social workers were looking after the prisoners. The colonel in charge of the whole affair told me: 'Tomorrow morning, starting at 4 a.m., we'll arrest all foreign Jews, around 800 people.' Then I hurried to find any Jewish representatives I knew and we went everywhere telling people, 'Leave, don't remain at home, hide.' The next morning instead of 800 people they found only 29.

Germaine's commitment to Jews and Judaism and to the State of Israel continues to this day.

Resistance is not be pinned down merely to the passive and the active, but arises in every situation and circumstance of the lives of the resisters – out of their occupations, their religious beliefs, their political convictions, out of the personality of each resister, out of the kind of society they came from. Among the great variety of resisters to the persecutions of Jews are whole nations, or at least, the majority of the people in them, such as the Bulgarians, the Italians. and the Danes.

The situation of the Bulgarian Jews is described briefly by Matei Yulzari (1967:275). Of all the Slavic peoples who came under German domination in World War II, the Bulgarians stand alone in their concern for the safety of their Jewish compatriots. The Bulgarian Orthodox Church; the professions; the army officers, the underground radio station; the political parties, including the Communist, Social-Democrat, leftist Zionist and agrarian parties, were all united in the singular determination to protect Bulgarian Jewry from the pro-Hitler Fascist majority in parliament, and the fate that befell the Jewish people in other occupied countries. The anti-Jewish decrees had been issued and the cattle cars were already waiting to transport the victims to the extermination camp. But thanks to the Bulgarian people they remained empty. Bulgarian Jews fought alongside their non-Jewish compatriots in a mighty partisan movement that inflicted a heavy blow on the Nazis and aided in the country's liberation. In Bulgaria there was no separate Jewish resistance and partisan movement, as was the case in Poland and France. The Jews had for centuries shared the historic destinies of all other Bulgarian people, and they now fought shoulder to shoulder for the freedom of their common nation. In Bulgaria today there is hardly a city without a street named after a Jewish partisan hero who fell fighting the Nazis.

The case of the Italians is the unusual story of another people who lived under Fascism, and who had been grievously harassed by the Inquisition in the Middle Ages and the early modern period. But the Italian populace, particularly the priests and the nuns, generally came to the aid of their Jewish compatriots after the Germans invaded Italy in 1943. Since a great many Europeans collaborated with the Nazis when their countries were occupied, what accounted for the fact of Italian resistance to the persecution of the Jews in this period? After all, the Fascist dictatorship under which the Italians were living had preceded and influenced the nature of Nazism in Germany, except that it was not antisemitic until strongly pressured by the Germans The answer lies in the diminishment of the power of the Catholic hierarchy and the abolition of the Inquisition, together with the emergence of the Risorgimento, in the mid-nineteenth century, particularly in Piedmont, as well as the assimilation of the Jews that proceeded thenceforth untrammeled. The comparison of the political development of Italy and Germany shows the contrast in their respective attitudes toward the Jews in the twentieth century.

In his essay "Potassium" Primo Levi (1984) reveals that he, his family and their friends did not leave Piedmont when the Racial Laws were passed in 1938; Piedmont was their country, where they still felt at home. I

> If looked at from close by and in detail, things did not after all seem so disastrous: the Italy around us, Piedmont and Turin, were not hostile. Piedmont was our true country, the one in which we recognized ourselves; the mountains around Turin, visible on clear days, and within reach of a bicycle, were ours, irreplaceable, and taught us fatigue, endurance, and a certain wisdom. In short, our roots were in Piedmont and Turin, not enormous, but deep, extensive, and fantastically intertwined.

Jewish roots were indeed deep, going back 500 years, covering the events in Piedmont with which the lives of the Jews were "intertwined," as described by Renata Segre in her three-volume book *The Jews in Piedmont* (1986–1990). As Murray Baumgarten notes in Chapter 7, Piedmont welcomed the Jews who settled there in the fifteenth century, bringing the silkworm trade with them. But while they were welcomed by the rulers of Piedmont, the Dukes of Savoy, they were strenuously rejected by the Catholic Church. The Inquisition, established in the thirteenth century to stamp out heresy, also harassed the Jews, and their instruments, the mendicant Dominican and Franciscan orders, became the mortal enemies of the Jews.

As pawnbrokers, the only occupation open to them, the Jews obtained the money that they were required to pay the Dukes for protection. They incurred the hostility of the people who had to repay their loans, a hostility deliberately fostered by the friars' antisemitic sermons.

The Jews were forced to attend these sermons, which vilified them, and the aroused church-goers attacked the Jews violently, sometimes murdering them. In addition, the Jews had to wear a distinctive badge, and their Hebrew books were often burned. Their children, some as infants, were abducted and raised as Catholics and the parents had no legal recourse. One father of a two-year-old boy, who had been abducted and baptized by a servant, was so beside himself with grief and rage that he refused the money that the Duke offered him in compensation, though he later took it, as he was advised to do, to avoid additional injury to the family. Jewish adolescents were seduced into converting by grandiose clerical promises. The Jews were accused of blood libel and well-poisoning, and blamed for the periodic plagues. When individual Jews were accused of crimes, particularly of offenses against the Christian faith, the entire community was punished, a tactic the Nazis adopted.

The Jews resisted persecution by negotiation, by hard bargaining when the Dukes required money, and occasionally some of their handicaps, such as the wearing of the invidious badge, were removed. They could also negotiate successfully when the Dukes later urged them to start businesses in areas that needed economic development, and in such cases they were granted greater religious freedom and protection against the molestation of their children. In one way and another, the Jews from time to time were able to get rid of some of their social disabilities, and were even permitted to carry weapons. But when they were finally ghettoized early in the eighteenth century and isolated from the bulk of the Italians, which had been the Inquisition's goal since their arrival in Piedmont, they were very badly off until their emancipation in 1848.[2]

By 1848 the Risorgimento was well under way in Italy, as was also the unification of Germany. In nineteenth-century Germany no figure comparable to the radical Mazzini in Italy gained prominence and wielded the influence he did. Piedmont evolved from being Italy's most reactionary state to the liberalism it attained under Mazzini's influence. Italian unity resulted from the interplay of actions taken by Piedmontese liberals and the democratic movement based on revolutionary ideology, whereas a conservative Bismarck, dedicated to raw power, guided the Prussian military and diplomatic activities that unified Germany. In Prussia, as in Piedmont, a moderate liberal movement was under way before Bismarck came to power, but he decisively defeated it, while Cavour stimulated liberalism in Italy. Shortly after 1871 Bismarck initiated the purges of progressive German judges, more than 80 percent of whom later became Nazi party members. Although Piedmont and Prussia were similar states in the late eighteenth century, with the Risorgimento, and the political and cultural revolution it brought about, Piedmont emerged radically different from Prussia. A few years after unification Piedmont became integrated into Italy whereas Prussia dominated Germany up to 1918 (DiScala, 1995:116–117).

In 1870, when France withdrew its troops from Italy during the Franco-Prussian War, Italy seized the remainder of the papal possessions it had earlier captured. The power of the Church, while still significant in the 11,000-room Vatican, was greatly diminished. "The Church greeted unification with anger because the new state had absorbed most of the papal possessions. Pius IX excommunicated the Piedmontese leaders responsible for annexing papal territory" (Ibid., 125).

The Inquisition had been abolished in the eighteenth century, and in 1848 Piedmont became the first region in Italy to emancipate the Jews, along with the Protestant Waldensians. With the Risorgimento, the aristocratic, clerical class was dispossessed. Italy was united by anti-clerical liberals at the expense of reactionary clerical and potentially antisemitic factions. By contrast, "in Germany the 1870s and 1880s had shown a surprising resurgence of antisemitism, which was not condemned by the government or the educated classes" (Fine, 1997:5)

The high degree of assimilation of Italian Jews may also have worked against the growth of antisemitism in all classes. "Italian Catholics, unostentatious and irregular in their observance of religion, were not deeply concerned about individuals, Jews and atheists alike, who did not share their beliefs" (Zuccotti, 1987:279). As a result of the Risorgimento the papacy lost Rome, and Italian Jews were integrated into Italian culture, to which they made significant contributions in politics, business, banking, insurance, the professions, education and the military.

In the twentieth century antisemitism had no deep roots in Italian society or in the Fascist movement. "Contrary to Il Duce's expectation, a wave of disgust and passive resistance followed the enactment of the antisemitic laws [in 1938]. In general the antisemitic campaign caused surprise in the country and prompted many people to turn against fascism" (DiScala, 1995:252). These are among the people who rescued their Jewish compatriots during the German occupation of Italy.

Summaries of the Individual Chapters

Martin Cohen, in chapter 2, describes the extent of world-wide Jewish armed response to the Holocaust, which was greater than 1.5 million men and women. Considering the rather small number of Jews left in the world after the Holocaust, quite a lot of them fought the Germans in World War II. So where does the Jewish antipathy to Jewish resistance come from? Cohen cites Nechama Tec's statement that there was both a serious omission and a serious distortion of the subject: "The omission is the conspicuous silence about Jews who, while themselves threatened by death, were saving others. The distortion is the common description of European Jews as victims who went passively to their deaths." The silence, says Cohen, is due to the general ignorance about Jewish resistance. The view of the Jew as victim is "historically derived."

The resistance in the ghettos is examined by Eli Tzur (chapter 3), and by Eric Sterling (chapter 4).

"Understanding the finality of the 'Final Solution' did not automatically lead to the willingness to fight it" in the Warsaw ghetto, writes Tzur. "This required a spiritual process, connected with charismatic leadership, relevant ideology, and extant organizations that could be transformed into resistance units." Tzur describes the processes whereby in the course of one year resistance changed from spiritual opposition to armed rebellion. On April 19, 1943 the Jews of Warsaw rose up in the first revolt of the civilian population in Europe.

Eric Sterling relates how in Vilna the United Partisan Organization (FPO) built its resistance under the jurisdiction of *Judenrat* leader Jacob Gens, who feared that the people would shift their allegiance to the FPO. Threatening to kill the remaining inhabitants of the ghetto, the Germans demanded that the FPO leader Yitzhak Wittenberg be handed over to them. This was done, but Wittenberg committed suicide. The Germans killed most of the surviving Jews anyway, but when the Red Army attacked Vilna the FPO, which had fled to the forest, exterminated the Germans by the score.

If the Jews who escaped from the ghettos into the forests were lucky enough to reach western Belorussia (Belarus), where the Bielski partisans were located, they had a good chance of survival, according to Nechama Tec in chapter 5. After their parents, two other brothers, and scores of relatives and friends were murdered by the Germans, the three remaining Bielski brothers organized a partisan detachment which accepted all Jews, regardless of age, sex and state of health. Even those who did not contribute to the maintenance of the detachment – the elderly, the sick and the children – were fed. The Bielski partisans sent guides into the nearby ghettos to bring people into the forest. By the summer of 1944, when the Red Army took over the area, the Bielski partisans numbered over 1,200 individuals, the largest armed rescue of Jews by Jews in Nazi-occupied Europe.

In chapter 6, Judith Tydor Baumel, describes the mission undertaken during World War II by three women parachutists in Palestine, as members of three dozen youthful Jews who attempted to alleviate the plight of Jews by parachuting down in Nazi-occupied countries. Two of the women were among the seven parachutists who lost their lives. Of the three only the poet Senesz achieved national fame and Baumel discusses the changing attitudes toward her heroism in Israel.

Murray Baumgarten discusses Primo Levi's resistance to the Holocaust in chapter 7. Using Levi's own books, which he felt compelled to write when he returned to Italy from Auschwitz, Baumgarten concentrates on those thoughts and actions of Levi which enabled him to withstand the German destruction of identity and the will to survive. Levi learned to develop the crucial power to refuse consent to the German attempts to dehumanize the Jews.

In chapter 8 (by Ami Neiberger) and chapter 9 (by Nathan Stoltzfus) the key factor is family. Neiberger describes the formation of family groups among women prisoners in Auschwitz and the important role these groups played in their survival. According to Stoltzfus, German women married to Jews stayed married not because their husbands were Jewish, but because they were family. He points out that Rosenstrasse, "the only incident of mass German protest against the deportation of German Jews," proved that if the Germans had protested against the marginalization of the Jews, countless German Jews could have been saved.

In chapter 10 Margaret Collins Weitz documents the activities of women who resisted the persecution of Jews by both the Nazis and Pétain's Vichy government. Since the definition of resistance emphasized armed encounters, women were absent from postwar Resistance historiography. But women of all ages and from all walks of life alerted the French public about the antisemitic program of the Vichy government, as well as of the Nazis, carried secret communiques, coded and decoded, sheltered the pursued, and nursed the wounded.

In chapter 11 Wayne Bowen describes the activities of the Spanish soldiers of the *División Azul* (Blue Division) in protecting Jews and Russian civilians from the worst excesses of the Nazi racial war. In the fall of 1943 Franco's withdrawal of the Blue Division from the Eastern Front, in line with Spain's neutral position, was a death sentence for those

Jews who were being helped by the Spanish soldiers. However, throughout the summer and fall of 1944 Spanish ambassadors in Berlin, Bucharest, Budapest and other European capitals managed to save thousands of Jewish lives.

The measures used by the Danes to rescue their Jewish compatriots from the "Final Solution" depended on the interplay among the following factors: the operation of the Danish Folk High School system, the resistance of the Danish Lutheran Church, the underground press, and the cooperative economic system, according to Myrna Goodman in chapter 12.

James M. Glass examines the situation of Jewish children in chapter 13. Glass relates the horrific German assaults on Jewish children to the lack of mass Jewish resistance, the structure and values of the Jewish ghetto leadership, and the role of religious belief in the environment of the mass murder of Jews.

I have read that the resistance to the persecution of Jews in the Holocaust was undertaken only by individuals, solitary individuals, voices crying in the wilderness. But this book describes the resistance as ranging from the concerted efforts of entire nations, or at least the majority of the people in them: Denmark, Bulgaria and Italy; to a whole division of 40,000 Spanish soldiers; to a partisan detachment of 1,200 Jews in the forest; to three dozen Jewish parachutists from the Yishuv; to the Jewish women who formed families to defeat the Nazis' goal of death; to the women in the French Resistance who rescued Jews; to the German women who refused to divorce their Jewish husbands; to the resistance of Communist, Zionist, Bundist Jews in the eastern ghettos; to the incredible resistance of some Special Squads and also some inmates of the death camps; to the German and Polish people who saved a few thousand Jews in caves, cellars and attics; to the resistance of Primo Levi, who refused to consent; and finally, to the million and a half Jewish men and women who fought in the armed services of all the countries that opposed the Nazis and beat them. These examples are only the tip of the iceberg of those who resisted the persecution of the Jews in the Holocaust.

Notes

1. I want to acknowledge the help I received from Professor Murray Baumgarten in the writing of this introduction. Murray, my friend and

Introduction

colleague, is a gifted teacher of English literature and Jewish studies, a sophisticated scholar, the author of books and articles about these two fields, and the editor of the journal *Judaism*. I am very fortunate that in the midst of his very busy life he took the time to critique my introduction. This collection contains his splendid article on Primo Levi.

2. On February 7, 1998 the op-ed page of *The New York Times* carried a communication by David I. Kertzer, professor of anthropology and history at Brown University, entitled "Secrets of the Vatican Archives," partially reproduced here:

Pope John II has apologized many times for the role that Christianity played in the rise of antisemitism through the ages. But now the church is encouraging a much more thorough examination of that history. Last month, Joseph Cardinal Ratzinger, head of the Sacred Congregation for the Doctrine of the Faith, announced that the archives of the Roman Inquisition would now be open to scholars. . . .

Among the earliest acts of the Inquisition . . . was the order, in 1553, that all copies of the Talmud be located and burned. The office of the Inquisition also enforced an order, promulgated later in the 16th century, that called for the Jews of the Papal States to be evicted from all but a few towns, where they were restricted to ghettos. Records of the Inquisition's conduct in the 19th century may prove especially revealing, as this was a critical moment in the church's treatment of the Jews. Despite the trend elsewhere to give Jews full civil rights, the church held to its vigorous enforcement of age-old restrictions. All social contact between Jew and Christian was forbidden. Jews were not allowed to own homes or land, and were to be confined to the ghettos. . . .

In 1858 the Inquisitor of Bologna learned that an illiterate Christian servant employed by a Jewish family had sprinkled water on their infant and recited the baptismal formula. The case was a simple one for the Inquisition: a baptized child was a Christian, and a Christian child could not be raised by Jewish parents. Therefore the Inquisitor ordered the boy, Edgardo Mortara, taken off to a monastery in Rome. The boy's parents naturally objected. Napoleon 111, Catholic Emperor of France, protested strenuously, as did Protestants and Jews in Europe and America. The furor contributed to the demise of the Papal States shortly thereafter. . . .

Clearly, the church is undergoing great change, although not without resistance from within. More than a few members of the hierarchy strenuously oppose the recent efforts to cast a critical eye on the church's history. The most heated debate today revolves around the question of how the Vatican, and Pope Pius XII in particular, acted during and after World War II. What could the Pope have done to save the Jews from the Nazi horror? To what extent did the church aid the escape of Nazi war criminals? . . .

The explanation of what made the Holocaust possible is to be found in no small part in the files of the Inquisition. These documents will deepen our knowledge of how for centuries the Roman Catholic Church conditioned the European population to view the Jews as inferiors. So scholars can now open the dusty folders that include new information on cases like that of the Jewish boy of Bologna. In allowing this to happen, the Vatican has taken yet another significant step in coming to terms with its past.

References

DiScala, Spencer M. (1995) *Italy: from Revolution to Republic, 1700 to the Present*. San Francisco: Westview Press.

Fine, David J. (1997) "Solomon Schechter and the Ambivalence of Jewish Wissenschaft," *Judaism*, Winter:3–24.

Glass, James M. (1997) *"Life Unworthy of Life"*. New York: Basic Books,

Levi, Primo (1961) *Survival in Auschwitz*. Trans. Stuart Woolf. New York: Macmillan Publishing Co.

—— (1984) *The Periodic Table*. Trans. Raymond Rosenthal. New York: Schocken Books.

—— (1989) *The Drowned and the Saved*. Trans. Raymond Rosenthal. New York: First Vintage International Edition.

Mark, Ber (1967) "The Herbert Baum Group, Jewish Resistance in Germany in the Years 1937–1942" in Yuri Suhl (ed.) *They Fought Back*. New York: Crown Publishers: 55–68.

Paulsson, Gunnar S. (1995) "The 'Bridge over the Oresund': The Historiography on the Expulsion of the Jews from Nazi-Occupied Denmark," *Journal of Contemporary History*, Vol. 309, 431–464.

—— (1997)"Resistance and Choices," *The Holocaust List, Internet*, Oct. 27.

Phayer, Michael and Eva Fleischner (eds), R Pibière, Germaine (1997) "I will not be a Bystander," in *Cries in the Night: Women who Challenged The Holocaust*. Kansas City: Sheed & Ward; 65–86.

Segre, Renata, (ed.) (1986–1990) *The Jews in Piedmont*. 3 vols, Jerusalem: The Israel Academy of Sciences and Humanities and Tel Aviv University.

Suhl, Yuri (1967) "Little Wanda with the Braids," in Yuri Suhl (ed.) *They Fought Back*, New York: Crown Publishers, Inc.

Tec, Nechama (1997) *Jewish Resistance: Facts, Omissions and Distortions*. Washington, D.C.: Miles Lerman Center for the Study of Jewish Resistance.

Weisblum, Giza (1967) "The Escape and Death of the 'Runner,' Mala Zimetbaum," in Yuri Suhl (ed.) *They Fought Back*. New York: Crown Publishers Inc.

Yulzari, Matei (1967) "The Bulgarian Jews in the Resistance Movement," in Yuri Suhl (ed.) *They Fought Back*. New York: Crown Publishers Inc.

Zuccotti, Susan (1987) *The Italians and the Holocaust: Persecution, Rescue, Survival*. New York: Basic Books.

Culture and Remembrance:
Jewish Ambivalence and Antipathy to
the History of Resistance
Martin Cohen

I have an ancient dream:
Jew, you were a warrior once;
Jew, you were a victor once!
O, how strange that seems!

(Morris Rosenfeld, 1905,
trans. Hershl Hartman)

The scholarly work of Rabbi Elijah Schochet (see Schochet 1994) periodically takes him to Vilna (Vilnius, Lithuania). On one trip he took a tour of the countryside. His guide, an older Gentile man, posed the question: "Why don't you Jews who come here from America ever ask about the Jewish partisans?" The man even took the Rabbi to task for the ignorance of American Jews on the topic of Jewish resistance, stating that it appeared that Jews didn't even want to hear about it (Schochet 1997).

This is not unique to Jews. Histories of resistance movements can be fragile. That is one of the underlying messages of Edgerton's works on African resistance (1988; 1989). American Jews and Gentiles remain generally unaware of the extent of Jewish resistance to the Holocaust. There is a tendency to downplay the role of Jewish resistance, and even an apparent antipathy toward the issue in some Jewish quarters. Yet many American Jews are embarrassed and ashamed by the image of the Jew as a passive victim.[1]

Both former resistance fighters and some scholars have been alarmed by this lack of knowledge. Shalom Yoran wrote his autobiography of resistance shortly after the war, but was only moved to have it published recently in response to what he saw as the general ignorance regarding

Jewish resistance (1996a; 1996b).[2] Tec, in the introduction to her book on the Bielski partisans, states that her research into the Holocaust made it clear to her that there was both a serious omission and a serious distortion: "The omission is the conspicuous silence about Jews who, while themselves threatened by death, were saving others. The distortion is the common description of European Jews as victims who went passively to their deaths" (Tec 1993:vii).

The extent of world-wide Jewish armed response to the Holocaust is known to have been greater than 1.5 million men and women (Kowalski 1984:12,15). Over half a million Jews fought in the armed forces of the United States.; over half a million Jews in the Soviet forces; 100,000 Jews fought with the French; 75,000 fought in the forces of Great Britain, plus another 30,000 Jews from Palestine who were under the command of the British; 60,000 were with Polish forces; 20,000 fought in Yugoslavia; another 200,000 were in the various armies of Canada, South Africa, Australia, New Zealand, and from elsewhere (Kowalski 1984:15). The allied armies had between 250 to 300 Jews in ranks equivalent to general or admiral (Kowalski 1984:12). Additionally, somewhere between 50,000 and 100,000 fought as partisans in the forests of the East (Foxman 1984:86; Kowalski 1984:12,14). These figures do not include the Jews who fought in resistance in the Netherlands, Belgium, the Scandinavian countries; nor do they include Jews engaged in various forms of ghetto and camp resistance, armed or unarmed.

I have formally interviewed five survivors of the Holocaust, four of whom are women. I have also had fewer formal conversations with other survivors and the children of resistance fighters. My informants come from various backgrounds, ranging from those affiliated with the Jewish Labor Bund, Hashomer Hatzair (left-wing Zionist) to Revisionist Zionist (right-wing).

One woman of Hashomer Hatzair background was in an organized partisan unit under a Jewish commander. I interviewed her by telephone. Another woman, whose family was Revisionist Zionist, was too young to join a partisan unit, but her brother organized local resistance in their community in eastern Poland. After her brother's execution by the Nazis, she engaged in personal acts of defiance. On more than one occasion she was able to rescue partisans from the Germans, acts that resulted in her receiving the Hero of the Soviet Union medal.

Another woman I spoke with came from a Bundist family (Jewish Labor Bund). She wanted to participate in armed resistance but was unable to (having been rejected by Polish partisans and trapped in a ghetto in which there was only one hidden revolver), so she engaged in various forms of "moral" resistance. Moral resistance in her case meant "when the enemy tries to destroy your humanity, remaining human is resistance." In the ghetto, the young people, both Bundists and Zionists, organized themselves into cells in the hope of someday offering resistance. She was a cell leader. They met in the evenings after curfew and kept up each others' spirits. If someone got hold of an extra bit of food, such as a potato, they went to great lengths to make sure it was divided up evenly. They risked their lives by passing out flyers calling for resistance (and were taken to task by the *Judenrat*). They also tried to maintain communication with the outside. Later, when this woman was in a concentration camp, moral resistance included seeing that the meager rations were fairly distributed. On one occasion, when she was whipped before the assembled prisoners, she clenched her teeth and would not allow herself to cry out in pain, following an example set earlier by her brother.

Another woman I interviewed was too young herself to have participated in resistance. She is the widow of a man who was "conscripted" at age 12 in Hungary by a secret Zionist organization that provided him with military training.[3] I met with her and she gave me a copy of a brief typed memoir from her husband. She also allowed my wife and me to view her husband's taped testimony for the Shoah Visual History Foundation.

I met with one male survivor and his wife in their home on a number of occasions. He lived in a *shtetl* (village) in Belorussia before the war. A few months after the Germans invaded and drove the Russians out, he and his younger brother went to the forest to join up with partisans. He fought in various partisan units until the Red Army liberated the area. Told he could go home, he chose instead to join them and marched through to Berlin.

In addition to working with survivors, I have also drawn on my own informal experiences in the Jewish community, as well as formal and informal discussions and interviews with a number of other Jews, including some of my informants in another ongoing project. I have made use of this information to examine various possible explanations for the limited awareness of Jewish resistance.

There are several factors that I believe contribute to the apparent ambivalence and antipathy to Jewish resistance. These include, but are not limited to: (1) the historically derived view of the Jew as victim; (2) avoidance of the topic by both American Jews and survivors; (3) how we define resistance; and (4) postwar politics. While these are separated here for analytical purposes, they actually form part of an interconnected complex.

Martin Cohen

The Jew as Victim

The image of the Jewish victim reinforces the idea that resistance was not a Jewish response to the Holocaust. Popular media and literature have helped promote this image, which has developed over the past 2,000 years. This image derives little from pre-Diaspora Jewish history, which includes mythohistorical templates for resistance.

The medium of film helps contribute to this image. When a major Hollywood director/producer made his "Holocaust film," he portrayed Jews as helpless.[4] Their survival depended on the heroism of a Gentile. The Jewish film archive at Brandeis University (perhaps the largest such archive in the world) has few documentaries on Jewish resistance (*The Partisans of Vilna* being a rare exception). The most frequently requested films of the Holocaust in the archives are documentaries of Gentiles rescuing Jews (Finkelstein 1996).

Most Jews, most Americans, have seen several photographs from the Holocaust. When I ask American Jews about this, two specific images come to mind: One is the photograph of the little boy in the Warsaw ghetto with his arms raised, the other is one of the many shots of stacks of emaciated corpses. Practically no one, unless they have gone out of their way to research the topic, has seen any of the many extant photographs of Jews bearing weapons or wearing uniforms. One of my informants has two photographs of himself in the forest. One of these hangs in the Yad Vashem in Jerusalem. Many such photographs can be seen in the four-volume set on resistance edited by Kowalski (1984; 1985; 1986; 1991) as well as a few others in Tec's book on the Bielski partisans (Tec 1993).

Whether media drives culture or reflects it in this case is unimportant. Either way, the attitude presented in media typifies how American Jews view the Holocaust. One common explanation given for the ignorance of resistance is that the destruction of the Jewish people was the major event of the Holocaust, and while there may have been resistance, it was small in comparison to the victimization. The response can be reduced to the rhetorical question: "How can a few resistance fighters be compared with the tragedy of 6 million victims?"

Such a question at first leaves one gasping in agreement. The victims were up against the most well-organized and efficient plans for genocide ever developed (so unthinkable that it was not difficult to hide the full knowledge of its intent from many of the victims almost up to the end). At the same time, the Nazis had what appeared to be almost immeasurable force. Despite the scale of the events, the victims are commonly seen as passive rather than overwhelmed. One must remember that the Nazis also overwhelmed most of Europe, from the English Channel to beyond the Russian border, and from the Arctic Circle to North Africa, but we do not today have an image of the passive and weak European. We recall underground and resistance movements in France, Scandinavia and Holland, but we forget that they represent a tiny fraction of these populations. Even in these cases, we ignore Jewish involvement. Foxman (1984:95) points out that while Jews represented less than 1 percent of the French population, they made up 15 to 20 percent of the French underground. This included wholly Jewish groups, such as the *Fortresse Juive* which became the *Forces Armées Juives,* Jewish battalions in the Maquis, and various organizations of Jewish Zionist youth and Jewish Communist youth.

If resistance really is eclipsed by the scale of events, then why are the stories of Gentiles rescuing Jews so popular? The numbers game doesn't work here. The number of victims, as well as the number of active persecutors (both Nazis and collaborators), greatly outnumber the relatively few Gentile rescuers. One of my informants insists that some Gentiles greatly exaggerate the aid they gave to Jews. She goes as far as attending local talks from one such "righteous Gentile" whom she knew during the Holocaust, letting her know in advance that she will challenge her if she strays too far from the truth. "If they gave a Jew a crust of bread once, and we were thankful if they did, they became a 'hero'."

Smoliar (1959) argued that this numbers game was based on a false view of the Holocaust. He claimed that armed resistance was the tip of the iceberg, while the daily activities of ghetto and camp survival also became a part of resistance. Food was smuggled into ghettos when the Nazis tried to starve them, people were smuggled out; escapes were planned and efforts were made to keep up morale. Smoliar points out that the victim, passive at the moment of execution, may have succeeded in resisting the enemy for months or years prior; and only at the end showed the effects of starvation, exhaustion and psychological manipulation in his "passivity." I would also add that the figure of 6 million represents between 1.5 to 2 million children, as well as a disproportionate number of the elderly, victims who cannot be called "passive" just because they were unable to offer direct resistance. Helplessness should not be confused with passivity. To put this in perspective, one of my informants pointed out that there were 6,000 Jewish children in her region before the Holocaust, and only 5 are known to have survived. During one six-month period of the war, 3 million Soviet soldiers were captured by the Germans, 2 million of them were put to death (Kowalski 1984:13). No one has yet to call them "passive."

The image of the Jew as a passive victim of the Holocaust draws on a long history. Jews in Europe have lived for much of the past 2,000 years with a reputation for avoiding violence. Hilberg, who systematically denies or downplays Jewish resistance, insisted that the Diaspora created a "Jewish reaction pattern" of compliance in response to force (Hilberg 1978:14). In summation of this, he wrote, "A two-thousand-year-old lesson could not be unlearned; the Jews could not make the switch" (ibid., 666).

The Israeli writer Amos Oz described the feeling of discontinuity between the Diaspora Jew and the Israeli Jew. During his childhood in Jerusalem four or five years before the founding of the State of Israel, during World War II, there was a sense that "a new race was being bred of new Jews who had undergone a certain mutation," Jews who were strong and heroic, and "Diametrically opposed to the traditional Jew of the Diaspora" (Oz 1995–96:50).

There is no doubt that this image arises in part out of historical circumstances. As a stateless people, Jews had no military. Further, Jews did attempt to avoid conscription into the Tsar's army. This was no shame, as this army often had little purpose other than to serve as a bloody playground for aristocratic officers, and at one time conscripted Jews as young as 12 years of age were subject to five years in cantonist battalions followed by 25 years of regular military service. In fact, those unfortunate enough to be put in uniform did not earn a reputation for cowardice in the military, and some distinguished themselves. Other historical events helped create this image, including the Inquisition and the various waves of pogroms. If Jews carried the image of victim, it was because Jews were, in fact, victimized. How passive they were in the face of victimization varied by time, place and opportunity. The desire for resistance certainly surfaced at times, as in the legend of the Golem (a kind of Jewish Frankenstein monster who defended the Jewish community of Prague), which can be seen as a myth of wish-fulfillment.

The Jews of Europe have also long perceived themselves as non-violent. This is expressed in many ways, including the self-description of the Jews as the "merciful children of the Merciful." Schochet (1997) has suggested that religious scholarship, rather than aggressiveness, became the image of Jewish masculinity.

The Yiddish writer I. L. Peretz challenged the passive and humble "ideal of goodness that had a powerful grip on the folk imagination" (Wisse, 1991:48–49). "Bontshe Shvayg" (Bontshe the Silent) was first published in 1894 (Peretz 1990).[5] This was just three years before the founding of both the Jewish Labor Bund and political Zionism; both movements were conscious responses to Jewish passivity. In this story, Bontshe (who represents the Jewish people) dies and faces a tribunal in heaven. His life began with a botched circumcision and ended in an ignoble death, with a multitude of miseries and indignities in between. The tribunal recounts how he was cheated and mistreated throughout his life, and yet remained silent and passive. Finally the voice of God interrupts the trial. Bontshe is offered whatever he wants of paradise. "All heaven belongs to you. Ask for anything you wish; you can choose what you like." Bontshe stood there dazed, and finally demanded his due: "a warm roll with fresh butter every morning." "The judges and angels hung their heads in shame. The prosecutor laughed."

Less than fifty years later, Red Army Lieutenant Alexander Pechersky turned the story of Bontshe around (Pechersky 1967). Captured by the Germans, he was sent with a group of other Jewish soldiers to work in the death camp of Sobibor. One day on work detail, a German guard challenged him to split a stump in five minutes. If he succeeded, he was to get a packet of cigarettes, if he failed, he would receive twenty-five lashes. He met the challenge, but refused the cigarettes, claiming that he didn't smoke. Shortly after, the guard brought him half a roll with margarine. Pechersky again refused, visibly angering the guard. A few weeks later, a mass escape took two-thirds of the prisoners beyond the camp's fences and led to its destruction. Pechersky was one of the leaders of the revolt.

In the tumultuous times of the early part of the twentieth century, the Jews of Eastern Europe found themselves in a rapidly changing world, and despite the explicit moral of the story of Bontshe, they began to look upon Bontshe's passivity in a different light; "his sweetness apparently reminded readers of the old values of humility and moral containment" (Wisse 1991:50). After pogroms and war, and finally the Holocaust, "the benign interpretation of Bontshe became almost irresistible, and the story entered the canon of literature inside out" (Wisse 1991:51). In fact, the story was given another twist after World War II by Isaac Bashevis Singer in his short story, "Gimpel the Fool" (1972). Singer resurrected Bontshe in his character Gimpel. But here Gimpel's passive nature leads to a long and satisfying life, while those who deride, cheat and abuse him end up far less fortunate. Passivity, in light of the Holocaust, was once again raised to the level of a Jewish virtue.[6]

The historically derived self-image of passivity stands in stark contrast to the mythohistorical template for resistance in the story of Hanuka.

Hanuka is a celebration of resistance that has been modified into the celebration of a miracle. For 2,000 years it was relegated to the status of a "minor" holiday, and was at times repressed. (Other, "major" holidays have fallen by the wayside in that time; who today observes the Fast of Gedalia or celebrates the Feast of Nicanor?)

Gaster ignored Hanuka's "minor" status by proclaiming that it is "the only *important* Jewish festival that is not mentioned in the Bible" (Gaster 1953:233, emphasis added). The sources for the historical events commemorated are in the first and second Books of the Maccabees in the Apocrypha, and in the writings of the Greek historian, Polybius (ibid.).

Hanuka is essentially the celebration of a second century BC military victory against the Greco-Syrian Empire under the rule of Antiochus IV, who declared himself Antiochus Epiphanes (God manifest). Antiochus attempted to Hellenize the nations ruled by his empire, denying them the cultural autonomy granted by his predecessors. When the Temple of Jerusalem was recaptured in 165 BC, the Maccabees proclaimed a week-long celebration, and called it "Hanuka" or "dedication." The common explanation for the eight nights of lights is the miracle that only a day's supply of olive oil was available for rededicating the temple, but it lasted for the eight days necessary to press and prepare more oil. This is only one of three Talmudic explanations, and it first appears 500 years after the events. The lights (not even mentioned in the Books of the Maccabees) probably have more to do with the time of year, around the winter solstice, when festivals involving lights and fire are quite common. There was a pre-Hanuka solstice festival that made use of the symbolism of fire among the ancient Hebrews.

By the time the Maccabees came to power, more Jews lived outside of Israel than within. When Israel fell under Roman rule, all Jews lived under foreign rule. A number of unsuccessful resistance movements continued within Palestine until the Jews were dispersed. This made Hanuka, the celebration of a military victory against an outside ruling power potentially dangerous. So the compiler of the Mishnah, Rabbi Judah the Patriarch, suppressed references to both Hanuka and Purim (also an occasion that commemorates a kind of victory) (Gaster 1953:248–249). The continual problem of this military aspect of the holiday may also be responsible for the shift of emphasis to the lights (Gaster 1953:248–249). It is likely that rabbinical and community leadership had a vested interest in keeping this celebration of military victory both "minor" and focused on non-military elements of celebration.

The "rediscovery" of this part of the Hanuka story by Jewish historians of the nineteenth and the beginning of the twentieth century seemed to

capture the imagination of some segments of the Jewish communities of
Europe and North America. It was the inspiration for Morris Rosenfeld's
verse quoted at the beginning of this chapter. It seems that more than one
Jew who escaped from the ghetto into the Belorussian forests during the
Holocaust envisioned Judah Maccabee when they saw the figure of the
Jewish partisan commander Tuvia Bielski on horseback (Tec 1993:4).

The conditions of Jewish history may have at times made any open
militancy impractical or dangerous. Active resistance often gave way to
negotiation (and negotiation can range from total capitulation to extreme
forms of non-militant resistance). Yet active resistance did occasionally
occur. In fact, it was on the rise during the fifty years that preceded
the Holocaust, as Zionism, socialism and Communism inspired various
members of the Jewish community. For example, a successfully planned
and executed resistance to a small pogrom at the end of the last century
was described by Jacob Marateck (Wincelberg and Wincelberg 1976:11–
20). Marateck also referred to his own participation in what might have
been the Jewish Labor Bund (although no organizational name is
identified): "I returned to Warsaw and once more became involved with
the Jewish revolutionary movement, both as a kind of labor organizer
and when necessary . . . as what today you would call a 'terrorist'"
(Wincelberg and Wincelberg 1976:4). He also described his first militant
experience as a paid labor organizer in Warsaw. Again, no organizational
name is given, but the man who trained him was a "hard-boiled Lithuanian
bundist" (Wincelberg and Wincelberg 1976:75).

Pogroms, in which Jews truly were victimized, have added to this
image. But less well-known are the responses. The event described by
Marateck was not unique. The Bund organized self-defense groups. There
is a photograph of one such group in Odessa in 1905 (Gitelman 1988:22).
Over 2,000 pogroms occurred between 1918 and 1921, but again, Jews
did form self-defense groups, as pictured in Gitelman (1988:102–103).
Gitelman (1988:107) also quotes an eyewitness who described a Red
Army company made up entirely of yeshiva students from Proskurov,
including some wearing earlocks. They joined the Red Army after
Petliura's riots, motivated by vengeance (Shapiro 1952:168).

One of my informants described an antisemitic riot that took place in
the late 1930s in Vilna. The police only decided to put down the riot
when the Jewish butchers of the city appeared on the streets, armed with
the tools of their trade and ready to confront the mob.

In short, Hilberg's contention that the history of the Jews made them
incapable of resistance in all circumstances is both unfounded and contradicted by the reality of Jewish resistance before and during the Holocaust.

The image of the passive Jew is a generalization that has helped create our false concept of the Holocaust Jew.

Avoidance

Avoidance of the topic of Jewish resistance has taken many forms and has many causes. The entire topic of the Holocaust was not always discussed as openly as it is now. Most survivors in the United States did not talk much about it in the early years after the war. Most Americans Jews no longer wanted to hear about the Holocaust. There has been, and remains, both organizational and scholarly avoidance of the issue of resistance.

Holocaust survivors tended to avoid the topic in the early years after the war. One particularly outspoken informant claims that survivors were quiet because when they initially tried to talk to American Jews, it was clear no one wanted to hear them. The American wife of one informant believed that this was in part due to the guilt that many American Jews had about not acting to rescue the victims, either because they were ignorant of the genocide or because they wouldn't take an active role in petitioning the US government to intercede in some way (such as letting in more refugees or bombing the camps and/or rail lines to the camps). Survivors of resistance had additional reasons to keep quiet, which will be presented in the next section.

Today the topic of the Holocaust is out in the open. Synagogues observe Yom HaShoah, movies make millions and speakers are in demand. But the partisan and ghetto fighter are nowhere to be seen. In the words of one informant: "Today it seems that if we weren't in the camps, then we weren't survivors of the Holocaust." When she argued with certain leaders in the community that Jewish heroes should be recognized, she received replies such as "all survivors are heroes."

This may be partially due to the self-image of the Jew as victim and its correlate of the Jew as less brutal than other people. As the same informant as above recounted, "When I said to my rabbi, 'You know, Jews killed Germans,' he said, 'God forbid!'" A former partisan stated it thus: "The world started looking at the Jews as martyrs. And here comes a Jew who says he fought. That's not good. No one wanted to talk to me at all. Because I killed. You understand?" (Finkelstein and Cohen n.d.:1). When another informant tried to discuss his partisan activities with men his age at a Jewish community center, they quickly changed the subject to their own military service during World War II, stating that it was the Americans who saved him and the other survivors.

Organizational avoidance of resistance seems to exist in the United States as well. One informant has over the years attended many ceremonies commemorating the Holocaust. She reports that she has never heard a word of remembrance for Jewish resistance fighters at any such ceremony. When Finkelstein and Cohen met with officials of an organization that funds educational projects on the Holocaust to apply for a grant, the officials "physically recoiled" when they heard that they wanted to document the lives of surviving Jewish partisans (Finkelstein 1996). More than one of my informants have implied that Jewish victims elicit more donations than Jewish heroes.

I have discussed some Holocaust issues with a few rabbis in the Los Angeles area. Some have been very considerate and helpful. One even helped me contact an informant. Two rabbis were not so helpful. One, a prominent rabbi in a Hasidic sect, seemed willing to discuss the concept of *kiddush hashem*[7] in relation to the Holocaust, when he was suddenly called away from the phone. He promised to call me right back. Instead, he did not return my subsequent phone calls. Another rabbi, associated with an institution that receives public and private funding, was also called away from the phone, promised to call me back and, again, neither called nor returned my calls.

One of my informants wrote an essay in Yiddish, which he wanted to read in his synagogue on Yom HaShoah. He went to his rabbi's office and presented his request. The rabbi denied the request because "no one knows Yiddish anymore." When it was pointed out that many members of the temple did in fact know Yiddish, the rabbi demanded in anger that he leave his office. I cannot determine if this is a rejection of Yiddish, Jewish resistance, or both. This attitude is not universal, as I have been asked to teach a course and speak on the topic of resistance by the rabbi of a local synagogue.

On the scholarly side, the first main work on the Holocaust was Hilberg's hugely ambitious work (Hilberg, 1978). As previously noted, resistance is all but ignored in this work. Hilberg mentioned resistance primarily to draw attention to its absence. I relied on a copy of Hilberg's book that I checked out of the library at UCLA. On pages 662–669, where he summarizes his view of the lack of Jewish resistance and the victims' compliance in being victimized, an anonymous reader penciled in his or her counter-arguments and questions.

Suhl took every opportunity to point out that Hilberg relied almost exclusively on German sources, not only ignoring Jewish sources, but ignoring parts of the same German documents he cited when they contradicted his view of resistance (Suhl 1967:45, 125, 134, 238–239).

It should be noted that Dawidowicz (1986) in *The War against the Jews 1933–1945* gives a bit more credit to Jewish resistance than Hilberg did. She even took him to task for the section mentioned above, stating that his "knowledge of Jewish history is not equal to his rashness in generalizing about it," and that his work was flawed by his "uninformed comments and distorted conclusions about Jewish behavior, especially in pp. 662–669" (Dawidowicz 1986:435).

On the other hand, Dawidowicz has also argued elsewhere, with some merit, that resistance has been exaggerated and redefined by both Zionists and leftists for their own ideological benefit; although she did not see the passive victim as the logical alternative (1981:130–135). Feingold (1995:54–58) also argues that resistance was not plentiful, and that the literature that emphasizes it also exaggerates and redefines it, based on some misplaced sense of Jewish honor.[8]

Avoidance of the topic of Jewish resistance has several causes: it is a subset of the general early tendency to avoid discussing the topic of the Holocaust; Jewish resistance contradicts organizational agendas, and it goes against the historically derived Jewish self-image of non-violence and passivity. This avoidance and even antipathy, especially within the organizational leadership of the Jewish community, bears much of the responsibility for the limited general knowledge of Jewish resistance.[9]

Defining Resistance

Some people have come to accept an overly strict definition of resistance when applied to the behavior of the Holocaust Jews. The late husband of one of my informants was recruited by a Zionist organization and given military training. However, when a man approached him with news of his family's whereabouts, and offered to lead him to them, he armed himself and left. Since he never participated in organized resistance, he felt he did not resist the Nazis, despite the fact that he engaged in at least two gun battles with German soldiers. He did not consider self-defense to be resistance.

Feingold (1995:56) argues that "those who seek to find a widespread Jewish resistance must redefine what is meant by resistance." In fact, it appears to be just the opposite; the definition applied to other people should be applied to the behavior of Jews as well.

There is little disagreement about the French Resistance (although disproportionately Jewish, as described above). Yet the French response was relatively small, late in organizing and did not change the fact that many French people collaborated with the Nazis. Much of the work of the French underground consisted not in armed resistance, but in disseminating information, keeping up spirits and waiting for either liberation or the right time to act. What ghetto lacked these actions? Some ghettos even had hidden printing presses.

Underground activity was vital in virtually every ghetto. Smuggling food and medical supplies occurred in direct defiance of the Nazis, at the risk of death. Yet without an illegal supply line, ghetto populations would have so quickly withered that there would have been no need for death camps. Smoliar (1959) argued that maintaining a supply line when completely surrounded by the enemy is a major military feat. We would consider this resistance under any other circumstances, so we must here as well.

Postwar Politics

The post-war political climate in the United States is responsible for a particular kind of avoidance. The Cold War and McCarthyism put a chill on many of the survivors of resistance, and perhaps made leadership in the Jewish establishment uneasy about partisan survivors as well.

When I asked one informant about her early experiences in the United States, she immediately said, "You have to understand, we were with the Red Army." When I asked her if she had been a Communist, she said no, and identified her background as Hashomer Hatzair. Another informant, a recipient of the Hero of the Soviet Union medal, also spontaneously suggested that the Cold War caused many to keep their silence.

Hershl Hartman, of the faculty of the International Institute for Secular Humanistic Judaism, was a reporter for the *Morgn Frayhayt* in the late 1940s. He conducted dockside interviews in Yiddish with arriving "displaced persons." He approached groups of young people and asked them what camps they had been in. When they replied that they hadn't been in any camps, he asked if they had been partisans. They did not reply, but exchanged smiles with each other. Further exchanges included: "How did you survive?" "We survived." As to where they stayed, they answered, "the forest." This most likely meant they were partisans. It seems they knew about the rising tide of McCarthyism before landing on our shores (it should be noted that immigration officers were present at the docks and making use of Hartman's Yiddish to question the new arrivals) (Hartman 1996).

Politics has clearly entered into at least one institution's portrayal of the Holocaust. The Museum of Tolerance in Los Angeles has Pastor

Niemöller's famous lines on one wall. The line that begins, "When they came for the Communists . . ." is missing.

It is probable that the leftist presence in Jewish resistance has been one of the reasons Jewish institutions have been slow to recognize resistance. Jews in the United States have endured antisemitic charges of both dual loyalty and disloyalty. The excesses of Cold War politics no doubt heightened sensitivity to such accusations among many Jews and Jewish institutions. Jewish institutions may have had a stake in downplaying the Jewish presence on the political left, either here or in Europe. While many American Jews trace their family histories back to prewar Poland, few realize that the Jewish Labor Bund was the largest Jewish institution in prewar Poland and quite probably a part of their heritage.

Post-war politics has informed other aspects of Jewish American responses to Holocaust history. Jewish writers in the United States were very slow to criticize the fact that until the actual liberation of the camps, the US military did not engage in any act directly to aid either Jewish resistance or bomb either the camps or railroad lines that fed into them. It is known that the government buried information about the Holocaust such as Jan Karski's report. Karski, a Polish Catholic, risked his life to meet with Jewish leaders, to visit ghettos, and even secretly to steal into and out of Sobibor in order to present a credible report to the Polish government-in-exile and Allied leaders in London and Washington. While I have heard of recent criticism that Jewish writers and scholars in the Soviet Union and Poland may have exaggerated the role of Communists and the Soviet Union in aiding Jewish partisans, we must not remain so smug as to dismiss the effect of the Cold War on American Jewish writers and scholars as well.

It is impossible to determine how much avoidance of the topic of Jewish resistance is motivated by politics since such motives are not usually stated, but it is clear that this was another important cause for the combined antipathy toward and ignorance of Jewish resistance.

Jewish ambivalence to the history of resistance in the Holocaust seems to range from ignorance of resistance among people who would welcome this knowledge to an antipathy among those who choose to ignore or deny it. The contrast between the actual history of Jewish resistance and Jewish recognition of this history can be found in the comparison between a good university research library and a typical Judaica bookstore. In the library, one will find dozens upon dozens of books documenting Jewish resistance, most of them out of print. In the bookstore, one will find books on Jewish history and on the Holocaust, but few, and often no books on Jewish resistance.

Notes

1. Some Jewish communities in other countries have a greater awareness of Jewish resistance. Thanks to Yad Vashem and different political circumstances in Israel, the stories are more widely known there. Jacques Lazarus ("Capitain Jacquel") has assured me that Jews in France are as aware of this part of their history as the non-Jewish population is of the French Resistance (Lazarus 1995). On the other hand, the Yiddish writer Hersh Smoliar was met with the idea that Jews were passive victims upon his return to Moscow after the war (Smoliar 1959). He took it upon himself to correct this notion through his writings on resistance in Minsk, some of which have been translated into English (Smoliar 1966; 1989). Bauer (1984:47) and Gitelman (1988:207) both state that the underground in the Minsk Ghetto sent 10,000 armed Jews to the forest in order to fight. Gitelman (1988:207) also points out that they set up family camps of women and children hidden in the forest.
2. Yoran appeared last year at a signing for his book (Yoran 1996a) at a large bookstore in a community with a dense Jewish population. Only a trickle of customers talked to him or purchased his book. The signing had been well publicized in the largest Jewish periodical in Los Angeles.
3. There is no clear identification of the organization, which took the name of the Maccabees. Since there was no Zionist organization that formally went by this name it is not possible to identify the actual group. They seemed fairly well equipped, and it is known that the British made use of Zionist/Palestinian volunteers, so it seems possible that this was a British-backed group. The people who took him were dressed in the uniforms of Hungarian Fascists, a tactic known to be used by Zionists in Hungary during the war (Foxman 1984:98).
4. The only exceptions I know of are *Escape from Sobibor* (made for television in 1989) and *Hanna's War*. Both are fairly obscure films that have received none of the publicity that accompanied *Schindler's List*.

5. To write about the Jewish self-image of passivity during the first half of the twentieth century up to the Holocaust without mention of "Bontshe Shvayg" would be like writing about attitudes toward slavery and abolition up to the American Civil War without mention of *Uncle Tom's Cabin*. Peretz documented the Jewish life of his time, as well as having a tremendous influence in the directions Jewish culture was to take in the twentieth century. Wisse (1991:xiv) argues that the only other writer to have a greater influence on modern Jewish culture was Herzl. Indeed, when Peretz died in 1915, over 100,000 mourners attended his funeral in Warsaw (the father of one of my informants in another project was brought by his parents at the age of 7 to this event). Wisse (1991:xvi) argues that "The most compelling, and poignant, proof of Peretz's influence came in the ghettos during the Second World War." She points out that there were at least "sixty commemorative gatherings in his name" in the Warsaw Ghetto (Wisse 1991:xvi).

6. Bontshe as a proper role model rather than a hideous reflection is evident in the Yiddish expression "ikh vil dokh nit mer vi Bontshe – a heyse bulke mit putter" ("I don't aspire to any more than Bontshe – a hot roll with butter") (Wisse 1991:51).

   In the 1960s my wife's family watched the film *The High and the Mighty* on television. The movie then became central to discussions and even family games (my wife's father spent his whole career in aviation). Finally, her grandfather who spoke more Yiddish than English, pronounced: "Let others fly, I got what to eat." This was a proper reflection of the values in which he was raised.

7. *Kiddush haShem* translates literally as "sanctifying the name" and is also the traditional description of martyrdom in Judaism. It includes accepting the will of God and dying for the sake of Judaism. A classic example is the story of Hannah and her seven sons during the Maccabean uprising. Hannah and her sons were captured, and her sons were put to death one by one because she refused to renounce Judaism. Her sons bravely begged her to hold fast to her faith. In downplaying the military aspects of Hanuka, this story often shared center stage with the miracle of the oil, while the military features of this victory stayed in the shadows. Ultra-Orthodox and Hasidic movements are mixed in their response to the concepts of resistance and martyrdom in terms of the Holocaust. The late Lubavitcher Reb, Menachem Schneerson, claimed that the Holocaust was God's just punishment to redeem the Jews, who had strayed too far from His word. On the other hand, one Lubavitcher rabbi assured me that the

death of even a Jewish atheist in the Holocaust was an act of *Kiddush haShem.*

8. Feingold (1995:58) also argues that Zionism, and especially "its left-wing groups" uses its history of resistance (which he admits is to their credit) for political purposes. In Israel today resistance is viewed far differently than in America and may well be exaggerated as it is claimed by various political factions as their own (Hartman 1996). I saw a post on the Internet in 1994 in which the history of the Warsaw Ghetto Uprising was rewritten to downplay the role of Zionists and emphasize the role of Bundists; one can be assured the opposite occurs as well.

9. A great exception to the claim of organizational avoidance is to be found in the US Holocaust Memorial Museum in Washington, D.C., which is establishing a center for researching resistance. They are also in the process of including resistance as a variable in their database catalog of recorded testimonies from survivors. This is a recent and singular change in the response of Jewish institutions in the United States.

References

Bauer, Yehuda (1984) "They chose life," in Isaac Kowalski (ed.) *Anthology of Armed Jewish Resistance 1939–1945*, Vol. I, pp. 43–52. Brooklyn: Jewish Combatants Publishers House.

Dawidowicz, Lucy S. (1981) *The Holocaust and the Historians.* Cambridge, MA: Harvard University Press.

—— (1986) *The War Against the Jews 1933–1945.* New York: The Free Press.

Edgerton, Robert B. (1988) *Like Lions they Fought: The Zulu War and the Last Black Empire in South Africa.* New York: The Free Press.

—— (1989) *Mau Mau: An African Crucible.* New York: The Free Press.

Feingold, Henry L. (1995) *Bearing Witness: How America and its Jews responded to the Holocaust.* Syracuse, New York: Syracuse University Press.

Finkelstein, Eileen (1996) Personal communication.

Finkelstein, Eileen, and Elizabeth Cohen (n.d.) The Jewish Partisan Project. Proposal for a film and video documentary.

Foxman, Abraham H. (1984) "Resistance: 'The few against the many'," in Isaac Kowalski (ed.) *Anthology of Armed Jewish Resistance 1939–1945*, Vol. I, pp. 85–105. Brooklyn: Jewish Combatants Publishers House.

Martin Cohen

Gaster, Theodore H. (1953) *Festivals of the Jewish Year*. New York: William Morrow & Co.

Gitelman, Zvi (1988) *A Century of Ambivalence: The Jews of Russia and the Soviet Union 1881 to the Present*. New York: Schocken Books.

Hartman, Hershl (1996) Personal communication.

Hilberg, Raul (1978) *The Destruction of the European Jews*. New York: Octagon Books.

Kowalski, Isaac (1984) "Foreword," in Isaac Kowalski (ed.) *Anthology of Armed Jewish Resistance 1939–1945*, vol. I, pp. 11–16. Brooklyn: Jewish Combatants Publishers House.

Kowalski, Isaac, ed. (1984) *Anthology of Armed Jewish Resistance 1939–1945*, vol. I. Brooklyn: Jewish Combatants Publishers House.

—— (1985) *Anthology of Armed Jewish Resistance 1939–1945*, vol. II. Brooklyn: Jewish Combatants Publishers House.

—— (1986) *Anthology of Armed Jewish Resistance 1939–1945*, vol. III. Brooklyn: Jewish Combatants Publishers House.

—— (1991) *Anthology of Armed Jewish Resistance 1939–1945*, vol. IV. Brooklyn: Jewish Combatants Publishers House.

Lazarus, Jacques (1995) Personal communication.

Oz, Amos (1996) "Chekhov in Hebrew: Learning to read at the far end of the world," *The New Yorker*, Dec. 25 1995 and Jan. 1, 1996, pp. 50–65.

Pechersky, Alexander (1967) "Revolt in Sobibor," in Yuri Suhl (ed.) *They Fought Back*, pp. 7–30. New York: Schocken Books.

Peretz, I. L. [1894] (1990) "Bontshe Shvayg," in Ruth R. Wisse (ed.) *The I.L. Peretz Reader*. Trans. Hillel Halkin. New York: Schocken Books.

Schochet, Elijah Judah (1997) Personal Communication.

—— (1994) *The Hasidic Movement and the Gaon of Vilna*. Northvale, NJ: Jason Aronson.

Shapiro, L. (1952) *Bakalakhat LaRusit* [In the Russian Cauldron]. Jerusalem: Lustigman.

Singer, Isaac Bashevis (1972) "Gimpel the fool," in *Gimpel the Fool and Other Stories*. Trans. Saul Bellow. New York: Farrar, Straus & Giroux.

Smoliar (also Smolar), Hersh (1959),"The lambs were legend, the wolves were real." Trans. Hershl Hartman. *Jewish Currents,* vol. 12, April:122–126.

—— (1966) *Resistance in Minsk*. Trans. Hyman J. Lewbin. Oakland, CA: Judah L. Magnes Memorial Museum.

—— (1989) *The Minsk Ghetto: Soviet-Jewish Partisans against the Nazis*. Trans. Max Rosenfeld. New York: Holocaust Library.

Suhl, Yuri (1997) Editor's postscripts to papers in Yuri Suhl (ed.) *They Fought Back*. New York: Schocken Books: 44–50, 115–127, 132–135, 238–239.

Tec, Nechama (1993) *Defiance: The Bielski Partisans*. New York: Oxford University Press.

Wincelberg, Shimon, and Anita Wincelberg (1976) *The Samurai of Vishograd: The Notebooks of Jacob Marateck*. Philadelphia: The Jewish Publication Society of America.

Wisse, Ruth R. (1991) *I.L. Peretz and the Making of Modern Jewish Culture*. Seattle and London: University of Washington Press

Yoran, Shalom (1996a),*The Defiant: A True Story of Jewish Vengeance and Survival*. Trans. Varda Yoran. New York: St. Martin's Press.

——— (1996b) Personal communication.

−3−

From Moral Rejection to Armed Resistance: The Youth Movement in the Ghetto

Eli Tzur

In August 1995 the first post-Communist president of Poland, Lech Walesa, presided at the commemoration of the statue of Poland's founding father, Josef Pilsudski. Opposite the statue stand the arches of the Unknown Soldier's tomb, covered with plaques listing the battles fought by the Poles since the dawn of their history. One plaque is dedicated to the Warsaw ghetto uprising, a military act performed by the Jews cut off from their Polish compatriots. As a military operation, the Warsaw ghetto uprising was of limited importance; as an historical event it is a symbol of its era. World War II was a total war, which abolished the difference between the front lines and the rear, soldiers and civilians. The Warsaw ghetto uprising was the first revolt of the civil population in Europe and, like all the subsequent uprisings, it was an act of the people. But it was organized by a close-knit body of resisters.

Resistance as a social phenomenon was a natural outcome of total war and differed from state to state according to national traditions and status in the Nazi empire. Resistance was generally one pole of the social spectrum when the opposite pole was the trend of cooperating with the Germans or adapting in order to survive of the majority. These features of resistance were transformed in the Jewish world, mainly because the Jews knew they were doomed to destruction, regardless of their views or acts. But this desperate awareness, which contradicted human consciousness about mortality, could not be accepted by the whole of the Jewish population; it was the dividing line between the Jewish resisters in the Warsaw ghetto and the inmates of other ghettos. Understanding the finality of the "Final Solution" did not automatically lead to the willingness to fight it. This required a spiritual process, connected with charismatic leadership, relevant ideology, and extant organizations that could be transformed into resistance units.

In 1944 resistance in Hungary acted mainly as an agent for rescue by hiding; in Belgium and France, it opened escape routes; in Poland, the Soviet Union and Lithuania it centered upon armed resistance. The development of the Jewish resistance was a prolonged process, which culminated in full-scale activity after the almost total annihilation of the Jewish population. Jewish guerrilla units appeared only after the destruction of the ghettos, and were composed of the escapees from these ghettos.

This chapter focuses on armed resistance and on those ideological factors leading to resistance. During the first two postwar decades most Holocaust research centered upon the phenomenon of resistance, neglecting many other facets of Jewish Holocaust experience. This concentration stemmed from three main factors. One was the need to reconstruct Jewish national pride, deeply damaged during the war years. The second was a desire to place the European Jews within the framework of the general anti-Nazi combatants. The third was the political infighting within the Jewish political arena, which used the issue of resistance in order to strengthen the status of various parties, particularly from the Zionist and non-Zionist left wing. During the later period the term "resistance" was substituted by a more ambivalent term of "day-to-day stand," which included not only active resistance but also every type of civil disobedience to the Nazi authorities. Even if this new outlook was historically correct, it pushed research into the resistance phenomenon into a corner. The importance of resistance dwells not only in its size and effectiveness, but in its psychological impact on ordinary Jews who didn't participate in the resistance movement but were affected by it in their everyday activities during and after the Holocaust. This interpretation of resistance endows it with ideological significance and therefore it is impossible to view resistance without its ideological connection.

The resistance movement, as opposed to acts of desperation or revenge, was a prolonged psychological and ideological process, formulated at some stage into an organizational framework. This process could develop only from an active ideology which presented its holders in opposition to the existing circumstances and believed in the possibility of changing the cultural and political ecology. Therefore the resisters usually had a previous history as members of anti-establishment groups. In Polish–Jewish interwar society this task was fulfilled by the left-wing organizations, many of them Zionist. The left-wing Zionist youth movement (the so called "pioneer movements") opposed the Jewish communities as corrupt and stagnant, the Polish social regime as anti-Jewish and anti-social, and the prevailing culture as harmful to the education of a "new Jew." During the war years this total negation of the existing society and its culture was translated into active participation in the resistance. The resistance, its ideological background and its youth movement roots, are the main theme of this chapter.

Memorial literature abounds with stories of people who fought to survive and of those who fought to revenge the murder of their families. In many cases resisters merged a response to national abuse with a striving for social change. While few Jewish political entities were absent from the armed resistance, this chapter deals with the history of an organization for which the struggle against the Nazis was an ideological issue. This organization was notable for the predominance of youth groups and the hegemony of the Jewish non-religious left. The qualities of youth, such as the physical ability to survive hardship and the resilience to accept the unacceptable, were advantages. The lack of family obligations, another advantage, arose pragmatically from the communes, based on common kitchens, in which the young people lived. In most of the Polish ghettos the Jewish resistance encompassed political parties with their youth organizations and youth movements. In interwar Poland the absolute majority of the Jewish youth movements belonged to the Zionist left wing, of which the oldest, largest and ideologically most extreme was Hashomer Hatzair (the Young Guard).

The Jewish youth organizations initially appeared on the eve of World War 1 and developed throughout the war years, influenced by the Polish scouting movement, the German Free Youth Movement, particularly the Wandervogel, and the Zionist movement. Soon after World War 1 ended, some of these groups opted for work within the Polish Jewish community, while others, swayed by the nationalist fervor of the Polish population, emigrated to Palestine. Members of emigrating groups decided that only the kibbutz offered an appropriate framework for settlement, thereby moving toward a leftist ideology, later expressed in Marxist terms. The ideological upheaval created a series of splits in the original youth movement which, in the mid-1920s, charted the map of the youth movements in Poland.

For the Jews in Poland the 1930s were a period of decline, marked by a prolonged economic crisis and, after Pilsudski's death, a crisis of legitimacy in the Polish state. Among the Jews a gap grew between those who weathered the economic crisis and those who were pauperized. The economic crisis and the political instability reinforced latent Polish antisemitism. The impoverished Polish peasants and the middle class moved from boycotting Jewish shops to small township pogroms, the most famous of which occurred in Przytyk. The local Jews defended themselves, usually with the help of the self-defense groups mobilized from the radical anti-Communist Socialist Bund. This pattern strongly influenced the behavior of the youth movements during the Holocaust. On the eve of World War II, large sections of the Jewish population, including almost all the youth movements, felt alienated from their compatriots. But with the outbreak of the war the youth movements played an important role, especially in the Jewish resistance. "The rebellion was the handwork of all Jewish youth movements, the climax in the life of a generation of Jewish youth, a historical proof of its unparalleled idealism, of its self-sacrifice and dedication."

Although many youth movements participated in the events, Hashomer Hatzair played a special role. From its ranks came some of the major figures of the Jewish resistance, including the commander of the Warsaw ghetto uprising, Mordechai Anielewicz. With its leftist ideology it bridged the gap between Zionist and non-Zionist socialist and Communist parties. Its intellectual traditions were responsible for the survival of its archives and underground press on a larger scale than those of any other organization. To guide us in the hell of the Holocaust, I have chosen the Virgil-like Shmuel Braslaw, the chief ideologue of the movement and an intimate friend of Anielewicz.

The Invasion of Poland and the German Conquest

On September 1, 1939 German troops invaded Poland. The Jewish youth movements had based their *modus operandi* on the event of war, expecting their graduates, including group leaders, to be mobilized. The Hashomer Hatzair in Poland nominated a new national command, including women and men under the call-up age, which included many of the future Resistance leaders such as Anielewicz and Braslaw. All the plans were based on the assumption that the war would follow the pattern of World War 1 on the Western Front. After the initial German success, the battle line would stabilize in Central Poland, enabling the youth movements to organize themselves under the new wartime conditions.

In reality, Poland became the first victim of the "blitzkrieg." Amidst the German bombardments the Polish civil defense commander announced that the men in Western Poland due to be mobilized should move to the East to be organized into military units. These groups joined the pre-mobilized men, and the mobilization plan deteriorated into a mass movement of refugees, which prevented the Polish army from moving to the front. Above the clogged roads the German planes strafed the helpless civilians, thus increasing the chaos. Among these masses were members of Hashomer Hatzair, including Anielewicz and Braslaw, who left the capital with the would-be soldiers.[2] Braslaw carried the movement's banner on his body, and was wounded by robbers.[3] By the time the refugees arrived in the East, Poland had ceased to exist.

In accordance with the secret clauses of the Soviet–German agreement, the Soviets occupied Poland's eastern provinces, and the Jewish inhabitants and the flood of refugees looked upon them as their salvation. The Jews viewed Russian society not only as their savior, but as a political system without ethnic discrimination. Within a few months, however, many discovered that the Soviets regarded the middle classes, to which the majority of the Jews belonged, as a social enemy, who were exiled to Siberia. But even before this stage, the Zionists, including the socialist wing, discovered that the Communists viewed them as an ideological enemy, to be eradicated. The Hashomer Hatzair refugees from Warsaw, who had just survived the terror of escaping to the East, had to provide an answer to the dilemma posed by the Soviet presence, for their ideological education had depicted the Soviet system as the future of the world. However, their fidelity to the idea of Zionism never wavered.

The concrete solution was to move from the Soviet-occupied regions of Poland to Vilna (today Vilnius), the capital of Lithuania, occupied by the Soviets and then transferred to the Lithuanians, and the only visible outlet to the free world. Toward the end of 1939 Vilna became the haven of Jewish parties, including Zionist youth movements. For many, the decision to move to Vilna presented an ideological dilemma, as Soviet rule was now seen as a paradise lost.[4]

In Vilna, where the contacts with the outside world, including Palestine, were renewed, the leaders of the youth movements discussed the resurrection and immediate goals of the movements in divided Poland. The Hashomer Hatzair senior leaders decided to reestablish the movement in Soviet-occupied Poland. Aware of the possibility of NKVD persecution, the organization planned to stay underground to avoid frontal clashes with the authorities. The goal, surviving until Soviet policies or circumstances would change, was based on the view that existence was more important than ideological sympathies.

Before the war, the Nazi authorities in Germany supported Hahalutz, the umbrella organization of the Zionist youth movements, as an instrument for the rapid removal of Jewish youth from the Reich. Following the German pattern, the Hashomer Hatzair leaders in Vilna and Palestine formulated the following objective: "We presume that in a short time there will be tremendous opportunities to build a mass organization, moved by a hope of emigrating to Palestine. Those who organize this spontaneous movement will control it."[5]

In order to resurrect the movement and organize emigration, two pairs of volunteer activists, who did not look obviously Jewish, were sent to Warsaw: Tosia Altmann with Mordechai Anielewicz, and Joseph Kaplan with Shmuel Braslaw. Typical of a youth of 20, Braslaw volunteered to return, a decision which mixed sentiment with ideology, Although he longed for his parents, who remained in Warsaw, he also wanted to fight against Nazi Germany, which he saw as the epitome of wickedness, anti-humanism and antisemitism.

Braslaw and Kaplan arrived in Warsaw at the beginning of March, 1940. Their initial goal was to rebuild the Warsaw Hashomer Hatzair organization, which had officially ceased to exist during the first week of September, 1939. The young members, many of whom had participated in Warsaw's defense, were confined to their homes with their families by the German curfew. The idleness following the hectic activity in September led to loneliness, and they reestablished their groups. The Vilna leaders moved from place to place, reorganizing the movement, although their activity was curtailed by the German ghettoization of the Polish Jewish population, which prevented contact between groups in different towns. However, a system of contact was maintained through underground couriers, who were mainly girls with a non-Jewish appearance. This was the only way to keep the youth movement together, to carry out ideological and organizational changes. The life of the couriers was poetically described by the chief courier, Tosia Altmann, in an underground publication: "On dark rainy evenings one knocks on unlit windows, and steps through doors with a whisper – the movement's command . . . In the all-embracing chaos we searched for a road of our own".[6] These contacts had a profound impact, and in ghettos such as Lodz, where the Jews were completely isolated, the local organization continued to act according to the guidelines they developed.

The movement distributed two gospels everywhere: Hashomer Hatzair is back, and it organizes its members to leave Poland. The movement collected data on candidates for emigration, and looked for routes outside the country. When it became clear that no legal ways existed, its emissaries began to search for an illegal border crossing, presumably to Slovakia. But in the summer of 1940, amidst the ghettoization of the Polish Jewry, the dream of mass emigration petered out. The major issues remained on the agenda of Hashomer Hatzair: to create an educational message and to adapt ideology to the new circumstances.

Moral Guidance under Wartime Conditions

The war and the ensuing defeat destroyed the edifice of the moral world for Polish youth. For the young Jews who, during the Warsaw blockade, had temporarily felt themselves to be partners in and contributors to Polish society, the moral collapse was even harsher. For the first time in their history Polish Jews were put outside the framework of Polish society, outside Polish history, becoming an unseen people. The ghetto walls completed this process. Combined with the hunger and epidemics of ghettoization, a deep moral crisis was created among the Jewish youth, as described by Shmuel Braslaw, in his first printed article:

> Today the leading imperative of youth is survival. Principles and ideals have disappeared. The slogan "eat and drink as we live today and no one knows what tomorrow will bring" rules supreme in the world of the young generation . . . In this way a slave's soul is molded and his backbone crouches in kowtow. Our young people learn to doff their hats when encountering Germans, smiling smiles of servitude and obedience. And deep in their hearts burns a dream: to be like them – handsome, strong and self-confident. To be able to kick, beat and insult, unpunished. To despise others, as the Germans despise us today.[7]

In this article Braslaw dwelt on the link between moral apathy and mental servitude, and the admiration for naked power, and claimed that this combination evolved in a particular human type which he saw among the ghetto police.

The youth movement, presented as an antithesis to this attitude, actively opposed its moral nihilism and servitude. The values the movement emphasized, such as "rowing against the current," were embedded in the tradition of Jewish humanist socialism, and crystallized the problematic of Jewish existence under the Nazi terror. From its early beginnings, Hashomer Hatzair ethics opposed the adult world based on bourgeois norms, and used education to create a counter-culture to the surrounding society. This mental abyss deepened when the movement concentrated on activity in Palestine while declaring detachment, the so-called "negation of the diaspora," from the problems of Jewish society in diaspora. Under the conditions of being cut off from Palestine and enclosed within the ghetto, together with all the Jews, the detachment from the Jewish establishment was translated into a cultural definition: "For us, 'going against the current' is traditional, as we always have done it . . . We are fighting alone, against the ruling terror, the all-pervading fear . . . We fight against the mood of the mob running amok in the fit of 'grab and eat'." Another article in the same publication describes the difference between the Fascist ideology and the movement's principles: "Today the revolutionary imperative is freedom of conscience, the preservation of the human principles fought by Fascism, which can be achieved only by dedication to the ethics of Hashomer Hatzair."[8]

The term "against the current" was associated with two spheres of the movement – ideology, and the code of behavior of an individual member and his age group. Ideological disputes were the realm of the small leadership stratum, and mainly influenced relations with the political sphere, while the educational code molded the members' everyday life. Before the war this sphere included informal education, scouting games and social activities, which aimed to develop the member's individual character and group cohesion. Informal education, a prominent item in the movement's agenda, became more important in the ghetto, as the Germans forbade all official educational systems. In the Lodz organization, the only locality where documents of day-to-day activities survived the war, in answer to the questions about the need for education, one of the young women, in April, 1943, wrote the following: "In the ghetto we suffer harsh conditions: constant hunger and the search for food . . . Where hungry people always return in their thoughts to the gray reality . . . I find time for geography, history, life in Palestine."[9]

In Warsaw the older members of the organization participated in a long seminar, which took place daily in November, 1941. The lecturers were the most prominent intellectuals of the ghetto, and one of them, the historian Emanuel Ringelblum, left a brief description: "I gave the lectures a number of times in the Hashomer seminar . . . Looking at the youngsters' shining faces, one could forget the war around us. The seminar took place across from a German army post, but they often forgot it ."[10]

The informal education served the manifold purpose of selecting the cadres, clarifying their positions, finding an aim in life in an atmosphere of apathy and escapism from the squalid reality. For the younger members the goals were achieved by scouts' games, some sounding improbable in the ghetto reality, like tracking in the ghetto confines. The most important educational instrument was the ghetto itself. In Warsaw all the youth movements organized its graduates in kibbutzim centered upon communal kitchens. The kibbutz quarters were the center of organizational activities and the meeting place of the leadership, besides being the feeding center of the members. The existence of a communal entity was *per se* a message of group solidarity and cohesion.

In Warsaw the groups established food banks to which every member donated a slice of bread or a potato for the less fortunate. In the hungry ghetto this act was not only self-sacrifice by the young members, but also a denial of food for the whole family. Nevertheless, all the groups kept these food banks.[11] In the Lodz ghetto, when the Germans demanded 1,500 young workers in February, 1944, the *Judenrat* (Jewish council appointed by the Germans) decided to send the movements' senior groups. As these groups refused to deliver themselves up for the transport and their food cards were confiscated by the authorities, the members donated food in order to save their colleagues.[12] Thus the educational framework of "against the current" became the basis of Hashomer Hatzair resistance through the prism of its changing ideology.

The Changing Ideology

The traditional ideology of Hashomer Hatzair, termed the "stages theory," was formulated in 1937 with the founding of its kibbutz movement, and was based on three principles: Zionism expressed as a resettlement of the Jewish nation throughout Palestine and the neighboring countries; socialism, interpreted as national ownership of land and capital; and the hegemony of communal settlement in the kibbutzim. The first stage of the future development of the Jewish community was the early evolution of its economy by the common effort of Jews worldwide regardless of their class allegiance. The second and revolutionary stage would occur when Palestine became a socialist state with the active participation of the Arab masses. While accepting the goals of the Soviet system, the leaders nevertheless deplored its praxis.

The Warsaw leadership was split on the basis of age. Tosia Altmann and Joseph Kaplan, in their mid-twenties, wanted the previous ideological line to continue. Mordechai Anielewicz and Shmuel Braslaw, in their beginning twenties, demanded changes imposed by three main issues: the definition of the war, the redefinition of relations with the movement in Palestine and the formulation of the movement status in the ghetto community.

At the Vilna sessions the vision of the emerging war reflected the existing stage of the military struggle: a strictly military encounter between European powers aimed at acquiring territories and political influence. But Anielewicz and Braslaw saw the war as a total clash between the socialist and the Fascist ideologies, the war becoming the preamble of the world revolution. They presented these views at the movement convention in May, 1940.[13] Although the convention toed the line of Kaplan and Altmann, who preferred the continuity of the traditional line,[14]

Anielewicz and Braslaw continued their efforts to change this line. Braslaw's argument combined the fate of the Jews with the war situation: "When the . . . workers in uniform will be ready to aim their rifles against those who send them, the victorious army will move from the East . . . to bring freedom to the peoples . . . to create a better, socialist future . . . but meanwhile, we, the Jews of Poland, face annihilation."[15] Braslaw believed that only this picture of the future could save the movement from nihilism and apathy, and feared that any outside development would come too late for the Jews. Being aware of the Jewish weaknesses, he relied on the external powers, believing that the Soviets would avenge the death of Polish Jewry. In the ghetto's world of no hope and no solution, where the only possible action was passive survival, Braslaw's outlook appeared fresh and promising.

A few months later the movement accepted his approach: "The awakening bell of the approaching revolution . . . is the voice of the socialist state . . . the Hebrew people do believe that a day will come when the sun will shine through the dark clouds."[16] This ideological construction depended on a single fact – the German aggression against the Soviet Union. And in June, 1941 the German army did invade the Soviet Union. For the movement's leadership, this attack was proof of the righteousness of its way, and the beginning of salvation. As soon as the clandestine radio broadcast the news, the movement published a leaflet for all its members, which sent blessings to the Red Army which they believed would destroy the ghetto walls: "members of the movement, we call upon you to do your utmost to cause any damage to the German army, and to make propaganda among the masses. Long live the Soviet Union. Long live the socialist intervention and revolutionary war. Long live the national and social liberation of the Jewish nation in the Soviet Palestine."[17] As the movement predicted, the German invasion of the Soviet Union transformed the nature of the war, changing it from a military clash into an ideological struggle.

For Hashomer Hatzair, Palestine and its kibbutzim were the center of its ideology. The movement expected its senior members to go to Palestine and join a kibbutz because of the process called self-realization. Following the image of the development of the war into the revolution, Braslaw and his friends created a picture of the steps leading to the future Palestine: "Our main Zionist conception is the creation of the Jewish Palestine within the Soviet Union."[18] In the May 1940 council, Braslaw presented the new vision, connecting the future of Zionism with the Soviet victory: "Zionism cannot fulfill its program under British rule; its victory is totally connected to the socialist victory . . . our destiny depends on the victory of the revolution in Europe, which will lead to the solution of the Jewish question along our principles."[19]

This scenario, improbable as it seems today, derived from the fact that the traditional Zionist program contradicted the movement's new vision of the war and the Soviet Union, and the top leadership wanted to combine revolutionary socialism, maximalist Zionism and kibbutz hegemony. In the Lodz ghetto organization, isolated from the outside world, in a group newsletter one young woman described her image of Palestine: "I would like to build the motherland with my two hands, to till the land, live on kibbutz, change the wasteland to blooming gardens. After the work, return home singing . . . Then mother woke me up."[20] The idea of Palestine was used to escape the sordid ghetto reality, and became an instrument of survival. If in Lodz, where the movement stagnated at the earlier ideological stage, the idea of Palestine canceled the reality of the war, in Warsaw it was an instrument for mobilizing the rank and file to awareness of the war and for active participation in it.

The views of the Hashomer Hatzair on the internal scene influenced and were, in turn, molded by its attitude toward the external world, its relations with the Jewish authorities, with the *Judenrat*, (the Jewish Council appointed by the Nazis to rule the ghettos), and with the opposition parties. In Lodz, where the youth movements were organized in self-managed agricultural farms in the suburb of Maryszyn, it was popular with the youth movements, as revealed by their parade in September, 1940. The movements established a police force in Maryszyn, an obligation which only the Hashomer Hatzair refused to accept.[21] In Lodz, every occupation and activity depended on the goodwill of the *Judenrat*, a dependence which weakened opportunities for opposition to the authorities. In isolated Lodz, no meaningful resistance ever evolved.

If the Lodz organization was the symbol of barren continuity, the Warsaw organization, the center of the Polish movement, represented a new approach to the outside world. In Warsaw the ghetto dwellers were occupationally less dependent on the *Judenrat*; the total control of the workplaces emerged only in the summer of 1942. If the welfare system in Lodz stemmed directly from the *Judenrat*, in Warsaw there were volunteer welfare groups, such as ZTOS (Jewish Society for Social Assistance), which preserved their independence, partly because of the financial assistance of the American Jewish Joint Distribution Committee. ZTOS supplied the institutional roof for those opposition groups, like Hashomer Hatzair, which refused to cooperate directly with the *Judenrat*.. In 1942 ZTOS became the cradle of the emerging resistance movement, and also supplied the Hashomer Hatzair underground press organized by Braslaw.

The Hashomer Hatzair press was a continuous effort to educate, inform and guide its members, and to influence the outside world. Among the large number of ghetto underground presses, its publications played a prominent role; out of 250 underground publications in the Warsaw ghetto, it printed 36, the second largest number of publications after the Communists.[22] The newsletters were initially aimed at the members of the Warsaw local organization, but soon became a source of guidance to the country-wide movement and the ideological center. The publication of two anthologies, in 1941 and 1942, *Iton Hatnua*, shows the pressure from outside Warsaw to receive the new line and the importance it had for the leaders to promulgate it.

The new line endangered the movement's ties with its traditional partners in the Labor Zionist movement. Reliance upon the Soviet Union as the source of salvation and the prediction of a Communist Jewish Palestine contradicted the ideological line of almost all Zionist parties and was viewed as heresy. Hashomer Hatzair's ideology made it acceptable to the Communists, who started their guerrilla movement in the winter of 1942, while preserving its close relations with elements of the Polish scouting movement led by Irena Adamowicz. In the latter part of 1941 the tensions with other Zionist youth movements lessened and at the beginning of 1942 it became the lynchpin of the opposition, connecting the Communists and the socialist Zionist organizations. When the opposition established the Anti-Fascist Bloc in April, 1942, the first resistance alliance in Warsaw, Hashomer Hatzair, was one of its main initiators.

The Sources of Revolt

Hashomer Hatzair responded to the reality of the German occupation and the psychological breakdown of the Jewish community through moral opposition. The attitude of "against the current" revitalized the movement and was naturally accepted by the local leaders all over Poland. Two main unforeseen deficiencies were embedded in this concept: a totally introspective point of view, and no possibility of active policies outside the movement. But even for activist leaders, like Anielewicz and Braslaw, the meaning of those deficiencies was not clear, as their views focused upon building their movement. Only on the eve of the uprising did Anielewicz admit that the movement lost vital time on education, without preparing itself for the battle.[23] Facing the battle, Anielewicz preferred not to see that without moral preparation and social cohesion, the movement would fail to organize itself into a combat force.

In the First of May Order the High Command demanded of all the members that they do their utmost to avoid the press gangs which kidnapped passers-by on the ghetto streets for German Army work teams. This attitude was a practical outcome of the "against the current" mentality, based upon avoidance. Two months later, following the news of the Nazi invasion of the Soviet Union, the members were called upon to sabotage German military effort and to assist the Red Army.[24] In spite of the militant wording, the actual meaning did not differ from the previous declaration. Even in November 1941, at the general assembly of the Warsaw organization, in which more than 500 persons participated, the Order of the Day called for the movement to "rebel against the reality and not to surrender . . . to guard the purity of the banners and to continue the moral preparation for pioneers in Zion."[25] Even then the movement still presented the rebellion in moral terms and hoped for active salvation from outside forces.

Holocaust historiography views the German invasion of the Soviet Union as a watershed, the beginning of the physical annihilation of European Jewry. The rumors of the mass massacres of the Jews filtered to Warsaw and were reflected in the Order of the Day of November 23, which mentions massacres in Minsk, Kiev and Odessa. As direct testimony of events in Lithuania was given at the meeting, the order emphasized the deaths of the Hashomer Hatzair members in Lithuania.

The German advances in the East enabled the High Command in Warsaw to renew the severed ties with the movement in the East, especially with the Vilna organization. The encounter between the radical ideology from Warsaw and the belief that the massacres in the East were just the beginning of a total destruction of European Jewry, as was happening in Vilna, culminated in the first call to the Jewish population "not to go as sheep to the slaughter." The underlying essence of this call was a belief that the Jews had only two options, to die with dignity or die without dignity. Only this view could justify an anti-Nazi rebellion, as in any other condition an armed rebellion could result in a massacre of the Jews, a German revenge for the Jewish provocation. Only this belief, in Vilna and later in Warsaw, could encourage people to fund resistance movements in the ghettos. The text of this manifesto was written by a movement leader in Vilna, Abba Kovner, and read by him and by Tosia Altmann at an assembly of the Zionist youth movements on New Year's Eve of 1942. In the wake of the Manifesto united Partisan organizations emerged in Vilna, while Altmann returned to Warsaw to bring the new tidings. But the Warsaw Jews, including the Hashomer Hatzair leadership, preferred to believe that the events in the East were unthinkable in Warsaw.

The mental change was a result of the rumor about the last battle of the eastern township of Nowogrudek, where the Jews fought the Germans, dying in their endeavor. Research shows that the Battle of Nowogrudek never occurred in reality, but the myth appeared as an answer to an acute need to show an alternative to passivity, to translate the Vilna message into concrete reality. It appeared at the right psychological moment, as the decision was being made to revolt. The watershed was not limited to Hashomer Hatzair, as in March 1942; Zionist political parties met the Bund representatives in order to discuss the establishment of a resistance movement, a meeting that proved fruitless. Hashomer Hatzair refused to participate in this meeting, which had been arranged under the aegis of political parties.

The publication of the Nowogrudek essay in *Jutrznia*, the movement's only newsletter aimed at the broad public, shows that the mental process of moving from spiritual opposition to armed resistance was over and that the movement presented the new message to the ghetto population. The length of this process was the sign of the youth movement's imminent feature: to strive for consensus after a prolonged, meandering debate. The internal results of this debate appeared in the first, hesitant organizational steps, such as the subdivision of the senior groups into five-men sections and the establishment of an arsenal. In the spring of 1942 the movement kept a single revolver in a secret cachet, shown to all important visitors.[26] Future plans centered upon transferring the combat sections to the forest, where the movement's partisan unit would fight in the formation of the Communist group. This conception of future activities was the base of cooperation with the Communists in the ranks of the emerging Anti-Fascist Bloc. While the various groups in the ghetto formed preliminary plans of armed resistance, the German blueprint for annihilating the Jews of Warsaw was ready. On April 18 German police units entered the ghetto and arrested sixty eminent political figures of the opposition. For Hashomer Hatzair's leadership, convinced as were their comrades in Vilna that any German act led to the total liquidation of the Jewish people, the limited German acts of terror signaled their intentions. In the wake of the German arrests, the Warsaw organization was dissolved: the senior groups were reorganized into combat teams and the juniors were sent home. The process, which began with the return of the Vilna quartet to Warsaw and the movement's reconstruction, made the full circle. Braslaw, according to contemporary evidence, may have been the initiator of this move.[27]

During the summer of 1942 the Warsaw Hashomer Hatzair ceased to exist as a youth movement, without yet becoming an armed resistance movement, as the Anti-Fascist Bloc disintegrated without an apparent heir. The summer of 1942 marked the end of the thousand-year Jewish history in Poland, as the trains rolling toward the four extermination camps – Chelmo, Treblinka, Sobibor and Belzec – brought Jewish multitudes to their sudden death. The turn of the Warsaw ghetto, numbering almost half a million inhabitants, the so-called "Great Action," began on July 22, 1942. During this operation more than 250,000 were sent to their deaths. On the eve of the ghetto blockade Anielewicz left the ghetto on a tour of the local organizations in the province to bring them the message of an armed resistance. In the footsteps of his meetings with the members of the movement, local resistance cells appeared. His visits helped to crystallize the ideas of armed resistance, ideas that were born autonomously, but were often not clearly defined. Places detached from the movement's mainstream did not transform their ideology.

Shocked by the German brutality in Warsaw, the day after the action began, public figures from almost all the political formations, including Hashomer Hatzair, represented by Kaplan and Braslaw, met to decide upon their response to the German actions. The meeting ended in discord between those who proposed active resistance to the German acts and those who opposed it. A week later, on July 28, representatives of the Zionist-Socialist youth movements decided to establish the Jewish Combat Organization (JCO).

The new organization had to decide upon the means, territory and weapons to be used for the fight against the Germans. Hashomer Hatzair had an advantage over other founders of the JCO, being connected both with the Communists, who were aware of its pro-Soviet organization, and to the Polish scouts, who now joined the general underground Home Army (Armia Krajowa). Therefore it was natural that the JCO emissary to non-Jewish Warsaw came from the movement's ranks. In spite of these connections, until the end of August the organization received few revolvers and hand grenades from the Communist sources. The question of how and where to fight the Germans split the JCO command. The majority adhered to the plans developed at the Bloc, of sending fighters to the forests to wage guerrilla warfare against the Germans. But the groups smuggled from one ghetto encountered the Germans and did not survive. This tragic reality strengthened the conviction of those who wanted to fight as urban guerrillas on the streets of the ghetto.

Braslaw supported the idea of the urban guerrillas, but for different reasons. From the onset of the action he tried to convince the ghetto inhabitants to refuse to obey German orders to show up at the embarkation site, to refuse to step on the trains, and by these simple acts of obstruction, to paralyze the German operation. With a group of movement members he tried to glue leaflets containing this message to walls, but was attacked by the inhabitants who feared that this was an act of *agents provocateurs*.[28] Disillusioned, Braslaw did not believe in the popular uprising, but demanded that the organization members fight the Germans and the Jewish police by any available means. He saw the Jewish population marching without any sign of resistance to the trains and from there to Treblinka. Toward the end of August the destination of the trains was clear, as members of the Bund and Hashomer Hatzair returned from there and reported what they saw. Braslaw demanded an act of defiance before the last of the Warsaw Jews disappeared in the fire pits of Treblinka. He therefore demanded acts of resistance that would save the abused Jewish honor. Braslaw pushed for immediate actions, a hectically demanding activity that did not fit the few and minor acts of JCO. He led an arson attack on abandoned houses to prevent Jewish property from being collected by the Germans and discovered a cachet of jackknives, but he saw in his deeds a minute symbol of defiance. His mood was captured and immortalized by Ringelblum, for whom he personified resistance. In all his copious notes, in spite of their acquaintance, Ringelblum mentioned Braslaw in a terse note entitled "The Resistance": "The young remained alone on the battlefield, the romantics and visionaries. Shmuel could not live after the ghetto tragedy."[29] Braslaw's mental attitude was compounded by the new material conditions in which he and other senior members of the movement found themselves. During the Great Action the only means of survival was receiving a labor card from one of the factories, "the shops," in the ghetto's territory. Braslaw and other senior members of the JCO were employed by A. Landau, whose daughter Margalit was a member of Hashomer Hatzair, and who became the first member of the movement to execute a police officer. During most of the day Braslaw was confined to the shops, thinking about the Jewish tragedy and planning action to avenge it.

On September 3, a German police patrol arrested Joseph Kaplan, who had been denounced by a member of the group sent by the JCO outside the ghetto to join the partisan movement, and who fell into German hands. Learning about the arrest, Braslaw hectically tried to organize Kaplan's release. A German patrol passing on one of the ghetto streets stopped Braslaw as he was hurrying to organize the rescue, checked the contents of his pockets, and finding one of his jackknives, shot him on the spot. At night his comrades removed his corpse and buried him on the edge of an abandoned football stadium near the Jewish graveyard. Kaplan was executed as he was transferred from the prison to the deportation point. On this day of disasters the Germans discovered the tiny arsenal of the JCO.

A few days later the Great Action petered out, and the remnants returned to the ghetto streets. Only now did the spiritual change which the Hashomer Hatzair members underwent at the beginning of the year became common to all ghetto survivors. From now on, the feeling was that never again would the Germans be able to transport the Jews of Warsaw without resistance. Only after the Great Action did the JCO become a general resistance movement, as the left-wing political parties, including the Communists, joined the organization. The new character of the JCO, and the supply of weapons from outside the ghetto, meager but on a much larger scale than before, enabled the organization to fight against the Jewish authorities nominated by the Germans, and to become the real force in the ghetto. On Passover Eve, April 19, 1943, the ability of the organization to fight, and the readiness of the population to resist, were put to the ultimate test as the armed uprising broke out.

Although Shmuel Braslaw died half a year before the uprising, his name appears on the list which the JCO sent after the rebellion to the Polish Government in Exile, enumerating the casualties of the uprising.[30] On the same date, in the Lodz ghetto, the members of the Hashomer Hatzair organizations read the proclamation of the local command: "Even now we believe that the liberation will come. It will not arrive as an armed uprising but as an inner struggle in which our weapons are patience, self-control, and hope."[31] The Warsaw ghetto uprising, confined within the ghetto walls and isolated from the Polish population, was doomed to fail. In spite of its preordained failure, the uprising had an impact throughout the world, including the German command, the Polish resistance and the public opinion of the free world. Although the ghetto uprising was followed by other civilian uprisings, it differs from them in one major way. While the other uprisings took place on the eve of the liberation of these populations by outside forces, the ghetto rebellion took place as an act of final defiance. When the other uprisings tried to influence the immediate future, the Warsaw ghetto uprising tried to mold the perspective of the future historians of the Jewish Holocaust in Poland.

The historiography of the Warsaw ghetto uprising tended to attribute the actions of groups participating in the JCO to a natural wish to resist the German policy of a "Final Solution." The participation in uprising was seen as a determined result of the ideology of the rank and file. According to the underground publications of various groups, there is a tendency to interpret the term "resistance" as armed fighting. As I have tried to show, the definition of resistance changed from spiritual opposition to armed resistance during a period of about a year. This change was an outcome of ideological radicalization, relative freedom of contacts with the outside world and the personal charisma of the leaders. In those places where isolation prevented contacts with the center in Warsaw, this change did not occur and the local organizations continued to follow the traditional line. In the case of Hashomer Hatzair, the ideological radicalization was connected with growing sympathy with the Soviet Union, even at a time when the Soviets were seen as a loyal ally of Hitler. The ideology was conditioned by the youth movement's education, but it caused political isolation in the ghetto, which permitted the internal development of the movement without external interference.

In all ideological, political and educational processes the figure of Shmuel Braslaw is prominent and crucial. Believing, from the outset of the war, in the total bestiality of the German regime and its determination to exterminate the Jews of Europe, he tried to prepare himself and his movement for the final battle and looked for comrades-in-arms. Mentally he found himself in the impossible situation of one condemned to death, surrounded by people refusing to accept the fact of mortality. The dichotomy between him and his closest entourage and the surrounding Jewish public opinion created his political extremism and, at a later period, his total despair. From his point of view, the Warsaw ghetto uprising was a victory because it saved the last property of the human being who had lost everything – human dignity. In spite of his Marxist fervor, at the end Braslaw fought for a virtue that does not appear in Marxist manuals – national honor. Throughout his ghetto period he tried to express this attitude in Marxist terms, but the dividing line between him and his movement and the Jewish nationalists was the belief that Jewish national honor is an expression of a basic human dignity. One can therefore say on his unmarked grave, *ecce homo*.

Notes

A.R. Ringelbaum Archives.
A.M. Moreshet Archives in Givat Haviva, Israel.
C.A.H.H. Central Archives of Hashomer Hatzair, Givat Haviva.

1. Kaligsberg 1974:138.

2. Shmuel B.: In Warsaw's organization, M'maamakim, Kaunus, January, 1940
3. Sh. Braslaw to Fima Braslaw, Ukmerga, 3.2.1940, in possession of F. Braslaw, Kibbutz Amir, Israel.
4. (Braslaw) (1941).
5. Z. Gayer to the Palestinian executive of Hashomar Hatzair Vilna 13.2.940 C.A.H.H., H-3.28(3).
6. T: In the movement, El-Al, Warsaw, April 1941.
7. S. "Plomienie," September 1940.
8. Iton Hatnua b'.
9. A M. D.I 198.
10. Ringelblum (1989).
11. Aliza Melamed's testimony, A.M. D.23.
12. A.M. D.I. 218.
13. Iton Hatnua b'.
14. Iton Hatnua b'.
15. S. "Plomienie", September 1940.
16. Order of the Day for May 1, Neged Hazerem (against the stream), 3(14), April 1941, Spring 1942.
17. A. R. Ring /1/111/1922.
18. Iton Hatnua b'.
19. Ibid.
20. A.M. D.I. 264.
21. Decisions of the Council of the agricultural groups 15.9.1940 (A.M. D.I. 286).
22. The Jewish underground press in Warsaw, 5 vols. Yad Vashem, Jerusalem.
23. Ringelblum (1989:14).
24. The H.C. Manifesto, Ring /I/III/1922.
25. The Order of the Day, 23.11.1941.
26. Gutman (1963:197–200).
27. Aliza Melamed's testimony, M.A. D.2.3, p. 35.
28. Tzukerman (1982:98) Tel Aviv: Am Oved.
29. Ringelblum (1993: vol. 1, p. 399).
30. B. Mark, Walka I Zaglada Warszawskiego Getta, aneks 1.
31. Order of the Day for Passover, April 21, 1943, A.M. D.I. 258.

References

Braslaw, Shmuel (1941) Vilna, Iton Hatnua b', *Anthology of Underground Hashomer Hatzair publications*, Warsaw, Spring.

Gutman, Yisrael (1963) *The Rebellion of the Besieged.* Sifriat Poalim.

Kaligsberg, M. (1974) *Di Iidishe Yugent Bevegung in Poilen.* New York: Yivo.

Ringelblum, E. (1989) *Mordechai Anielewicz and his Movement Hashomer Hatzair.* Yalkut Moreshet, May.

—— (1993) *Diary and Notes from the Warsaw Ghetto.* Jerusalem: Yad Vashem.

Tzukerman, Y. (1982) *Pages from the Legacy, the Days of September* (in Hebrew). Tel Aviv: Am Oved.

The Ultimate Sacrifice:
The Death of Resistance Hero
Yitzhak Wittenberg and the Decline of
the United Partisan Organization
Eric Sterling

In his Holocaust drama *Adam*, the Israeli playwright Joshua Sobol explores the most pivotal moment and the most critical dilemma in the Vilna ghetto – the decision whether Jewish resistance leader Yitzhak Wittenberg should have been turned over to the Nazis. Abraham Foxman calls the incident, known as "Wittenberg Day," "one of the most tragic chapters in the annals of the [H]olocaust" (Foxman 1967:153). Wittenberg (Sobol uses the *nom de guerre* Adam Rolenick) was the charismatic leader of the FPO (Fareynegte Partizaner Organizatsye, known in English as the UPO – United Partisan Organization), a Jewish armed resistance group that planned to lead a revolt against the Nazis within the Vilna ghetto, in an effort to salvage the lives and dignity of the remaining 20,000 inhabitants of the ghetto, including themselves. They hoped to lead the Jews to safety in the forest, where they would join the partisans who had already stationed themselves there. The ghetto resistance movement began on January 23, 1942 – after approximately 33,500 of the 57,000 Jews in Vilna were executed in 1941 and buried in huge excavated pits located in the Ponar mountains, with the surviving Jews being herded into the ghetto (Bauer 1982:160). The FPO members cleverly and courageously smuggled weapons into the ghetto in order to battle the Nazis soldiers, led by Gestapo officer Bruno Kittel, who lived outside the ghetto; consequently, the FPO members bided their time and attempted to increase their membership and armaments. When Kittel discovered the presence of the armed resistance in the ghetto and the identity of Wittenberg as the commander, he immediately demanded that Gens, the head of the Vilna ghetto, turn the FPO leader over to him. Kittel became concerned because only three months earlier the Nazis experienced difficulties in suppressing the Warsaw ghetto uprising (which began on April 19, 1943); he determined therefore that he would prevent another such revolt in this ghetto in Vilna, Lithuania, by arresting and murdering the resistance leader.

In this chapter, I explore the moral and political dilemmas faced by Jacob Gens, members of the FPO, and Wittenberg himself, using various historical sources, such as chronicles and eyewitness accounts written by resistance members, Sobol's play, *Adam* (which focuses on Gens's and the FPO's decision to turn Wittenberg over to Kittel) and an interview I conducted with the dramatist. Sobol, one of Israel's greatest playwrights, researched the incident exhaustively in preparation for his documentary drama. He portrays two lingering controversies in his play: whether the Jews in the Vilna ghetto should have relied upon military resistance or submissive compliance in their struggle against the Nazis, and whether Gens, the Vilna Jews, and the FPO should have turned Wittenberg over to the Nazis, thus destroying the possibility of armed resistance within the ghetto. Although the opposing sides of both of these complex dilemmas are plausible and the information from various historical accounts is sometimes contradictory, I believe that Gens made the wrong choices when he advocated passive compliance and when he turned over Wittenberg to the Gestapo because he must have known that the Nazis planned to liquidate the ghetto shortly thereafter, as part of the "Final Solution," and that armed resistance was the only hope for the 20,000 Jews who had thus far escaped death.

The FPO began as a resistance organization, consisting of a union of leftist, moderate, and right-wing Zionists, Communists, and the anti-Zionist Bundists (Bauer 1982:252). The group amassed fifty machine guns, fifty grenades (the first four of which were smuggled into the ghetto by the Mother Superior of the nearby Benedictine nunnery), thirty revolvers, several rifles, and several thousand bullets (Foxman 1967:151); the fighters intended to confront the Nazis when the German soldiers attempted to liquidate the ghetto. The members of this clandestine organization decided that when the destruction of the ghetto was imminent, they would protect the 20,000 Jewish citizens and either lead them to safety in the forests or at least allow them to die with dignity. The FPO considered it useless to wait for the Nazis to decide their destinies, especially because they knew the fates of those Jews whom the Nazis transported to Ponar; instead, they wanted to control their destinies by preparing themselves for an armed conflict. Wittenberg and other FPO fighters such as Abba Kovner wanted to create "a revolt [that] would have historic and national significance and might also enable many people to escape" (Arad 1982:106). During a memorial service on January 1, 1942 (three weeks before the creation of the FPO), honoring those who died at Ponar, Kovner presented his now famous manifesto. Yitzhak Arad quotes from the speech that Kovner delivered to his fellow resistance fighters:

> No one returned of those marched through the gates of the ghetto. All the roads of the Gestapo lead to Ponar. And Ponar means death. Those who waver, put aside all illusion. Your children, your wives, and husbands are no more. Ponar is no concentration camp. All were shot dead there. Hitler conspires to kill all the Jews of Europe, and the Jews of Lithuania have been picked at the first line. *Let us not be led as sheep to the slaughter!* . . .
> Brethren! Better fall as free fighters than to live at the mercy of murderers. Rise up! Rise up until your last breath. (Arad 1981: 232, my italics)

Kovner's words signify his courage and resolve; he firmly believed that the Nazis intended to exterminate the Jews in the ghetto and that armed resistance was the only logical choice.

Kovner's position, like that of the other FPO members, also demonstrated altruism. Yitzhak Arad, the renowned resistance fighter, had attempted to recruit members of the FPO to join him and his fellow partisans in the forests, where they would have a significantly better chance of survival. Wittenberg and the other FPO members understood that their organization could function better in the forests than in the ghetto because they could work with far fewer restrictions and pressure. In an interview, Sobol said:

> When I spoke to survivors of the ghetto and also when I read the diaries, I got the impression that the Nazis were almost always unpredictable . . . The ghetto was a world closed upon itself, like a semi-porous membrane. You cannot go out, but everything can come in. And the people had the feeling that they could be invaded at any moment by the Gestapo, by the Lithuanian militia, by selections . . . The Jews in the ghetto were living under the constant threat of imminent death, where values like justice or normalcy or the value of human life don't exist anymore. (Sterling 1995)

Nonetheless, the resistance members refused to escape to the forests because they envisioned themselves as protectors of the Jews in the ghetto; they believed that if they left the ghetto to save their lives, they would be deserting their fellow Jews. The resistance fighters of the FPO refused to escape to the forests before the organized revolt because, as Wittenberg noted, "[t]o take to the forests is tantamount to seeking personal safety and saving one's own skin" (Ainsztein 1974:491), and such an action would endanger the lives of their family members who remained. Thus, the resistance built up its organization within the Vilna ghetto, which was under the jurisdiction of Jacob Gens.

Although Gens and the FPO considered the Nazis their common enemy, the ghetto leader became apprehensive that the Jewish resistance movement in the ghetto threatened his authority; Gens feared that the people might shift their allegiance from him to the FPO and that the resistance possessed more weapons (and thus more power) than his ghetto police. He also believed that if the Gestapo discovered the presence of an armed underground, they would immediately liquidate the ghetto, killing all 20,000 inhabitants. In *Adam*, Gens warns the resistance fighters that "[t]he local German command is of course dependent on orders from above. Their policy, since the uprising in Warsaw, is to liquidate all ghettos where they find evidence of an armed underground movement" (Sobol 1996:283). Like Lodz *Judenrat* leader Mordechai Chaim Rumkowski, Gens ignored the idea that the "Final Solution" would include his ghetto and convinced himself that the Jews would survive by working diligently and thus making themselves indispensable to the Nazi war effort. And like Rumkowski, the leader of the Vilna ghetto saw himself as a Moses figure who, through passive compliance with the Nazis, would ultimately lead the Jews out of the ghetto. Philip Friedman notes that Gens often compared himself "to Moses. He would say again and again: 'You Jews will see, I will lead you out of the ghetto'" (Friedman 1980:370). Joseph Tenenbaum adds that possibly "this glib Nazi collaborator [Gens] truly believed in his messianic mission to save the remnants of the Jews through organized surrender of the multitudes" (Tenenbaum 1952:344).

Under the pressure of torture, a Polish Communist named Kozlowski informed the Nazis that he had encountered Yitzhak Wittenberg, who had expressed an interest in obtaining weapons; thus the leader of the Jewish resistance in the Vilna ghetto came to the attention of the Nazis. Kittel, who supervised the ghetto, demanded that Jacob Gens turn Wittenberg over to him. Although Gens might have sympathized, to a small extent, with the FPO members, the ghetto leader found himself caught between helping the resistance fighters such as Wittenberg and maintaining his authority over the other Jews in the ghetto, including those with weapons – the ghetto police. Furthermore, although Gens may have wanted to aid the Jewish resistance in the ghetto, he had to obey the orders of the Nazi authorities, who observed him carefully. Gens might have wished to aid the FPO but realized that by doing so, he endangered the lives of the 20,000 Jews who remained in the ghetto, practically all of whom were unarmed. During a conversation with partisan Natek Ring, Gens confided that he was afraid to help the Jewish resistance because he was constantly watched by the head of the ghetto police, Salek Dessler – an informant for the Gestapo. Isaac Kowalski, a member of the FPO, noted that Gens told Ring that he wanted to help the underground, but "he was afraid of Dessler. "Dessler," he said to Ring, "was an out-and-out Gestapo man, and he was sure to learn sooner or later that Gens had been in contact with a clandestine group" (Kowalski 1985:II, 367). The ghetto leader feared that if the Nazis discerned signs of Jewish armed resistance and indications that he supported it, they would quickly liquidate the ghetto.

In an effort to protect the ghetto's Jews and maintain his own political authority, Gens decided to obey the order from Kittel and betray Wittenberg. Calling an emergency meeting for midnight on July 15, 1943, Gens invited the FPO leaders to his home, arranging for ghetto policemen, including Dessler, and the Gestapo to arrest Wittenberg there. When the Gestapo officers entered, Dessler pointed to Wittenberg and declared that he was the commander of the Jewish armed underground in the ghetto. As the Gestapo officers led Wittenberg away, FPO resistance fighters attacked them, liberating their leader. This confrontation was the first armed fighting between the Nazis and the FPO, and it demonstrated to Gens that he no longer monopolized total authority over the people within the ghetto while demonstrating to the Nazis that the FPO was a force they needed to destroy before it grew too powerful. The FPO acted impulsively and instinctively in their rescue of their commander, disregarding the inevitable consequences. Kittel now knew the power of the armed Jewish resistance in the Vilna ghetto and would certainly not allow the ghetto underground to continue.

After Wittenberg escaped from the Gestapo officers who had arrested him, he hid in the ghetto. Kittel apparently ordered Gens to deliver Wittenberg to him immediately – with the understanding that the Jews in the ghetto would otherwise suffer tremendous reprisals. Addressing a large crowd from his balcony, Gens declared that the Gestapo ordered "the surrender of Wittenberg alive within two hours. If he is not surrendered, the German tanks and planes will demolish the ghetto with bombs'" (Eckman and Lazar 1977:31). The threat created widespread panic in the ghetto, causing Jews to search the ghetto hurriedly in order to capture this man whose presence, they believed, jeopardized their safety. The Jews turned against Wittenberg and the underground resistance, demanding that the FPO leader surrender; in fact, they conducted a massive house-to-house search within the ghetto, for they would gladly deliver him to save themselves. Borrowing from historical eyewitness accounts of the incident for his play, Sobol dramatizes the fear that spread throughout the ghetto: people cry, "Jews in the houses. Jews in the hideouts. Listen! Help us find Adam Rolenick [Wittenberg]. Save the ghetto! Look around you in your houses, your hideouts, your shelters. He may be among you. Jews, save yourselves" (Sobol 1996:320). Like Gens, they would willingly sacrifice one life to save many. Because Wittenberg commanded the FPO and this organization enabled him to escape and was responsible for incurring Kittel's threat to bomb the ghetto, the Jews developed a negative opinion of the resistance movement, fearing it and considering it a threat to their own survival – not as source of protection or hope. They recognized that the presence of armed fighters increased dramatically the chances that the Nazis would liquidate the ghetto – an idea that frightened them because many of those who were forced to board the rail cars never returned or were heard from again. Furthermore, the Jews discovered that the Russian army, which had enjoyed recent triumphs over the Nazis, was moving toward Vilna. The Jews wanted to remain in the ghetto peacefully and indefinitely, hoping that the Russian army would eventually liberate them; consequently, they strongly disapproved of the idea of a resistance movement provoking the Germans. In an interview, Sobol says that "it was clear that the Germans were going to lose the war, and hope among the Jews was almost delirious. [Herman] Kruk, in his diary, speaks of the people in the ghetto as suffering from the disease of hope, saying that it was the worst disease in the ghetto" (Sterling 1995). Sobol and Kruk imply that the Jews became so hopeful that they became inactive, unwilling to take risks or to do anything that might provoke the Germans to liquidate the ghetto; such an attitude might have caused them to play into the hands of their enemies and might have contributed to their decision to hand over Wittenberg.

Furthermore, the Jews in the ghetto willingly sacrificed Wittenberg because they lacked faith in the ability of a Jewish resistance to defeat the Nazis. Many historians agree. Yehuda Bauer says, "A rebellion meant certain death for everyone. A slave labor economy provided at least the possibility of survival" (Bauer 1982:252). Abraham Foxman asserts that the resistance group believed that

> they should lead the fight in the ghetto itself in order to show the world and posterity that the Jews revolted against their German oppressors and died an honorable death. The proponents of this view were well aware that they could not count on the support of the non-Jewish population. In no country was the Jewish underground treated on an equal footing with the recognized national

independence organizations. . . . They realized it would be a struggle without hope, a struggle for honor and history, and not life. (Foxman, 1967:151).

But Bauer and Foxman cannot be sure that a revolt would have failed. Perhaps some Jews would die while many thousand more would escape. Actually, the FPO was quite optimistic about its chances of waging a successful revolt against the Nazis. The FPO planned to build up armaments and leave the ghetto when the Nazis attempted to liquidate it, escaping to the forest, which lay approximately 4 miles away. The FPO would lead 20,000 Jews who inhabited the ghetto into the forest, where they would then join the partisans. Although Holocaust scholar Reuben Ainsztein admits that the plan initially appears unrealistic, he believes that this plan seems more practical when one considers that the Jewish resistance fighters "counted on the Communist underground in the city being strong enough to organise at the same time large-scale sabotage and attacks on German military installations, which would create enough panic and disorganisation to allow thousands of Jews to escape" (Ainsztein 1975:497). It is noteworthy that 90–95 percent of the FPO members survived while only 2–5 percent of the rest of the Vilna Jews lived past the war (Kowalski 1985:II, 360). That statistic demonstrates the skill and resourcefulness of the ghetto resistance and their potential for success.

The people failed to realize that the elimination of the underground would greatly facilitate the liquidation of the ghetto because the Nazis would face no adversaries and could search for, and murder, Jews without the fear of being shot or ambushed. In Sobol's play, the FPO leader says that the Nazis "learned their lesson in Warsaw. They want to cripple our organization and liquidate the ghetto without resistance" (Sobol 1996:296). Lazar says that the FPO

> knew that Wittenberg's arrest was just a pretext on the part of the Gestapo. They wanted to begin destroying the armed force of the ghetto to make it easier to carry out the general destruction without fear of resistance. But how could we explain the bitter truth to the masses? How could we tell this to all the Jews, incited by the leaders who preached fraternal war on the very brink of destruction instead of calling the ghetto to fight together against the common enemy? (Lazar 1985:73–74)

Without the presence of the FPO, the Nazi soldiers could kill, pillage, and destroy with impunity. But Gens successfully turned his fellow Jews in the ghetto against the FPO commander, partly because he envied the

FPO's growing authority (at the expense of his own) but primarily because he feared that its power would incite the Nazis to liquidate the ghetto.

Ironically, the Jewish resistance fighters in the ghetto, who had prepared so diligently and courageously to fight the Nazis, discovered, to their dismay, that they would first have to attack their own people in the ghetto. The name of the underground organization is important – the *United* Partisan Organization. The resistance consisted of a gallimaufry of organizations (such as the Zionists and Bundists) who held different, and sometimes opposing, political views. But they wisely considered the Nazis their common enemy and consequently put aside their political differences, uniting together into one cohesive organization. Unfortunately, Gens fragmented the relationships between Jews in the ghetto during the dilemma surrounding Wittenberg, pitting Jew against Jew. Reuben Ainsztein says that Gens

> summoned the resistance leaders and this time succeeded in persuading them to hand over their leader. His chief argument was that the people of the ghetto were on his side because they believed that the German defeats in Russia and the collapse of Italy promised a quick end to the war and therefore it was only a matter of surviving for another few months to be saved for good. Consequently, if they refused to surrender Wittenberg, they would have to fight their own people. (Ainsztein 1974:511)

Lester Eckman and Chaim Lazar state that FPO members came to Wittenberg's hiding place and told him to surrender because "the entire organization was exposed and there was danger that it might have to fight its own brothers instead of the Germans" (Eckman and Lazar 1977:32). Disdaining the thought of killing their fellow Jews, the FPO members voted, with great reluctance, to hand Wittenberg over to Kittel. It is also ironic that the resistance fighters, who had altruistically declined the opportunity to leave the ghetto for freedom in the forests in order that they could protect their compatriots, found their organization destroyed, in part, by those Jewish citizens whom they wished to defend. It is also noteworthy that the decision to risk their lives by remaining in the ghetto derived primarily from Wittenberg, himself. In *Adam*, FPO member Rozin criticizes the people for turning against the resistance leader and the underground:

> Shame on you! Your beloved have gone the way of all flesh, and it was you who let go the father's hand, the mother's hand, the grandmother's, and the child's. . . . He who no longer feels that hand burning in his palm with pain,

he who no longer remembers turning his back on the beloved he abandoned to death, seeking instead life for himself . . . let him, let him dare raise his hand! You think you will live forever? So why the noise? Why the panic? (Sobol 1996:305 the playwright's ellipses)

Yet most of the frightened people still insisted that Wittenberg surrender to Kittel. Because the partisans lacked the public support for their underground organization, the FPO deemed that it had no choice but to turn Wittenberg over to the Nazis.

In his play, Sobol glorifies Wittenberg, suggesting that the FPO commander readily accepted the decision of his underground organization and of the Jews in the ghetto. In his introduction to the drama, Michael Taub says that

> in Sobol's play, the entire operation, the success or failure of the revolt hinges on the leader's resolve, on his willingness to risk lives for an honorable exit from history. In the end, Sobol's leader equivocates because he is a liberal man, a humanist who places people over ideas, individuals over lofty ideals . . . Clearly, no one can tell with any degree of certainty what would have happened had the revolt materialized. Adam, however, had no doubts that an armed conflict under existing conditions would have been militarily futile; it would only have filled some with a sense of revenge and Jewish pride. (Taub 1980:10–11)

Sobol's portrayal of Wittenberg's response to the FPO vote, however, differs greatly from historical truth because the leader failed to concur with their decision and believed that an armed resistance from within the ghetto could succeed. Upon learning that the FPO members voted to turn him in, Wittenberg escaped from them because he initially proved unwilling to accept their decision. He claimed that the ghetto would be destroyed in any case, and it was best to begin the revolt immediately against the Germans. When he was caught again, he reluctantly agreed to surrender to the Gestapo because he lacked the support of Gens, the people and even the FPO, which voted to turn him over to Kittel. The disappointed resistance commander declared, "It has never happened that an organization would surrender its leader. Any party which acts this way is bankrupt" (Friedman 1980:377). Wittenberg strongly disagreed with the decision, not so much for selfish reasons but rather because he understood that his death would destroy the armed underground in Vilna and consequently allow the Germans to liquidate the ghetto, murdering thousands of Jews without any hindrance or resistance. And his words proved prophetic. The hero committed suicide while in their custody.

Kowalski says, "Designating Abe Kovner as his successor, Wittenberg went to give himself up, to save the lives of the ghetto population. The next morning his body was found in the corridor of the Gestapo, limbs broken and eyes gouged out" (Kowalski 1985: II, 61–62). Yitzhak Wittenberg died a hero, without divulging the identities of any of his colleagues in the armed resistance.

Sobol begins his play with a scene in which Kittel interrogates Adam [Wittenberg]. Kittel arranges for a woman to be tortured within Adam's hearing, and the Nazi officer informs his prisoner that he will end the woman's suffering on the condition that Adam reveal to him the identities of the other important members of the resistance. If he reveals the names, the ghetto resistance will be crushed, but the woman will survive and be released (Kittel also promises Adam's release, yet it is obvious that his assurance should not be taken seriously). Yet if he continues to protect the underground by refusing to divulge the names of other resistance members, the woman will endure more pain. Adam selects neither option, however, because he bites his nails, absorbing the cyanide that he has received from Gens. This action releases him (and the nameless woman) from further torture and prevents him from betraying vital secrets about the resistance to the Nazis. Sobol employs this scene to symbolize the dilemma faced by Yitzhak Wittenberg just before his death – whether he should turn himself in to Kittel or remain in hiding within the ghetto. The two situations are alike in that both require the resistance leader to choose between betraying the FPO or innocent bystanders.

Most of the Jews in the ghetto were unarmed, and many did not even know that the clandestine FPO existed. Sobol believes that in Vilna there was a "special ghetto mentality where you were not interested in anything that hadn't to do with your immediate area, your immediate concerns. You didn't want to know" (Sterling 1995). This belief holds true when one considers the dangers that accompanied membership in the armed resistance. Most Jews worked diligently during the day because Gens pointed out that the Nazis would allow the ghetto (and thus its inhabitants) to exist as long as the Jews worked productively. The goal of most Jews in the Vilna ghetto was survival, so they wished to avoid antagonizing and provoking the Nazis. Joseph Glazman, one of the founding members of the FPO, remarked that the FPO would have been successful had it received the support of the people in the ghetto and if the people had united behind it:

> the Jews lacked a sense of collective responsibility. They did not understand that the fate of the individual depended on the fate of the whole community.

Everyone thought that no ill would befall him and he would be saved. This one had a non-Jewish friend who would save him; that one hoped that his money would take care of everything; a third was preparing a hideout for himself; and a fourth simply believed that he was invulnerable to death. If these Jews had only understood that all Jews are responsible for one another; if they had only understood that salvation of the individual is linked to salvation of the community, they would have concluded that only mass resistance could save the masses. Had the ghettos resisted, the Germans would not have pulled out forces from the front to carry out their extermination plans. Had the Jews invested in the purchase of arms the same sums they spent on arranging hiding-places or other private means of survival, their chances of survival would have been much greater. (Lazar 1985:54)

They disapproved of armed resistance within the ghetto because they feared that it would incite the Nazis to liquidate it. In his explanation of why the ghettos during the Holocaust often lacked a significant armed resistance, Israel Gutman says:

A powerful hindrance which carried great moral weight was provided by responsible public figures who issued warnings, exhorted and cautioned against rash and fateful acts by hot-headed and inexperienced youth. Well-known historians who had to their credit long and faithful service pointed out that the Jewish People had been through this sort of thing before, and that just as in the past this ancient people had often had to pay a heavy toll in blood to Moloch in order to save part of the nation, so now the imperative of history demanded acceptance of the inevitable so as to ensure the survival of part of the people. And since the Nazis had imposed collective responsibility and collective punishment, any attempt at revolt that did not lead to successful military results would in the end only hasten the doom of all the Jews. (Gutman 1989:171)

Gens employed the arguments of collective responsibility and collective punishment against the FPO, telling the people that the Nazis would retaliate against them for the actions of that underground. Gens preached that hard work, not resistance, was the means for survival.

Despite Tenenbaum's aforementioned comment labeling the ghetto leader a Nazi collaborator, there should be little doubt that Gens attempted to do what he could to help his people in the ghetto. His decisions and strategies, not his motives, were highly questionable. Because his wife was an Aryan Lithuanian, he could have avoided his internment in the ghetto, but he risked, and ultimately sacrificed, his life by taking an active role in the ghetto because he believed that it was his duty, his calling, to protect his fellow Jews in this dire situation. Despite his opposition to the FPO, he sometimes "personally assisted the Jewish underground, and if he was full of contradictions, so were the exigencies of the times in which he lived and ruled" (Tenenbaum 1952:344). And Gens genuinely believed that he was helping his people by sacrificing some in order to save others. In a dilemma similar to the problem faced by the Lodz ghetto leader Rumkowski, Gens, realizing that the Nazis wanted some Jews removed from the ghetto (in order to murder them), acquiesced because he felt that if he refused, the Germans would kill double the number they had requested — or even liquidate the ghetto. In a passionate speech to the people in the ghetto, Gens defended his position:

> *I take count of Jewish blood, not of Jewish honor.* When the Germans ask me for a thousand persons, I hand them over, for if we Jews will not give them on our own, the Germans will come and take them by force. Then they will take not one thousand but thousands, and the whole ghetto will be at their mercy. With hundreds, I save a thousand; with the thousands that I hand over, I save ten thousands. You are refined, learned people, you do not come in contact with the ghetto scum. You will come out with your hands clean. If you survive, you will be able to say, Our conscience is clear. But I, Jacob Gens, if I survive, I shall come out of here unclean, my hands dripping with blood. Nevertheless, I shall willingly declare before a Jewish court: I did my best to rescue as many Jews as I could to bring them to the gate of redemption. I was forced to lead some to their death in order that a small remnant may survive; in order to have others emerge with a clear conscience, I had to befoul myself and act without remorse. (Friedman 1980:371)

Sobol believes that Gens acted more rationally than Rumkowski. The dramatist asserts that Gens believed "that there was no moral justification for what he was doing. He knew it. . . . He knew that he was the only person responsible for what he was doing and that he was functioning in a world in which morals didn't exist anymore. It was almost a foolish pretension to be moral" (Sterling 1995). Furthermore, Gens also noted that it would be less horrific if the ghetto police, as opposed to the Nazis, performed the selections. After the ghetto leader and the Jewish police conducted a selection in nearby Oszmiany, Yiddish philologist Zelig Kalmanovich noted, "Had the foreigners [Germans and Lithuanians] conducted the *Aktion*, the number of victims would have been larger. [Arad adds,] The ghetto community regarded the police action as a dictate of reality which had succeeded in saving as many as possible" (Arad 1982:347). Gens believed that if he satisfied the demands of the Nazis, the Germans might let the survivors live in peace. Like many Jews in the ghetto, Gens hoped, naively, that the Nazis would eventually satisfy their thirst for blood and spare the remaining Jews. Gens acted according to this hope even though several Vilna rabbis had warned him that his selections violated Jewish law. In *Mishneh Torah*, Maimonides states, "If a heathen said to you: Give us one of yours and we shall kill him, and if you don't we shall kill you, all shall die, but you shall not turn over one soul of Israel to them" (Friedman 1980: 370, 358). By selecting who should live and who should die, Gens not only comported himself as a tyrant, but also attempted to play a role reserved for the Lord.

Selections became a significant source of conflict between *Judenräte* and armed resistance forces in the ghettos during the Holocaust. The underground as well as other Jews in several ghettos complained bitterly about leaders who acquiesced – albeit reluctantly – to Nazi demands for selections. For instance, in his *Diary of the Vilna Ghetto*, librarian and ghetto historian Herman Kruk stated that "The greatest tragedy was that public opinion largely acquiesced in Gens' stand" (Arad 1982:347). Kruk believed that life was so precious that it was shameful to sacrifice willingly the lives of any Jews to the Nazis. This dilemma regarding the sacrifice of the few in order to save the many becomes crucial in the situation involving the fate of Yitzhak Wittenberg. One may say that Wittenberg was, himself, a victim of a selection, sacrificing his life so that others might live. Unfortunately, the sacrifice of Wittenberg, which Gens supported, also destroyed the armed resistance that might have saved many Jews' lives.

One may argue that detractors of Gens criticize him unfairly because he, living in the midst of this unprecedented tragedy, could not have foreseen that the Nazis would ultimately liquidate the ghetto anyway and that acquiescence to selections would prove a fruitless gesture. But Sobol mentions that by the time Kittel reached Vilna, "he had the reputation of having liquidated a few other ghettos and had become a specialist" (Sterling 1995). And Gens should have suspected that Kittel would liquidate the ghetto regardless of whether he turned over Wittenberg because Kozlowski's testimony under torture, along with the FPO's rescue of its leader, indicated that an armed Jewish resistance definitely existed in the ghetto. The Nazis would not tolerate the presence of such an organization, especially after the humiliation they suffered in defeating with difficulty the outmatched Warsaw ghetto fighters, so clearly they would want to destroy the ghetto.

Gens already knew that the Nazis could not be trusted. Although the ghetto leader believed that hard work and productivity to the German war effort would make the Jews indispensable, the Nazis kept asking for more and more selections. Only four months earlier, the Nazis had terribly deceived Gens, promising to relocate 5,000 Jews from Vilna to the Kovno ghetto. The Gestapo promised that these 5,000 Jews would thrive under better conditions in Kovno, and even allowed Gens to accompany them during the trip. In the midst of that transfer, Gens discovered, to his horror, that his ghetto policemen (who served as escorts) were replaced with Nazis, and the train traveled not to Kovno, but to Ponar, where the 5,000 were murdered. Gens returned to Vilna, stunned and disillusioned. Lazar says that during "the early morning, Gens and his police reached the ghetto. Everyone who saw them, trembling, ashen-faced, and depressed, understood immediately what had happened" (Lazar 1985: 55). Joseph Tenenbaum says that "The 'Kovno' ruse at last convinced some, if not all the people, of the futility of passive submission" (Tenenbaum, 1952:345). So it is most surprising that after he had been duped and had given his word to 5,000 Jews who paid for his gullibility with their lives, Gens still placed his trust in the Gestapo.

Although Gens stressed diligence as the key to survival, the ghetto leader also knew that Kittel, who also oversaw the Bezdany ghetto (25 kilometers away), destroyed those Jews. Sobol mentions in an interview that "Kittel heard that they [the Bezdany Jews] organized an underground movement in that factory, that these 200 young Jews were probably preparing to escape into the forest" (Sterling 1995). Therefore, Kittel arranged a party to congratulate the Jews of that ghetto for their hard work:

> Kittel was in high spirits. He spoke to them for over an hour and told them it was because of their work that they remained alive. He promised them that if they continued to work diligently, the Germans would treat them well. He pointed to the large jars [of expensive jam] and said that only soldiers at the front got such food. He continued to raise their hopes and even said that at the end of the war they would live in the Third Reich under the auspices of National Socialism and its great leader, Hitler. (Lazar 1985:69)

Kittel then left the room and began shooting them. The first shot was a signal to the Nazi soldiers who waited outside; they began shooting the Jews and then burned down the building, killing all of the workers whom Kittel had just praised for their hard work and to whom he had just promised survival. This incident, known to Gens, indicated that Kittel could not be trusted and disproved the idea that the Nazis would spare Jews in the ghetto if they worked diligently. Because he feared the growing authority of the FPO, Gens chose to ignore the seriousness of the Kovno and Bezdany incidents and to remind his people that Kittel had promised him that the Vilna ghetto would be spared. The Gestapo murdered the inhabitants of the Bezdany ghetto upon discovering that some of the Jews possessed weapons and that they were planning an underground organization. Now that Gens realized that Kittel discerned the existence of an armed resistance in Vilna, the ghetto leader should have anticipated the liquidation of the Vilna ghetto. One must wonder why an intelligent and rational man such as Gens would believe that Kittel would destroy one ghetto but spare the other. Perhaps the answer lies in Gens's desperation to maintain his power. Chaim Lazar, a member of the FPO, mentioned that the Bezdany Jews also planned an armed resistance but postponed their military action because they too succumbed to Kittel's promises. Lazar says, "Thus ended the story of Bezdany, a story of strong lads, armed and ready to fight, who did not know when to seize the opportunity" (Lazar 1985: 69).

The FPO represents, unfortunately, a similar disappointment – to some extent. After planning their revolt for eighteen months and continuously risking their lives by stealing and smuggling weapons, the members of the underground fled to the forest to join the partisans. As a result, a large number of those 20,000 Jews were led like sheep to slaughter – to the rail cars. Chaim Lazar reflects,

> In the death cars, on the journey from which none returned, they would later recall how they attacked us. They would remember the stones they threw at us and the clubs they hit us with. They would recall the human sacrifice who offered himself in vain, and the blind stupidity of the fraternal war in the presence of the common enemy, and perhaps they would find atonement for their sins (Lazar 1985:75).

On September 1, 1943 (only six weeks after the heroic sacrifice of Wittenberg), the Nazis sealed off the ghetto. Three weeks later (September 23), the Germans liquidated the ghetto, resulting in thousands of deaths. Thus, the planned armed resistance in the Vilna ghetto never occurred. But the underground was by no means a total failure because the FPO hindered the Nazi war effort and enjoyed some triumphs and some revenge.

The concepts of revenge and pride are intertwined because the Jews who avenged the destruction of their relatives and friends experienced a sense of pride and fulfillment, a feeling that they were exacting justice rather than passively being led like sheep to slaughter. In May 1943, after the FPO destroyed a Nazi military train transporting soldiers and weapons to the front, Wittenberg lauded the successful mission:

This was an act of partisan sabotage in the rear, causing the enemy considerable losses. The Germans, who felt safe in a place so far away from the front, have learned that the rear is not particularly safe and that an organized fighting power is operating underground. We heard that they have reinforced their guards along that railroad. Every soldier whom they have to keep here instead of sending to the front reduces their fighting manpower. (Lazar 1985: 40–41)

Isaac Kowalski relates – with great admiration – the defiance of Zalman Tiktin when the Nazis caught and tortured the sixteen-year-old for stealing hand grenades; Abraham Sutzkever also tells the story of Tiktin in his memoirs and notes that after the Nazis had shot Tiktin at least eight times, Kittel visited him frequently and offered him chocolate and other foods. Tiktin turned down the gifts and refused the Gestapo officer's demands to tell him for whom he had attempted to steal the ammunition: "'I stole them for you. Because you murdered my parents" (Sutzkever 1949: 72). Kowalski built his own printing press in that ghetto, disseminating many anti-Nazi leaflets. Furthermore, several members of the FPO slipped out of the Vilna ghetto and visited the Warsaw and Bialystok ghettos, informing them about what was transpiring in Vilna and suggesting that they revolt against the Nazis. Furthermore, the resistance fighters of the FPO, who eventually left the ghetto in disappointment, went to the forest and renamed themselves the "Avengers." The Vilna partisans avenged the loss of their commander, blowing up trains and burning bridges. Kowalski notes that "[w]hen the Red Army began its attack on Vilna, the Jewish partisans were the first to enter the city, engage the barricaded Germans in battle and exterminate them by the score" (Kowalski 1985: II, 62).

FPO member Schmerke Kaczerginski, a famous Jewish poet and friend of Wittenberg, memorialized the tragic death of the resistance organization leader. Kaczerginksi concludes this song, which became one of the most popular Yiddish songs in the ghetto, in the following way:

> The ghetto is restless,
> And Gestapo threatens
> Our Commander-in-Chief!
> Then Itzik spoke to us,
> His words were like lightning –
> "Don't take any risks for my sake,
> Your lives are too precious
> To give away lightly."
> And proudly he goes to his death!

The foe again crouches
Like beasts of the jungle,
My pistol is ready in hand,
My gun is my guardian,
My rescuing angel,
It's now my Commander-in-Chief. (Kowalski 1985:106)

References

Ainsztein, Reuben (1974) *Jewish Resistance in Nazi-Occupied Eastern Europe: With a Historical Survey of the Jew as Fighter and Soldier in the Diaspora*. New York: Harper & Row.

Arad, Yitzhak (1982) *Ghetto in Flames: The Struggle and Destruction of the Jews in Vilna in the Holocaust*. New York: Holocaust Library.

Bauer, Yehuda (1982) *A History of the Holocaust*. New York: Franklin Watts.

Eckman, Lester, and Lazar, Chaim (1977) *The Jewish Resistance: The History of the Jewish Partisans in Lithuania and White Russia during the Nazi Occupation 1940–1945*. New York: Shengold.

Foxman, Abraham (1967) "The Resistance Movement in the Vilna Ghetto," in Yuri Suhl (ed.) *They Fought Back: The Story of the Jewish Resistance in Nazi Europe*. New York: Crown: 148–159.

Friedman, Philip (1980) *Roads to Extinction: Essays on the Holocaust*. Ed. Ada June Friedman. New York: The Jewish Publication Society of America.

Gutman, Israel (1989) "Youth Movements in the Underground and the Ghetto Revolts," in Michael Marrus (ed.) *The Nazi Holocaust: Historical Articles on the Destruction of European Jews: Jewish Resistance to the Holocaust*. 9 vols. Westport, CT: Meckler: vol. VII, pp. 160–184.

Kaczerginski, Schmerke (1984) "Itzik Wittenberg," in Isaac Kowalski (ed.) *Anthology on Armed Jewish Resistance, 1939–1945*. 2 vols. Brooklyn: Jewish Commemorative Publishers House: vol. I, p. 160.

Kowalski, Isaac (ed.) (1985) *Anthology of Armed Jewish Resistance, 1939–1945*. 2 vols. Brooklyn: Jewish Combatants Publishers House.

Lazar, Chaim (1985) *Destruction and Resistance*. Trans. Galia Eden Barshop. New York: Shengold.

Sobol, Joshua (1996) *Adam*. Trans. Ron Jenkins. In Michael Taub (ed.) *Israeli Holocaust Drama*. Syracuse: Syracuse University Press. 268–330.

Sterling, Eric (1995) "Interview with Joshua Sobol." Catholic University of America. Washington, D.C. February 24.

Sutzkever, Abraham (1949) "Never Say This Is the Last Road," in Leo Schwarz (ed.) *The Root and the Bough: The Epic of an Enduring People*. New York: Rinehart & Company: 66–92.

Taub, Michael (1996) "Israeli Theater and the Holocaust," in Michael Taub (ed.) *Israeli Holocaust Drama*. Syracuse: Syracuse University Press: 8–18.

Tenenbaum, Joseph (1952) *Underground: The Story of a People*. New York: Philosophical Library.

–5–

Jewish Resistance in Belorussian Forests: Fighting and the Rescue of Jews by Jews

Nechama Tec

Targeted for total biological annihilation, Jews who lived under German occupation resisted the enemy by devising unusual strategies of survival. Some of these strategies took the form of illegal escapes into forests. How did the Jewish fugitives fit into the forest and how did they relate to non-Jewish forest dwellers? How did Jewish and non-Jewish partisans adjust to the woods, to each other and how did they cope with the Germans and the Nazi collaborators? To consider some of these questions I turn to another time and another place.[1]

The time is World War II, the early 1940s. The place is Western Belorussia, now known as Belarus. Much of this area is covered by thick, jungle-like, partly inaccessible forests. During the German occupation many fugitives and partisans lived in these wooded areas. The very presence of these illegal forest dwellers signaled a resistance to Nazi orders. Gradually Western Belorussia was transformed into an important center for the Soviet partisan movement and an equally important haven for the oppressed.

Until 1939 Western Belorussia belonged to Poland. By September 17, 1939, because of the German–Russian friendship treaty, it was transferred to the Soviet Union. In less than two years, as a result of the German–Russian War, control over this territory switched hands.

On June 22, 1941, Germany launched an attack upon the Soviet Union. Through this move, Hitler wanted to acquire new territories, to eliminate Communism as a political entity, and to come closer to the goal of Jewish annihilation. The German attack – a sudden, massive onslaught – caused the collapse of several Red Army divisions. In no time, the entire Soviet army was in disarray. Thousands of Russian soldiers ran into the Belorussian forests. Many more surrendered to the enemy.[2] German treatment of the Soviet POWs was ruthless. Many fell victim to mass executions while others died a slow death as concentration camp slaves.

Estimates for Russian POWs who perished run into millions.[3] Some POWs succeeded in running away into the Belorussian forests, where they met their comrades who had come there earlier.

The Soviet government was quick to recognize the potential benefits of their former soldiers: they could help Russia fight the enemy from within. Specially trained men were sent to the Belorussian forests to organize a guerilla movement. These government-sponsored organizers faced a formidable task. They found many more former army men than they had expected. Referring to themselves as partisans, these forest men were divided into small splinter groups. As a rule they lacked weapons, leaders and discipline. Often they would limited their activities to finding food and shelter. Only very rarely would these early partisans attack Germans and only when confronted by easy targets. The inducement in such cases would be the acquisition of arms. The men sent by Stalin could not control them.

By mid-1942, these former Soviet soldiers were joined by other prospective Nazi victims. At first, because the Belorussians had no strong sense of nationalism, they chose not to oppose the Germans and assumed a friendly posture toward their new masters.[4] The Nazis were successful in recruiting Belorussian volunteers for work in Germany. Only gradually, and only after the Belorussians had learned about atrocities committed against the Jews, against the Russian POWs, and about abuses of foreign workers, did they refuse to relocate to Germany. Short of laborers, the Germans used force. They would catch Belorussian men and send them to Germany. The Belorussians retaliated by running into the forests where they joined other forest dwellers or formed their own units.[5]

About that time, too, the early partisans were joined by Jewish fugitives. From the start of the Russian–German War, Jews and Communists became special targets of Nazi measures of destruction. It is estimated that within the first six months of the war with Russia the Germans had murdered over a million civilians, practically all of them Jewish. Jews who had eluded these initial onslaughts were forced into isolated ghettos, located in the most dilapidated areas of urban centers. Overcrowding, disease, starvation and death were the order of the day. Some of the Jews were periodically removed and murdered close to the ghettos. Those who had survived these purges had a hard time denying the grim reality. With hardly any options they eagerly searched for ways to counteract the Nazi terror. Understandably, the Jews welcomed rumors about fighting partisans. They clung to the idea that these forest fighters would help them. Encouraged by such expectations, some ghetto inmates escaped. Some were murdered on the way to the forests. Those who succeeded in entering the woods faced many hardships.

Only some of the ghetto runaways were young men. Of these young men, very few were armed: a definite disadvantage. Most of the Jewish fugitives were older men, women and children. Moreover, in prewar Poland, the majority of Polish Jews (77 percent) had lived in urban centers. They were therefore unprepared for life in the countryside.[6] Antisemitism, quite common among the non-Jewish partisan groups, added yet another serious obstacle to the survival of Jewish fugitives.

Largely because of who they were, the Jewish ghetto runaways, more so than others, were at the mercy of different partisan groups who, instead of fighting the enemy, would rob each other of anything they considered of value. Rivalry and greed would sometimes lead to murder. Caught in these conflicts, some of the Jews were robbed and killed. Others were stripped of their meager belongings and chased away. Only a minority, usually young men with guns, were welcomed into partisan units.

With time some ghetto inmates realized that in the forest only young men with arms had a chance of being accepted into partisan detachments. The majority did not know or preferred not to know that sometimes even armed Jewish men met with rejection and death.

And so, Jews who managed to run away from a ghetto had to cope with Nazis and their collaborators, with hunger, with disease, with harsh weather conditions and with partisan hostility. Each and all of these contributed to the fugitives' high death rates.

While different in terms of background, nationality and demographics, all early forest dwellers including the ghetto runaways, had much in common. None of them were making an ideological statement. All were preoccupied with self-preservation. All had come to the forest because they wanted to live, not because they wanted to fight.[7]

Because of the German defeat at Stalingrad the year 1943 became a turning point in the Russian–German War. At this stage, Stalin made a concerted effort to establish a firmer grip over the Russian partisan movement. More men from the Soviet Union were parachuted into Western Belorussia. Others came in planes that landed at secretly constructed airports, close to the woods. In these forests the Russians were definitely the dominant group. Nevertheless, even after the influx of these special organizers, the partisans managed to retain much of their independence and never submitted fully to Soviet control. Moreover, it seems that for the entire duration of the war, the combat activities of the Soviet partisans were highly exaggerated. Many anti-German moves were planned but never executed.[8]

In the shaky, life-threatening environment of the forest, the Jews struggled hard. Only some achieved a certain measure of independence. This was true for the Bielski brothers, the founders of a Jewish partisan unit, known as the Bielski otriad, a Russian term for a partisan detachment.

As peasants the Bielski brothers belonged to a small minority of Jews. The only Jews in the isolated village of Stankiewicze, they were very poor and badly educated, just like their Belorussian neighbors. Familiar with life in the countryside, they were independent. Already in the summer of 1941, the three Bielski brothers, Tuvia, Asael and Zus, refused to submit to the Nazi terror. Warned by Belorussian friends that they were about to be arrested because of their past ties to the Soviet authorities, they escaped. For safety, each brother went in a different direction. In exchange for food and shelter, each brother offered his services to Belorussian peasants. The three brothers belong to the minority of Jews who, from the very beginning, refused to became ghetto inmates.

In the summer of 1942, news that their parents, two other brothers, scores of relatives and friends had been murdered strengthened the Bielski brothers' determination to oppose the Germans in a more organized way. They decided to form an independent Jewish partisan detachment. For this they needed arms. A gun commanded respect; a gun promised food and safety. Soon each brother, with the help of non-Jewish friends, received a gun. Then in the late summer of 1942, with over thirty followers, they organized a partisan unit and appointed the oldest brother, Tuvia Bielski, as its commander.

A gifted, charismatic leader, Tuvia Bielski set out to neutralize the surrounding dangers by cooperating with the different partisan groups, especially the dominant Soviet partisan detachments. This cooperation extended to food collection and to joint military ventures. Different partisan groups were assigned to different villages from which they would confiscate provisions. Peasants were the main suppliers. Faced with armed men, the peasants had no choice but to part with their limited provisions. While food was gathered separately by each group, attacks on Germans and their collaborators, for the purpose of collecting arms and goods, for sabotage activities such as cutting telephone wires, blowing up bridges and trains, were performed jointly by partisans from the various units.

Tuvia Bielski assumed full control over external and internal policies and over all the organizational arrangements of the otriad. From the very start, he insisted that all Jews, regardless of age, sex, state of health or any other characteristics, would be accepted into the group. This policy met with internal opposition which saw in this measure a threat to the group's survival. With this opposition Tuvia argued that large size meant greater strength and greater safety. He never budged from this position. On the contrary, as the Germans stepped up the process of Jewish destruction, he became more determined to save lives. Eventually, because of his forceful personality and charisma, Tuvia convinced many of his followers of the need to rescue as many Jews as possible.

The Bielski otriad's brief history – from 1942 till 1944 – was filled with dramatic changes. At first, the group led a nomadic existence, moving from place to place. Toward the end of 1943, it established a more permanent base in the huge, swampy and partly inaccessible Nolibocka forest. At this stage the camp came to resemble a "shtetl," a small town, with factories and workshops.[9] Among them the gun repair shop had an honored place. It was headed by the locksmith, Shmuel Openheim, whose skill at repairing weapons and ability to create new parts were admired throughout the region. Eventually, his fame brought to the Bielski otriad Soviet newspapermen who were on a visit from Moscow. They were amazed. One of them said: "This is the first time that I have seen such an otriad. When I write about it in the newspaper in Moscow no one will believe me."[10]

The forest was generous with its materials. The carpenters were inventive, manufacturing all kinds of items; wooden parts for weapons, sandals for the summer, barrels that were used for the production of leather and much, much more. The blacksmiths were busy attending to the camp's horses and to horses from surrounding otriads. They also repaired wagons, particularly wheels.

Appreciated by all was the sausage factory. If for example, a Soviet detachment wanted sausages, they would deliver to the Bielski base a cow. For this they would receive an agreed amount of sausages. The rest of the meat, plus the bones, would stay in the Bielski camp and would be used in the collective kitchen. In the tannery, the skin of the same cow would be made into leather which would then be transformed into boots, saddles, belts and other items. These finished goods in turn would be exchanged for food, medication and arms.

The establishment of factories and workshops had several important consequences. It transformed the Bielski partisans into suppliers of services to the Soviet partisan movement; in itself a valuable additional connection. Also, in the forest antisemitism was often expressed in complaints that the Jews consumed too much food without contributing anything of significance, thereby depriving the rest of the partisans, the "real" fighters, of food. The services offered by the Bielski partisans helped neutralize some of these anti-Jewish sentiments. In addition, transactions which grew out of the workshops and factories improved the economic situation of the Bielski unit and reduced the number of dangerous food expeditions. Finally, too, the work itself might have improved the workers' psychological well-being.

The Bielski otriad, despite its many dramatic changes, retained certain basic characteristics and social arrangements. This was true for the community's social composition, its general lifestyles and prestige rankings. During the otriad's history about three quarters of its members were "older Jews," women and children. Similarly, the proportion of the young men, men capable of using weapons, fluctuated between 20 percent and 30 percent. Practically all of these young men had little education and before the war belonged to the working class.[11] Only a minority of the otriad's people had a prewar upper- or middle-class background.

At the start of the German occupation the Jewish male elite became special targets of the Nazi policies of annihilation. Many of them were murdered.[12] A few Jewish leaders succeeded in escaping. Those who stayed on and survived the initial waves of persecutions were ill-equipped for life in the forest. Only a few of them moved into the wooded areas.

Compared to the prewar elite, working-class men were more resourceful and better prepared for life in the countryside. Activities like riding horses or milking cows came easily to them. They were more likely to fight, more likely to go on food expeditions.[13] Because the skills of the male working class were valuable for survival they became important. This led to a switched ranking system. The prewar working class became the new elite. The prewar elite moved to the lower echelons of the forest community.

Aware of their newly acquired status, these former working-class men looked down upon those who had a hard time adjusting to the rough living conditions and to manual labor.[14] In fact they resented any behavior that signaled a higher-class background. One member of the prewar elite recalls: "Once my husband and I spoke Hebrew with each other and one of them told us 'Do not speak Hebrew, this is Russian territory and you are not supposed to speak Hebrew.' We did not. After that, when we wanted to speak Hebrew, we did it so that no one could hear us."

At another time the same woman was asked the following questions:

"Did you study, in high school?"
"I did."
"Did you study at the university?"
"I did."
"So what does it give you? Can you make a thicker soup out of it?"
"No."[15]

This anti-intellectual posture contributed to making politeness and good manners irrelevant, almost inappropriate. The use of coarse language became an established pattern. For the few who came from an upper- or middle-class background this could present problems. One of them remembers meeting an old friend in the forest who, already well-adjusted, greeted her with a string of vulgar words: "My ears stood up and I said to my husband, 'what will be?' He said 'we will get used to it.' I never got used to it. I could never use this kind of language."[16]

Similarly, when one of the well-educated and refined young women came to the forest some of the common women called her a whore, a frequently used expression. In her innocence, she argued that she was sexually inexperienced and therefore not a whore.[17]

In general within all the Russian partisan units and among all forest dwellers cursing was widely accepted, as was heavy drinking. Former members of the lower classes had no trouble adjusting to these patterns.

About the Bielski otriad the disapproving voice of the intellectual Shmuel Geler says that:

> People did drink before an expedition and after an expedition. In the winter people drank to feel warmer and in the summer not to feel the heat. Everyone did drink, even women. It was seen as proper behavior. Some partisans paid with their lives for this weakness. Sometimes they were attacked when they slept after a drinking spree . . . People saw these abuses, but did not talk much about them.[18]

Most agree that drinking made life easier. It helped them to forget.[19] Tuvia's wife, at that time not yet 20, admits to drinking: "a cup, a glass, but not more. All of us used to drink. I was never drunk. The doctor told me to drink, it kept away illnesses."[20] In fact, some feel that Tuvia's success as a commander was enhanced because in his continuous dealings with Russian partisans "he could outdrink them and he could curse like they did."[21]

While the Bielski detachment accepted all Jewish fugitives, no matter who they were, internally the group was stratified according to those criteria that mattered most to the group's existence and survival. The top elite were the Bielski brothers, their wives, some relatives and close friends. A part of this upper crust were also those who worked at the headquarters.

Next in importance were young men with guns. Below the young men with guns were craftsmen and artisans. The craftsmen and artisans enjoyed a more privileged position in the second year of the otriad's existence, in the fall of 1943, when the otriad built many workshops and factories. Within these various workshops and factories, the skilled workers had a higher social standing than the unskilled workers or those whose skills were of no use to the camp.

At the bottom of the social ladder were those who did only manual unskilled labor, such as kitchen duty, chopping wood, or taking care of the cows and horses.[22] In fact, the bulk of the people, those who had no special skills, no special functions and no guns, were at the bottom of the social ladder. These people were contemptuously called "malbush." Malbush, or malbushim in the plural, is a Hebrew term for clothes. No one seems to know how the term acquired its negative meaning.[23]

How did the different classes relate to the otriad's two most basic needs: safety and food? How did the people feel about the newly emergent strata and their privileges? Tuvia Bielski and those who belonged to the headquarters were in charge of the otriad's policies and activities related to safety and food. The young men with guns, the fighters, defended their people when attacked and indirectly protected them by participating in joint anti-German military moves.

Because so many members in the otriad were incapable of supplying themselves with food, the burden of feeding the people fell upon the young male fighters who devoted most of their energies to gathering provisions. Food expeditions were exhausting and dangerous, sometimes ending in the death of the participants.

In the second year of the otriad's existence, though still life-endangering, the actual delivery of provisions became more stabilized. Coming back from a food expedition the men

> would drive up in the wagons to the storage place and leave all the food there. If they had brought luxury items, like cream, eggs, etc., they could take them for themselves. This was their privilege. But the basic goods belonged to the camp. Then it was distributed. There was a special person who gave flour to the bakers, vegetables to the kitchen, etc.[24]

At first Tuvia tried to enforce the rule that everything collected during a food expedition had to be distributed equally to all members of the otriad. But when the food collectors refused to obey, without formally acknowledging defeat, Tuvia pretended not to see. Taking part of the provisions, before delivering them to the otriad, became a semi-legal activity. One of the participants describes how it was done:

When we would come back from a food expedition with 7–8 cows, about 3–4 kilometers before our base we would select the best cow, kill it, and divide it among the 10–12 of us who were a part of the expedition. We had people among us who knew how to slaughter and butcher a cow, take the skin off, cut up, and clean it. In the winter we would put the meat into the snow, it would be preserved this way.[25]

At this stage too the skilled laborers and artisans, because of their participation in factories and workshops, improved the economic conditions of the otriad as well as their own situation. Often unofficially, they were rewarded for their special skills with food. They, and all who directly or indirectly benefited from the unequal distribution of food, approved of the existing inequities.

In contrast, the malbushim, who ate only what was officially allotted to them by the otriad, reacted in a variety of ways. Some of them tried to make the best of the situation, saying: "We were not starving, we also did not have an abundance, some had more than others. We had enough. We would collect berries in the forest, mushrooms. This helped, too."[26] Others seemed to support this view by claiming that people were neither hungry nor full, that there was enough bread and that the bread was of excellent quality.[27]

Still others were less satisfied. In fact, quite a few of those I interviewed insisted that they were hungry.[28] One of them, who identifies herself as a malbush, recalled: "When I would come to the kitchen I was dizzy from hunger. I am telling you the truth. I don't accuse anyone. The Bielski family ate better. It was their right, it was coming to them."[29]

Resigned to their situations, some malbushim even rationalized their lot when they said that: "Those in power had to eat better. There is no equality in any place and there was no equality in the forest either."[30] Other comments took an interesting twist:

> I was not a communist, never thought that people should have the same. Those who did not go for expeditions would get soup, sometimes bread and potatoes in peels. There was no salt. If the cook liked you, you would get a piece of lung or some such object that was swimming in the soup. If he did not like you, you would get watery soup.[31]

No matter how people felt about it, food assumed a central place in the forest. For most people, the day started with a trip to the kitchen. In the morning the kitchen consisted of a huge hole filled with burning wood. Suspended over it and hanging from a tree was a big kettle. The kettle contained brewed chicory. This was a substitute for coffee. To this drink were added two boiled, unpeeled potatoes or bread. This was breakfast. After that people went to work.[32]

The midday meal in the Bielski otriad was more substantial. Shmuel Amarant, the historian, describes this event:

> Long lines of people carrying food containers would form around the kitchen. Those who came pushed and shoved to be at the head of the line, to receive the soup at its thickest. There was much fighting and quarreling about one's place in line. Sometimes, the daily bread portion was distributed at the same time. On festive occasions, such as May first, they would distribute portions of sausage.[33]

However, in the second and last stage of the Bielski otriad's existence, many of the people "availed themselves of the 'unlawful' opportunities to acquire extra food which they cooked near or in their huts. The camp kitchen gradually deteriorated to serving the 'weaklings' of the camp who had to resign themselves to accept whatever rations they were given."[34]

Being at the bottom of the social ladder had other serious effects. One woman, a member of the prewar intelligentsia, explains her situation and that of others like her:

> The intelligentsia was down, we were depressed. We were not worth much, they made fun of us, that we were malbushim. We were not fit for this kind of life. We had no experience with horses, nothing. The rest, the majority of the people, were uneducated, close to the soil . . . I had little in common with them. I really did not know them. I wanted to be closer to them, but they did not want us. I worked all the time so they would not make fun of me.[35]

A young girl, a teenager, describes her father, who used to have a high position in the brewery in Lida: "In the otriad he became a malbush, he did nothing . . . he was intelligent, educated, but not resourceful at all. He was dirty, neglected. He was not counted as a human. No one would have recognized him. There were many disappointed people like him."[36]

Speaking about her husband another malbush reconfirms what was said before while raising an additional question:

> My husband came without a gun. He was not a great fighter. He had a high school education and he finished a technical school in Vilna . . . How the heroes are made, is a question one always asks. In general, the intelligentsia was not prepared to fight. We had one, Baran, a common man, limited in many ways,

till this day we don't know if he was a hero or an idiot. He would only want to fight and wanted to go on the most dangerous expeditions. He was a great fighter, not afraid of anything.[37]

At the bottom of the class ladder, as the lowest-ranking members of the community, the malbushim were more apathetic, less interested in what was happening. They found it more difficult to elaborate on different aspects of the otriad. For example, three intelligent women, all former malbushim, could tell me practically nothing about the workshops. Each was almost unaware of their existence. Most malbushim were basically uninformed about the workings of the camp.[38]

In the forest physical strength, perseverance, fearlessness and courage were highly valued. No one associated these characteristics with being a woman. Instead in the rough, jungle-like environment of the forest, most men were convinced that women were unfit for combat and therefore a burden. Here, just as in society in general, gender cut across the stratification system in important ways.

Estimates for women's participation in the entire Soviet partisan movement range from 2 to 5 percent. The majority of women who had come to the forests were Jewish. They came to avoid death. In contrast, most Christian women stayed in the forest because of a special attachment to a man. Only a fraction of them was motivated by a desire to oppose the Nazis, and an even smaller fraction came because their lives were endangered.

In Soviet detachments women who did not become the mistresses of Russian partisan officers were relegated to unimportant duties. The closest they came to combat tasks was as scouts and intelligence agents. But even these jobs were performed only rarely.[39] Eagerness to participate, or special fitness, rarely tipped the scale in their favor. Instead, most women were assigned to service jobs in the kitchen: cooking and keeping the place clean.[40]

While the male partisans resented all women, their resentment was more strongly directed against Jewish women. Jewish women were doubly disadvantaged; as Jews and as women. In fact, of the Jewish women a large but unknown proportion perished on their way to and inside the woods. Of those who stayed alive, some found refuge in Soviet and some in Jewish detachments. A small fraction made it on their own, as a part of small scattered family groups.

Of those who were accepted into a Russian otriad the majority became mistresses of Russian partisan officers. However, in the Soviet otriads men who had Jewish mistresses were under special pressure to terminate their relationships. Some refused to give in, while others broke off their connections to these women.[41]

While most male partisans were eager to have sexual relations with women, they accused them of promiscuity. The very women they desired as sexual partners they viewed with contempt. In male conversations, for example, the word "woman" was often substituted by the word "whore."[42]

Defined as sex objects and excluded from participation in valued activities, all women in the forest were relegated to dependent positions. Of the Jewish women, in particular, only few gained entry into a Russian otriad. Those who could became sexually involved with Russian partisan officers. But not all who sought entry were ready to trade sex for protection. Perhaps more significantly, only a fraction would have qualified for such transactions. Most women lacked two basic requirements: youth and good looks. Special skills could overcome these barriers. A physician or a nurse or a good cook would be accepted into a Soviet detachment, even though she refused to become someone's mistress, or did not qualify as one.[43]

In contrast, the Bielski otriad had no membership preconditions. Here full membership was guaranteed to all Jewish women. But the road to the Bielski camp was filled with grave dangers. The suffering of Jewish women in the forest was more serious if they did not come directly to the Bielski otriad. Some lost their families while hiding in the woods. Others, on the way to the camp, were raped by Russian partisans. For practically all of these women the Bielski otriad was the last resort, the last hope. Here a woman had more freedom than in other, non-Jewish otriads. In the Bielski camp the same basic rules applied equally to men and women. Every individual was entitled to an official allotment of food. From the start, Tuvia insisted that even those who did not contribute to the maintenance of the otriad, the elderly, the sick and the children, had to be fed. He allowed no deviations from this rule. Despite this open-door policy and such protective measures, even inside the Bielski otriad there were some gender inequalities. The fate of men and women followed the established forest pattern: women were excluded from leadership and combat roles. Moreover, a woman's social standing was determined by the position of the man to whom she was attached. If she remained single, her ranking was low unless she had special skills – usually medical skills.

Though faced with continuous threats, throughout its brief history the Bielski otriad continued to grow and expand. In fact, after the otriad achieved a semblance of stability, the Bielski partisans expanded their rescue activities. In addition to accepting all Jews who reached them, they would also send special guides into the surrounding ghettos to bring people into the forests. Special scouts were also dispatched into the countryside and forests to search for Jewish fugitives in need of help. Those found were accepted into the Bielski unit.

Whenever news reached the Bielski partisans that local civilians had denounced or killed a Jew, some of the young fighters would pay them a visit, kill the guilty together with their families and often destroy their farms. Before moving on they would leave a written warning that the same fate awaited all others who would harm Jews. Eventually, the local population realized that the Bielski partisans were serious. This knowledge prevented some from informing on Jews. Some were even eager to help. The roads from the ghettos to the forests became safer, encouraging more ghetto inmates to escape. Finally, too, whenever Jewish partisans in Soviet units felt threatened, they knew that they could count on finding shelter in the Bielski otriad. Some actually did.

By the summer of 1944, when the Russian army took over the area, the Bielski detachment numbered over 1,200 individuals. Most of them were older people, women and children, precisely those whom no one wanted. The Bielski otriad represents the largest armed rescue of Jews by Jews in Nazi occupied Europe.[44] The history of this unit corrects a serious omission and an equally serious distortion. The omission is the conspicuous silence about Jews who, while themselves threatened by death, were saving others. The distortion is the common description of European Jews as victims who went passively to their death.

Notes

1. This chapter relies on qualitative data that come from the following sources:
   A. Archival materials; unpublished testimonies of people who participated in the activities described in this chapter. These testimonies are a part of the archival collections in Israel, Poland and the United States.
   B. In-depth interviews conducted with people who were directly or indirectly connected with the events described.
   C. Wartime documents relevant to the topic, found in different archival collections.
   D. Secondary sources relevant to the topic, including biographies.

2. While some of these Soviet soldiers might have been willful deserters, others could have been left behind because of the special circumstances. The Russians were retreating fast, in a chaotic way, and pockets of the army might have inadvertently stayed on. Arad describes the Red Army's limited means of transportation. See Arad 1982:30). Also, Hersh Smolar (1989:4–8) talks about the difficulties in eluding the advancing German army.
3. It has been estimated that in the first six months of the war the Germans took over 3,000,000 Soviet soldiers as prisoners of war. See Ziemke (1964:143).

   Basically, Nazi policies toward Russian POWs consisted in economic exploitation and murder. Of the two, economic exploitation was an intermediary step that led to death. Economic exploitation in turn was closely related to political and economic conditions. See Ainsztein (1974:243); Gilbert (1989:373).
4. For statements about limited Belorussian nationalism see Fitzsimmons et al (1960:17, 50); Vakar (1956:185).
5. Dallin (1980:199) cites several German SD reports written at different times that illustrate the Belorussians' change of attitude toward the German occupation: (1) July, 1941. "We are enthusiastically received on all sides"; (2) August, 1942. "The basic attitude is one of deep resignation"; (3) October, 1943. "In truth the bulk of the population is hostile." Some historians feel that in large measure German cruelty was responsible for the expansion of the partisan movement. See Michel (1972:185); Vakar (1956:185). Moreover, in a secret report the Nazi Major Daven writes: "The natives don't think that there is a Jewish problem at all. This is due to the Communist influence that perceives no racial differences" (YIVO, the Berlin Collection, Box 30, Occ E3a-14).
6. Lestchinsky (1947:319–338); Lestchinsky (1956–1957:243–269); Polonsky (1972).
7. Ideological and political concerns came later, when the partisan ranks were augmented by arrivals from the Soviet Union and by Poles connected to the Polish underground. Pinchas Boldo, Personal Interview, Haifa, Israel, 1990; Hersh Smolar, Personal Interview, Tel Aviv, Israel, 1989–1990; Vakar (1956:191).
8. Even after the Russian–German war turned in favor of the Soviet Union, it was quite a while before the Soviet partisans became an effective force. Some are convinced that the partisan fighting was much less extensive than officially claimed. Boldo, Personal Interview, Tel Aviv, Israel, 1987–1988; Oswald Rufeisen, a member of the

Ponomarenko otriad, is convinced that the partisan battles and heroism have been highly exaggerated. See Tec(1990:201–202).

9. Amarant (1973).
10. Eliezer Engelstern, Yad Vashem Testimony, No. 3249/233. Some people say that the parts Openheim made were more precise than the originals.
11. To be sure, these are rough estimates. They were offered by: Tamara Rabinowicz, Haifa, Israel, 1990, Personal Interview; Chaja Bielski, Personal Interview, Haifa, Israel, 1987–1991; Pinchas Boldo, Personal Interview; Raja Kaplinski, Personal Interview, Tel Aviv, Israel, 1987–1989.
12. In most communities the first victims were prominent Jewish men. For example, in Lida, on July 5, 1941, the Germans collected together 200 men, all members of the Jewish elite, and murdered them. "Lida" in *Encyclopedia Judaica* (1971), Vol. 11, pp. 212–213. In Nowogrodek, too, the first victims were leaders of the Jewish community. ("Novogrudok" in *Encyclopedia Judaica*, Vol. 12, pp. 1237–1238). Philip Friedman (1980:387–408) notes that many of the Jewish leaders were deported to Russia, while others escaped as the Germans were occupying the region. Kahanowicz (1986) writes that the initial massive killings of Jewish leaders created a leadership gap.
13. These distinctions were noted by most Bielski partisans. A few examples are: Shmuel Geler, Yad Vashem Testimony No.1556/112; Raja Kaplinski, Personal Interview; Riva Reich, Personal Interview, Tel Aviv, Israel, 1989; Cvi H. Isler, Yad Vashem Testimony, No. 1706/113, was very sensitive to these conditions and tried to participate in activities associated with the working class.
14. Cvi H. Isler, Yad Vashem Testimony.
15. Tamara Rabinowicz, Personal Interview.
16. Luba Garfunk, Personal Interview, Tel Aviv, Israel, 1989; Cila Sawicki, Personal Interview, Tel Aviv, Israel, 1989.
17. Sulia Wolozhinski-Rubin, Personal Interview, Saddle River, New Jersey, 1988.
18. Shmuel Geler, Yad Vashem Testimony.
19. Chaja Bielski, Personal Interview; Pinchas Boldo, Personal Interview; Abraham Viner, Personal Interview, Haifa, Israel, 1990; Lili Krawitz, Personal Interview, Tel Aviv, Israel, 1989.
20. Lilka Bielski, Personal Interview, Brooklyn, New York, 1989.
21. Sulia Rubin, Personal Interview. Saddle Rock, New Jersey, U.S.A., 1988
22. Amarant (1973)

23. These ideas were expressed by practically everyone I spoke to. A few examples are: Tamara Rabinowicz, Personal Interview; Chaja Bielski, Personal Interview; Pinchas Boldo, Personal Interview; Baruch Kopold, Personal Interview, Haifa, Israel, 1990.
24. Raja Kaplinski, Personal Interview.
25. Shmuel Geler, Yad Vashem Testimony.
26. Tamara Rabinowicz, Personal Interview.
27. Shmuel Geler, Yad Vashem Testimony.
28. Among those who say that they were hungry are: Riva Kaganowicz-Bernstein, Personal Interview, New York, New York, 1988; Hana Stolowicki, Yad Vashem Testimony, No. 3439/191; Cila Sawicki, Personal Interview, Tel Aviv, Israel, 1989. Hanan Lefkovitz, Personal Interview, Tel Aviv, Israel, 1988, also told me that when he visited the otriad people complained to him that they did not have enough food. Still it is true that in the Bielski otriad no one ever died of hunger: Jacov Greenstein, Personal Interview, Tel Aviv, Israel, 1984–1990.
29. Cila Sawicki, Personal Interview.
30. Shmuel Geler, Yad Vashem Testimony.
31. Luba Garfunk, Personal Interview.
32. Tamara Rabinowicz, Personal Interview.
33. Amarant (1973).
34. Ibid.
35. Cila Sawicki, Personal Interview.
36. Hana Stolowicki, Yad Vashem Testimony.
37. Luba Garfunk, Personal Interview. Baran was a legendary figure, fearless, brave, not very intelligent. Pesia Bairach, Personal Interview, Tel Aviv, Israel, 1990, talks about him in the same way. See also *Sefer Hapartisanim Hajehudim* (*The Jewish Partisan Book*) (1958), vol. 1, p. 402.
38. Riva Kaganowicz-Bernstein, Personal Interview; Cila Sawicki, Personal Interview; Rosalia Gierszonowski-Wodakow, Personal Interview, New York, USA, 1989.
39. Ziemke, Earl (1964:143).
40. Hersh Smolar, Personal Interview.
41. No clear-cut figures are available. These estimates were offered by several partisans. Among them: Moshe Bairach, Personal Interview, Tel Aviv, Israel, 1988–1989; Raja Kaplinski, Personal Interview; Lazar Malbin, Personal Interview, Tel Aviv, Israel, 1987–1988.
42. Hersh Smolar, Personal Interview. It is interesting that some women used these expressions as well.

43. Doctors and nurses were in short supply and they were readily accepted into partisan groups: Berkowitz (1962). Cila Kapelowicz reached the Bielski otriad after she escaped from the Mir ghetto and after the few relatives and friends she was with were murdered by Russian partisans. She lives now in South Africa. I interviewed her when she was on a visit in Israel in 1987.
44. For a discussion of the extent, efficiency and implications of rescue by the Bielski detachment see Tec (1993:204–209).

References

Ainsztein, Rueben (1974) *Jewish Resistance in Occupied Eastern Europe.* New York: Barnes & Noble.

Amarant, Shmuel (1973) "The Tuvia Bielski Partisan Company," *Nvo Shel Adam* (Expressions of a Man). Trans. R. Goodman. Published privately with the help of Misrad Hahinuch V. Tarbut.

Arad, Yitzhak (1982) *Ghetto in Flames: The Struggle & Destruction of the Jews in Vilna in the Holocaust.* New York: Holocaust Library.

——(1989) *The Minsk Ghetto Soviet Jewish Partisans against the Nazis.* New York: Holocaust Library.

Berkowitz, Ester Krynicki Gorodejski (1962) "Sichrojnes Fun Der Deitscher Okupacje" ("Memories from The German Occupation"), in N. Blumenthal (ed.) *Mir.* Jerusalem: Memorial Books, Encyclopedia of the Diaspora

Dallin, Alexander (1980) *German Rule in Russia, 1941–1945: A Study of Occupation Policies.* New York: Octagon Books.

Fitzsimmons, Thomas, Malof, Peter, and Fiske, John C. (1960) *USSR.* New Haven: Hart Press.

Friedman, Philip (1980) "Jewish Resistance to Nazism," in Ada J. Friedman (ed.) *Roads to Extinction: Essays on the Holocaust.* Philadelphia: The Jewish Publication Society.

Gilbert, Martin (1989) *The Second World War: A Complete History.* New York: Henry Holt & Co.

Kaganowicz, Moshe (1986) "Why No Separate Jewish Partisan Movement was Established during World War II," in Isaak Kowalski (ed.) *Anthology of Armed Resistance to the Nazis, 1939–1945.* 3 vols. New York: Jewish Combatants Publishing House:25–40

Kowalski, Isaak (ed.) (1986) *Anthology of Armed Resistance to the Nazis, 1939–1945.* 3 vols. New York: Jewish Combatants Publishing House.

Lestchinsky, Jacob (1947) "Economic Aspects of Jewish Community

Organization in Independent Poland," *Jewish Social Studies* 9, Nos. 1–4.

—— (1956–1957) "The Industrial and Social Structure of the Jewish Population of Interbellum Poland," *YIVO Annual Social Science 2.*

Michel, Henri (1972) *The Shadow War: European Resistance, 1939–1945.* New York: Harper & Row.

Polonsky, Antony (1972) *Politics in Independent Poland, 1921–1939.* Oxford: Clarendon Press.

Sefer Hapartisanim Hajehudim (1958) *The Jewish Partisan Book.* Merchavia: Sifriat Poalim, Hashomer Hatzair, Vol. 1.

Smolar, Hersh (1989) *The Minsk Ghetto Soviet Jewish Partisans against the Jews.* New York: Holocaust Library.

Tec, Nechama (1990) *In The Lion's Den: The Life of Oswald Rufeisen.* New York: Oxford University Press.

—— (1993) *Defiance: The Bielski Partisans.* New York: Oxford University Press

Vakar, Nicholas P. (1956) *Belorussia, The Making of a Nation.* Cambridge: Harvard University Press.

Ziemke, Earl (1964) "Composition and Morale of the Partisan Movement," in John A. Armstrong (ed.) *Soviet Partisans in World War II.* Madison, WI.: The University of Wisconsin Press.

6

The "Parachutists' Mission" from a Gender Perspective

Judith Tydor Baumel

Blessed is the match
    that is consumed in kindling flame.
Blessed is the flame that burns
    in the secret fastness of the heart.
Blessed is the heart with strength
    to stop its beating for honor's sake.
Blessed is the match
    that is consumed in kindling flame.[1]

(Senesz in Syrkin 1971: intro.)

This poem, familiar to almost all school children in Israel, is considered by many to be the ultimate echo of Holocaust resistance in Israeli commemorative culture. Its haunting melody fills the airwaves on Yom HaShoah (Holocaust Memorial Day); its text has become indelibly woven into the tapestry of collective Israeli memory. Bridging Holocaust and Rebirth, victims and fighters, Diaspora and Yishuv (pre-State Israel), "Blessed is the Match" has metamorphosed into the cultural symbol of the "Parachutists' Mission" during World War II in which Jews from Palestine attempted to alleviate the plight of their beleaguered brethren under Nazi rule. Between 1943 and 1945 over three dozen parachutists from the Yishuv were dropped by the British army behind enemy lines in a clandestine mission to aid the Allied war effort. Simultaneously, the young volunteers were sent by the Yishuv's leaders to assist Jews in occupied Europe, strengthen existing communities, organize resistance and rebuild the Zionist movement.

Three women took part in the operation, each sent to a different front: Hannah Senesz to Hungary, Haviva Reik to Slovakia and Sara (Surika) Braverman to Romania. Senesz and Reik were among the seven parachutists who lost their lives at the hands of the Nazis and their collaborators; Braverman returned to Palestine where she played a pivotal role in her kibbutz movement until retiring several years ago. Of the three, only the poet Senesz, author of "Blessed is the Match," achieved national stature. Within months of her execution in Budapest at age 23 a unique set of circumstances catapulted her into the front row of the Israeli national pantheon. Valiantly succumbing to the dictum stating that collective national consciousness absorbs but one hero per event, Reik attained posthumous immortality among a smaller circle centering on her kibbutz movement. Braverman, separated by a hairbreadth from eternal fame due to her survival, was relegated to the depths of public oblivion (Baumel 1996ª:521–546).

For over five decades the Parachutists' Mission has held a special position in Israeli public memory. Numerous press articles exposed the operation and the individuals involved to public scrutiny. Commemorative albums, memoirs and investigations have shed light upon the protagonists' lesser-known exploits while films, television docudramas and even newspaper caricatures have embedded certain incidents – and specific parachutists, notably Hannah Senesz – deep into the cultural consciousness of a generation fifty years removed from the operation (Senesz 1971; Shadmi 1973; *Hannah's War* 1988). Centering on the juncture of myth, symbol and ethos, this cultural awareness has been accompanied by a serious academic debate regarding the Mission's relative successes and failures, and a reinterpretation of its organizers' true aims.

"Warfare and military service have played key roles in national histories and in the fashioning of gender identities," write Marilyn Lake and Joy Damousi in an introduction to their recent study of gender and war (Damousi and Lake 1995:1). Since the mid-1980s, a rising consciousness in western society has elicited a number of studies examining women's participation in both World Wars, national struggles and underground resistance movements. This growing academic and public interest has also been expressed in the commemorative sphere, as is seen by the York Cathedral memorial to local servicewomen killed during the two World Wars and the recent feminist reinterpretation of Anzac Day in Australia. In contrast, the female experience of the Parachutists' Mission has largely been ignored, with no attempt having been made critically to analyze it from a feminist perspective or explore its impact upon collective memory from the vantage point of women's studies.

This chapter will meet that challenge by examining the Mission through a gender-sensitive approach, addressing motivation, performance, interpersonal relationships and impact upon collective public memory in the light of feminist consciousness. First it will concentrate upon the three

women involved in the operation, exploring feminist issues as they were
seen at the time the events being described took place. Then it will re-
map the canvas of memory in the light of a feminist agenda, by analyzing
the Mission's public image as depicted in Israeli historiography, and
commemorated in both "official" and popular Israeli culture. Concen-
trating on the crossroads of history, memory and feminist dynamics, we
will attempt to uncover a lesser-known dimension of Jewish resistance
during the Holocaust: the "female voice" of the Parachutists' Mission
from the Yishuv during World War II.

* * *

The Parachutists' Mission was the culmination of almost a decade of
intelligence cooperation between the Yishuv and British military authorities. Early cooperative projects were carried out during the spring of 1941.
However, only after late 1942 did cooperation with the Palestinian
"natives" become truly attractive to the British. Having shifted their sights
to the Balkans, British military authorities discovered that they had few
persons familiar with the terrain, fluent in local languages and committed
enough to be willing to risk their lives to further the war effort. Suddenly
the Yishuv's offer of European-born, loyal and committed volunteers
became an intriguing solution to an acute military need. In early 1943
the Jewish Agency approached two British intelligence units – the "A
Force" (counter-propaganda and smuggling Allied prisoners of war out
of occupied Europe) and the ISLD (Inter-Service Liaison Department –
wireless training) – and proposed the idea of joint missions in the Balkans.
Both British units agreed in principle to the proposal and thus the idea of
the Parachutists' Mission was born (Gelber 1983:187)

From March 1943 until autumn 1944, the units prepared groups of
Jewish volunteers from Palestine for clandestine European operations.
Our protagonists – Senesz, Reik and Braverman – then joined the ranks
of volunteers, eager to return to Europe, rescue their families, fight the
Nazis and further the Zionist cause. Like many, all three parachutists were
kibbutz members, representatives of their youth movements who had
joined the mission straight from the ranks of the Palmach ("striking
forces"), the elite local defense units. Similarly, their motives were con-
gruent with those of their male counterparts. Almost all parachutists were
European-born, with close relatives still living in Europe (Senesz in
Hungary, Reik in Slovakia and Braverman in Romania). Like Senesz and
Braverman, the majority were in their early to mid-twenties (Reik was

30); some were already married (Reik was separated), with children. Many were individualists like Senesz, trying hard to integrate into their chosen kibbutz, but not always succeeding. A second group consisted of those who were singled out by their Palmach commanders as being uniquely driven, like Braverman, a burning internal need igniting their initiative. Others, like Reik, were considered "difficult" (those with personal problems or in conflict with their kibbutz) or "outsiders" to the circles in which they lived. Most were relatively new immigrants and newcomers to kibbutz life; almost none held important positions in their kibbutzim. This collective profile is corroborated by a recent study of Palmach recruitment, which shows how national, economic, social and personal constraints molded kibbutz enlistment policy during the war (Kadish 1995:39–94; Gilad 1952:193–197).

Training took place on two levels. While the British arranged wireless and paratrooper drilling, Jewish Agency, "Haganah" (pre-State army) and kibbutz representatives indoctrinated the volunteers, trained them to form rescue and resistance networks among the surviving Jews, assist refugees and rebuild the Zionist movements in liberated areas. Senesz, Reik and Braverman were given the same treatment and training as their male counterparts; as Palmach graduates, they were familiar with military equipment and regulations. In the socialist Yishuv atmosphere which perceived men and women as equals, the men accepted their presence with few reservations, granting them no special privileges or dispensations. This attitude would later leave its mark upon the Mission's historiography.

Initially, the volunteers refused to be inducted into the British army. However, they were ultimately classified as officers in order to protect them if captured by the Nazis. This was of little benefit to the female volunteers. As the Nazis had adopted the Geneva conference ruling, which stated that women caught in uniform behind enemy lines were to be treated as spies and not prisoners of war, their chances of remaining alive if captured were negligible.

By the spring of 1944 several teams of parachutists were already in Europe awaiting final orders or preparing to jump. Senesz and her Hungarian group watched helplessly as their native land was overrun by the Nazis. In June, the young parachutist crossed into Hungary ahead of her contingent but was immediately imprisoned by the Hungarian authorities. In an attempt to break Senesz's spirit her mother was brought to the Budapest prison to meet the daughter who had emigrated to Palestine five years earlier. Both were shocked by the meeting: unaware that her daughter was in the country, Catherine Senesz now faced a young woman with bruised eyes and a broken tooth. The younger Senesz could not believe her eyes: Jewish Agency officials had promised that her mother would be spirited out of Hungary long before she arrived in order to prevent her being used as a Nazi pawn. "Forgive me, mother," she cried upon meeting the older woman.

Arrested within days both mother and daughter passed the summer months in the same prison, occasionally able to exchange messages or catch a glimpse of each other. They were later joined by Joel Palgi and Peretz Goldstein, the two other members of the Palestinian contingent who had also been captured by the Hungarian authorities. Catherine Senesz was released in September 1944, but her daughter was tried for espionage in the early autumn of that year. Denying that she was a British spy, Hannah defended herself with valor and accused her judges of treason, but was sentenced to death. Offered a pardon if she admitted her guilt, she refused the suggestion out of hand. On November 6, 1944 the 23-year-old parachutist was shot to death in the prison courtyard, eyes unbound as she faced her executioners. Forced to join the death march from Budapest, Catherine Senesz escaped and eventually reached Palestine where she was reunited with her son, Giora, and lived until her death in 1992.

Meanwhile, additional Yishuv volunteers completed their training and prepared for transfer to Romania and Slovakia. Surika Braverman from Kibbutz Shamir, "the blond bombshell" in the words of her British superiors, was earmarked for Romania. (Foot and Langley 1980:231). Braverman, a representative of the Zionist left-wing youth movement, Hashomer Hatzair, had not completed her training, unable to overcome her fear of jumping. Years later she recalled the seconds of frozen terror when she realized that she couldn't make the jump: "It was my turn to jump from the plane, but when the English sergeant shouted 'go!' I automatically moved backward and remained on the floor as those behind me jumped, one after another." So great was her fear that Braverman even refused to jump in tandem, sandwiched between two of her sympathetic co-trainees.[1]

Unable to parachute with her comrades, Braverman flew to Yugoslavia where she joined Tito's partisans en route to Romania. As Romania was liberated by the Red Army before her arrival, Braverman operated in Yugoslavia and returned to Italy where she worked with Jewish refugees until making her way back to Palestine. Largely forgotten by the public, Braverman's parachuting trauma earned her a timid, defeatist image, far removed from the reality of her life. This image was strengthened by the label which she herself quoted on many occasions: "the parachutist who didn't jump" (Rivlin 1995:34-39).

Training at a later stage, Braverman had met Senesz only briefly. "She was a sweet young girl," recalled Braverman, "full of enthusiasm but not particularly deep." Senesz had belonged to a different kibbutz movement, the labor-oriented Hakibbutz Hameuchad, and the two had no shared youth movement background. In Reik, Braverman found a kindred spirit, both personally and ideologically, and true friendship kindled during their Palmach training, long before the Mission had begun.

Unlike Senesz and Braverman who had joined the Mission directly from their kibbutz as young, unencumbered women, Reik's path to the Palmach was more complicated. Before emigrating to Palestine in 1939, she had married a fellow Hashomer Hatzair member in Slovakia, Avraham Martinovich, in part to provide her widowed mother with a pension (Shadmi 1973:25–32). The couple made their home in Kibbutz Ma'anit but soon separated. Martinovich left the kibbutz, continuing to pine for Reik who maintained contact with him until departing for Bari. Simultaneously, she had several romantic relationships, the most serious of which involved the son of a wealthy landowner from the nearby town of Zichron Ya'akov.[2] "Haviva was ostracized by her kibbutz," recalled Braverman, "and was told that she would have to choose between them and her 'capitalist' boyfriend whose family owned the Zichron vineyards." Sent to Braverman's Kibbutz Shamir for a cooling-off period, the two became friends, joined the Palmach and trained simultaneously for their mission. "Haviva wasn't a girl, she was a woman," declared Braverman. "She came to the operation with life experience and temperament. And despite bitterness over her kibbutz's ultimatum, she remained steadfastly loyal to Hashomer Hatzair."[3] Reik was assigned to the group which prepared for a drop in the free Slovakian enclave of Banska Bystrica, her native town. As the center of the Slovakian revolt of 1944, Banska Bystrica had drawn thousands of Jewish refugees, many of whom had participated in the fighting and were to be the target population for the parachutists' Yishuv-related mission. At the last moment, however, Reik was forbidden to join her male colleagues – Haim Hermesh, Zvi Ben-Ya'akov and Refael Reiss – as the jump was a "blind" one, in which the chances of discovery were great. Bursting with rage, Reik convinced her commanding officer to allow her to join the mission if she could find alternative transportation. Luck was with her and within a day she was offered a seat on an American plane bringing supplies to the liberated enclave. "Some luck," remarked Braverman, "when she was informed that she couldn't jump I told her 'enough, now come home with me. You've done all you could.' But she had to try every possibility. 'How could I let the others go without me when there isn't a representative of

Hashomer Hatzair among them?!' she replied. So she went and got killed."[4]

Reik arrived four days before her comrades who were astonished to find her in contact with the local Zionist leaders. Painfully aware of the conditions in which 5,000 Jewish refugees were living, Reik set up a communal kitchen and organized a duty roster to combat hunger and internecine political warfare. For six weeks she fulfilled a multitude of tasks, assisting downed pilots returning to Allied hands while simultaneously acting as nurturer, organizer and peacemaker. With the stronghold's collapse in October the parachutists, joined by local Hashomer Hatzair members, moved to the hills with a group of refugees, as the partisans refused to take all but the young and able into their camp. Within days Reik, Ben-Ya'akov and Reiss (Hermesh managed to escape) were captured by Ukrainian forces and incarcerated along with the refugees. Not having identified themselves as British officers, Reik and Reiss were murdered alongside 250 imprisoned Jews on November 20, 1944. The third member of their group, Ben-Ya'akov, was treated as a prisoner of war and transferred to Mauthausen where he was executed with a group of officers in late December of that year. The last of the group, Abba Berdichev, who had left for Romania in late October, was seized by the enemy before crossing the border, and was later murdered in Mauthausen (Hermesh 1971:191–192).

Thus, two of the three women parachutists – Senesz and Reik – lost their lives along with five of their male comrades. Within months the Parachutists' Mission had become widely recognized in Palestine as the Yishuv's main contribution in fighting Nazism and assisting European Jewry. At that time, the balance sheet of failures versus successes, which was later to form the nucleus of a political and historical debate, was still a moot point. The newly established State of Israel was in need of heroes, and the parachutists – particularly the young poet Senesz, whose valor became a symbol of the entire mission – had all the qualities necessary to meet this need.

* * *

I now turn to the image of the Parachutists' Mission, and particularly that of the female parachutists, as perceived by the collective national memory of the State of Israel. The tools by which this collective memory was created – official and popular historiography, literature, commemorative ritual, plastic representation and the like – give us a clue to understanding this collective perception, and particularly that pertaining to the complete picture of its protagonists. "The relationship between historiography and literature is . . . as tenuous and difficult to define as that between historiography and science," states Hayden White. "In part, no doubt, . . . because historiography in the West arose against the background of a distinctively literary discourse which itself took shape against the even more archaic discourse of myth" (White 1987:44). This juncture of myth, image, literature and history is the starting point for probing the memory of "women's voices" emanating from the Parachutists' Mission.

Concomitantly, the social and tangible aspects of collective memory came into play, reflecting the cultural perceptions of an event while simultaneously moulding its future image. As Susanne Kuechler and Walter Melion succinctly state: "memory is socially and culturally constructed . . . and operates through representation . . . modalities of recollection are historically based . . . and forgetting can be the selective process through which memory achieves social and cultural definition" (Kuechler and Melion 1971:7). In practice, it is often the move from verbal to visual formulations which bestows upon an act its final form, that which is indelibly imprinted upon a society's collective memory. As we will see in the case of the Parachutists' Mission, this was particularly true regarding gender-sensitive issues and sexuality, both factors having direct bearing on a total historical image.

The image of the Parachutists' Mission was imprinted upon the collective memory of Israelis in several stages, each mirroring that society's culture and values from the mid-1940s onward. I have delineated three stages during which the Mission's image evolved. The first step in de-gendering the parachutists' images – and particularly those of the female trio – was taken by the volunteers themselves, both during the Mission and soon after its tragic conclusion. Here we see how the protagonists set the tone for a lack of historiographical and literary male/female differentiation by their own attitude toward the Mission which made no social or military distinction between the tasks, responsibilities, and rewards of male and female parachutists. With the exception of the British prohibition on allowing female parachutists to participate in blind drops, no operational gender-related differences were evident during the Mission. The British assigned similar intelligence tasks to men and women out of necessity, as seen by Foot and Langley's description of the dozens of women sent by the MI9 on clandestine missions; the Yishuv did so out of an equality ethos which was a basis for the socialist society being created in the Yishuv (Foot and Langley 1980:187–190). This *de jure* equality was not altered by the traditional gender-related tasks (nurturing, protecting the elderly or feeble) which, for example, Haviva Reik carried out as part of her Zionist (as opposed to British) mission. Yet even when dealing with the European groups, which in all probability would have responded differently to female, as opposed to male parachutists – the local Jews whom they assisted, the authorities which imprisoned them, etc. – Israeli historiography makes no mention of anything but total equality (Rivlin 1995:34–35). I have therefore entitled this first period – the years 1943–1945 – "unawareness" of gender differences, a state which stemmed from a combination of British military necessity and socialist-Zionist ideological ethos.

The Yishuv's socialist ethos of equality continued to leave its mark on the second historical period, lasting from the late 1940s until the mid-1970s. These were the State of Israel's formative years during which a national culture, consisting of ethos, symbol and myth, took form; the period when everything was still imbued with a sense of the heroic, accompanied by heavy overtones of socialist-Zionist ideology. These were the years when the Parachutists' Mission became a national symbol. The fact that the parachutists' sacrifice took place on European soil was of little importance; they came from the Yishuv to rescue their endangered brethren and raise the banner of resistance among them.

This motif was particularly prevalent in the "official" Israeli historiography of the Yishuv's resistance efforts during World War II. *The Hidden Shield*, published in 1952, depicting the parachutists' heroism and providing the public with the "full" – but doctored – details of their lives (Gilad 1952:223–614). Here one sees how descriptions of the female parachutists – particularly Reik and Senesz – are doctored to an extreme, omitting any mention of personal data (such as Reik's marriage, Senesz's romantic attachments or her overriding desire to become a martyr) which might mar the public image that the designers of Israel's political and literary climate were trying to create. A fuller depiction of Senesz is found in Joel Palgi's book, *A Great Wind Comes*, written soon after the mission. However there, too, one senses an unwillingness to deal with interpersonal issues, in view of the greater need to set down the larger historical events for posterity, at least from Palgi's point of view (Palgi 1946:25–30).

The same lacuna is also found in the "popular" and "grassroots" cultures of the period. Despite the existence of a budding Israeli counter-culture emerging from the 1950s onward, the Parachutists' Mission's sacrosanct nature was unsullied by even the slightest question mark (Zerubavel 1995:96–137). This tendency carried over into commemorative ceremonies, where the texts read aloud were usually "official" ones, emphasizing Zionist sacrifice and placing little emphasis on the details of the protagonists' lives, with the exception of their Zionist zeal (Ben-Yehuda 1995:271–306).

In all these spheres, the female parachutists' inviolability was conveyed by their image which was first neutered and later imbued with alternative, non-threatening sexual/gender characteristics. Hannah Senesz, the "Israeli Joan of Arc," became the local vestal virgin, her purity surpassed only by her heroism. Alternatively, she was portrayed as the devoted daughter, with her mother playing a unique role in later propelling her into the pantheon of Israeli heroism. From the mid-1940s onward Senesz became the mission's icon, later making the transition from national political symbol to cultural and educational figure for all segments of Israeli society. This was expressed by the publication of her poems (rewritten for literary style and language) and diary (fifteen editions of which were published between 1945 and 1994); several plays dealing with her life; and finally, a plethora of books published in various languages. All of these took their code from "official" Israeli historiography, perpetuating her as the mission's symbol, the child-virgin image which became a symbol of national valor.

However, a closer look at Senesz's life shows this depiction to be lacking depth and content. Neither "official" nor popular accounts of this period make any mention of Senesz's personal life, as if she were dedicated from birth to the Zionist ideal, leaving no room for love or family life. In spite of what seems to be a detailed description of her literary development, no references, even veiled, are made to her relationship with Joseph Weiss, a friend from her Hungarian youth, who had been her early and most important literary sounding board. Weiss pursued her after emigrating to Palestine, declaring his (unreciprocated) love, penning her love letters published only after her mother's death (Weiss 1996:6–22). Any mention of this relationship might have marred the purist, sexless image which the Israeli political and literary consensus had obviously decided that a national symbol must have. Even her diary was censored, with references to her Hungarian childhood and personal life removed as they might mar the image of the almost "sabra" heroine, pure in body and spirit.

A similarly doctored, two-dimensional picture was painted of Haviva Reik. Here the task was more difficult as Reik was separated, but still legally married, her name appearing as Martha Martinovich on all British documents. It was this name which appeared under her official picture published in the kibbutz movement's newsletter, announcing her death while on a British mission. With very few exceptions, the marital facet of her personal history was strikingly absent in the Mission's historiography or literary portrayal. In those cases where it was impossible to obscure the fact, her marriage was described as a fictitious undertaking of short duration, contracted solely in order to obtain a pension for her widowed mother or emigrate to Palestine on a British certificate. These depictions appear ludicrous next to her sketches of a 1938 Vienna honeymoon which strengthened her desire to emigrate, or in view of letters she wrote to her husband after he left the kibbutz, penned with love and longing.

To compensate for this lacuna in her personal history, and in view of the fact that it would be ridiculous to portray her – a married woman of 30, with several tumultuous love affairs behind her – as a companion to the virginal Senesz, Reik was stereotypically depicted as the "mother" figure in the female parachutist trinity, denied her female identity and vibrant sexuality which was so important a component of her total personality. Even Reik's "official" commemorative picture is a photograph of a stern-faced woman in profile, dressed in a British army uniform (Newsletter 1945). Yet the dry, sexless image it projects is light years removed from the reality of her life. In descriptions provided by her family, friends, and colleagues, the stern countenance is replaced by that of an adventurous, laughing young woman, straddling a motorbike, as she appears in a picture found at the Kibbutz seminar bearing her name, Givat Haviva (Haim 1946:1). Thus, Reik's image, as inscribed for posterity by her kibbutz movement and later filtering down to the general public, hid more than it revealed.

The third female parachutist, Surika Braverman, falls into a special category. Returning unscathed from the mission, she became part of the amorphous body of surviving parachutists who as a group became part of Israeli collective memory. Unlike Senesz and Reik who literally became part of the map of the State of Israel when their kibbutz movements named postwar settlements after them, Braverman's name was known to few outside of her kibbutz movement, her only public distinction having been that of the timid young woman afraid to jump. Yet in reality, parachuting was the least important part of the mission, leading directly to the capture of two male parachutists in Romania and one in Italy. In Braverman's case, the fact that she began her mission with a conventional landing was used to imbue her image with a stereotyped female characteristic – timidity – thus fitting the two-dimensional pattern which I have discerned, particularly in the case of the female parachutists.

In truth, the beautiful parachutist was a trailblazer in breaking barriers for women in the Palmach, later to hold high-ranking positions in the military security committees of her kibbutz movement. Nothing could be farther from her reality than the image given to her by popular historiography, which she herself later adopted, due either to culturally induced guilt or to the pressures of her kibbutz society, which judged both men and women by an absolute success/failure scale, regardless of sex, long into the 1960s (Bar On 1985:25).

How can one explain the dichotomy between the three parachutists' historical/cultural image and the reality of their lives? Why was a concerted effort made to ignore their female sexuality when the same was not done to the male members of the Mission? How is female as opposed to male sexuality used in political image-building? Finally, is this a solely Israeli phenomenon or does it have parallels in the historiography of other cultures regarding the military roles of women in war?

One answer is rooted in the male attitude toward women's wartime roles. Françoise Thebaud states in her study of the Great War: "Fear was the dominant emotion in the male reaction to the mobilization of women" (Thebaud 1994:35). This apprehension may have carried over into postwar descriptions of women's military activity, resulting in a two-dimensional description which removed a threatening element from the scene: their sexuality. Another answer is specifically related to women who were active in resistance, facing what Helene Eck calls "equality with respect to risk and reprisal" but not "an acknowledged equality of merit" (Eck 1994:219). Particularly in Eastern Europe where this equality was expressed in traditionally male spheres such as combat, fighting women became "good comrades" and not feminine beings. Older women were depicted as "mothers," as in Eastern European iconography of World War II (Baumel 1996:100–126). The same tendency may have evidenced itself in the descriptions of Senesz, Reik and Braverman.

The term "comrade" brings us to a specific Israeli issue: Socialist-Zionist ideology. As Dorit Paden-Eisenstark summed up: "since the beginning of the century, when the first kvutzot and kibbutzim were established in what was then called Palestine, the Jewish community in Israel became known as a society in which women had achieved full equality with men in all fields of life" (Paden-Eisenstark 1975:492). Within the pioneering society, this equality was accompanied by a dogmatic, almost defiant refusal to acknowledge gender differences, and particularly expressions of female sexuality, which was often culturally seen as more threatening to the well-being of society than its male counterpart. One example was the enforced collective bathing and sleeping arrangements on kibbutzim, lasting until the member's late teens. Another was the denial of gender differences between male and female soldiers, which resulted in Yishuv military leaders convincing themselves that the enemy would treat both sexes in the same manner, a belief overturned only when front-line female soldiers' bodies were mutilated at a massacre near Kibbutz Gevulot in 1948 while those of male soldiers were not.

The implicit threat of female sexuality can also explain the difference in historical/cultural treatment of the male and female parachutists. While all parachutists were neutered to an extent, only in the case of the female parachutists was an effort made to imbue them with alternative non-threatening female characteristics (virgin, daughter, mother, etc.). Concomitantly, no efforts were expended to deal with any facet of the three women's sexuality which could have contaminated their public image. Consequently, public commemoration of the Parachutists' Mission, as expressed in a national "cult of the fallen soldier," reinforced the image of Senesz as daughter-virgin and Reik as sacrificing mother. Even the burgeoning Israeli counter-culture was unwilling to take up that challenge, preferring to wrap itself in the "unawareness" of the previous period.

As the 1950s and 1960s unfolded, the edges of a Socialist-Zionist ideology began to soften and blur; not so the treatment of the parachutists, which rigidly maintained the stance of earlier years. I therefore characterize this period as one of "unwillingness" to recognize the gender-related aspects of the Parachutists' Mission, a more active position than the "unawareness" manifesting itself during the war years.

The third historical period, beginning in the late 1970s and lasting up to the mid-1990s, is characterized by a general change in the perception of western culture regarding woman's wartime roles. With the growing awareness of women's studies and feminist issues, and the development of research on "nature versus culture," "work versus family" and "public versus private" (Bock 1991:1–23), the female military experience was also reexamined from both the historical and cultural aspects. Female bonding, sexuality, unprecedented freedom from social conventions, financial independence and liberation of the body had all been latent topics in the postwar social discourse which preferred to concentrate upon equality, sacrifice and ordeal. Now they were granted a legitimate place in the examination of women's military experiences, particularly of those serving with the Allied powers (Condell and Liddiard 1987:22–47).

A similar awareness of women's issues slowly infiltrated Israeli society, politically expressing itself in a growing feminist movement and culturally evidencing itself in an increasing academic tolerance of feminist studies. As scholars began examining hitherto uncharted areas, it would have been natural to expect a similar scrutiny of the parachutists' mission. Yet the

critical examinations of the mission appearing in Israel during the 1980s
and 1990s continued to focus upon national and ideological issues, leaving
women's issues off the agenda. While various historical and sociological
topics were being reexamined from the feminist perspective, the Parachutists' Mission remain rooted in the stereotypes developed during the
late 1940s and early 1950s. Why?

One possibility takes its cue from the depth of Israeli collective national
memory. In the winter of 1994 the Israeli public was presented with an
"alternative Senesz" when the docudrama *The Kastner Trial* by Motti
Lerner was broadcast on Israeli State television. The three-part drama
provoked a public outcry even before its screening took place. Already
in the promotions the public was treated to the preview showing how
Senesz had broken during a Gestapo interrogation, telling them how to
find her two comrades. Before the serial was broadcast, Senesz's brother
Giora, backed by complete public support, petitioned the Israeli Supreme
Court to serve Israeli television with an injunction forbidding the episode
to be shown. Although the Court supported Lerner's claim for artistic
freedom, the Broadcasting Authority, not wishing to offend its viewers
outright, ultimately cut the scene from the serial.

Neither Giora Senesz's petition nor the Supreme Court's verdict
showed the depth of public sentiment demanding that Senesz's canonical
image be preserved, that of the myth upon which they had been raised.
This became evident in the scope of both the academic and public debates
about the revisionist depiction of the young heroine. For several weeks,
almost every newspaper in Israel carried stories, editorials and letters to
the editor, berating the attempt to besmirch the "untouchable virgin of
Israel." Indeed, several times during the following months, both the
official State channel and Israel's cable TV broadcast Menahem Golan's
epic, *Hannah's War*, in an attempt to compensate the public for its
unwillingness to shatter the myth, thus reinforcing the canonical version
of Senesz's story. Although the entire Mission (and particularly its
initiators' motives) came under public scrutiny, no individual parachutist
could be besmirched. In view of the depth of public sentiment, even an
experienced scholar might balk at the thought of publicizing a recently
unearthed remark, said to be Senesz's last words before execution: "I'm
only sorry that I die a virgin."[5] This is hardly a Zionist credo, such as the
last words attributed to the mythical Israeli hero Joseph Trumpeldor, "it
is good to die for one's country."

A second explanation is rooted in the sphere of documentation. Until
Senesz's uncensored diary and letters were published in 1994 and
Reik's complete files at Kibbutz Ma'anit were recently made available

to scholars, the primary source of information regarding the parachutists' images were memoirs and oral documentation: those of the mission's surviving members, their British and Yishuv commanders, friends and comrades. While the commanding officers usually provided researchers with "official" and rather dry versions of the Mission (the only exception being British commander Tony Simmond's open admiration of Braverman's looks), the others were usually more generous with information, up to a point.

"Of course we felt ourselves women," replied Braverman to my question about her experiences with Reik while training in Cairo. "We used to do all the usual things, talking long into the night about our plans and dreams, my need for adventure, Haviva's desire for children, our relationship with the men on the Mission. We may all have been comrades, but there was no doubt that the men treated us as women, at least when we were off duty."[6] Braverman recalled how the parachutists were ordered to camouflage themselves in order not to be recognized by friends and relatives in Europe after landing. "Haviva took it the farthest and one day she dyed her hair and bought a large hat to cover her face. The men didn't stop commenting about it." The fact that the male volunteers' attitude to their female counterparts was not as "comradely" as it appears in the missions' "official" historiography was hinted at by Haim Hermesh, the only survivor of the hapless Slovakian contingent. "Haviva was unique, and she was without doubt a *woman*. An organizer, a courageous fighter and a woman who had a tremendous effect upon the men with whom she worked."[7]

Only in one sphere did I come across a marked reticence among the surviving parachutists, and particularly Surika Braverman: "She was a normal young woman," remarked Braverman curtly to my questions about Reik's romances. Attempting to approach the subject from another direction, I again came up against a brick wall. Only after I told Braverman what I already knew of Reik's vineyard romance did she agree to fill in the few missing gaps. "It was all very complicated," she said, "connected to Haviva's attitude toward herself, her kibbutz and Hashomer Hatzair. As it affected a number of people, those of us who knew the truth decided that it would help no one to talk about it after Haviva was dead."[8]

The decision "not to speak ill of the dead" (as if acknowledging sexuality would be considered outré in the parachutists' inner world) also guided the creation of several other parachutists' public images, not only the female ones. In my conversations with the parachutists, I learned of another member's European liaison with a non-Jewish female partisan and his decision to marry her and bring her to Palestine after the war. He did not survive. Yet another conversation centered upon the relationships between the parachutists, some platonic, others less so. All the conversations were illuminating in view of the official stereotyped image of the mission with which every historian, nay, every schoolchild in Israel, was so familiar. All provided me with a different vision of the parachutists' mission, not only in terms of its gender aspects.

These conversations bring me to a third explanation for the unchanging image of the mission: that of moral dilemma. "As long as there are people still alive who will be hurt by stories of the parachutists 'real lives', do you really have to tell everything?!" remarked Braverman in exasperation. "So 'history' will 'suffer' for a few more years, but do the widows, brothers and sisters of the fallen, their friends and families, have to be told precisely how 'human' their loved ones were?"[9] While writing this chapter I often recalled these words as the historian in me wrestled with my moral conscience. "At least wait until Haviva and Hannah's last surviving relatives are gone," she once said. "The world waited fifty years for the stories, they can wait a few more," she concluded decisively. How ironic that Senesz's and Reik's surviving siblings died within days of each other during the winter of 1995–1996, weeks before Joseph Weiss's love letters to the young Hannah were published.

In view of the juxtaposition between a rising consciousness of women's issues in Israel and a marked reticence to delve into the reasons which shaped the mission's image, I have entitled this period "unable": scholars were already aware of the importance of the gender component in historical narrative but were still unable to probe it with respect to the Parachutists' Mission, thus perpetuating the timeworn, two-dimensional images of "comrades" Senesz, Reik and Braverman, which had evolved fifty years earlier.

The word "remember," states Nachman Ben-Yehuda in his history of the "Masada Myth," can be understood in two different ways. One is to "recollect"; the other is to "commemorate" (Ben-Yehuda 1995:272). Yet the two are inexorably intertwined in a perpetual circle. How one recollects an event affects its commemoration, influences which elements are stressed and which are neglected and thus forgotten. The image of the Parachutists' Mission in Israeli historiography and literature is the best proof of this connection. Consequently, the collective Israeli perception of the mission, particularly that of its female participants, remains stereotyped Yishuv imagery at best. Senesz is the virgin warrior, Reik is the universal mother and Braverman is the fearful phobic, if she is remembered at all. Yet as we have seen, the complete picture is so different, so much richer and fuller; in which the parachutists, both male and female, were human beings, with the accompanying drives, impetuosities, desires and failings. None of this detracts from the importance of their actions or mars their heroic image. Only now, fifty years after the Mission's end, are the first glimpses of the "real" parachutists coming to light, in terms of gender consciousness, political awareness and human frailties, without the moralistic overtones of the previous decades. For only a mature society, willing to face an intellectual and emotional challenge, is capable of dealing with the figure behind the myth instead of preferring a two-dimensional, sanitized version of a politically correct hero or heroine.

Notes

1. Author's interview with Surika Braverman, Kibbutz Shamir, September 6, 1993.
2. Author's interview with Haviva Reik Shklarsky (Haviva Reik's niece), Haifa, September 8, 1993.
3. Author's interview with Surika Braverman, Kibbutz Shamir, September 6, 1993.
4. Author's interview with Surika Braverman, Kibbutz Shamir, September 6, 1993.
5. Author's interview with a friend of Hannah Senesz at Kibbutz Sdot Yam, September 9, 1993, who requested anonymity.
6. Author's interview with Surika Braverman, Kibbutz Shamir, September 6, 1993.
7. Author's interview with Surika Braverman, Kibbutz Shamir, September 6, 1993.
8. Author's interview with Surika Braverman, Kibbutz Shamir, September 6, 1993.
9. Author's interview with Surika Braverman, Kibbutz Shamir, September 6, 1993.

References

Bar On, Y.(1985) "The Parachutist Who Didn't Jump". (Heb.) *Dvar Hashavua*, Feb. 1, p. 25.

Baumel, J.T. (1996a) "The Heroism of Hannah Senesz: An Exercise in Creating Collective National Memory in the State of Israel", *Journal of Contemporary History* 31, pp. 521–546.

Baumel, J.T. (1966) "Rachel Laments her Children: Representation of Women in Israeli Holocaust Memorials", *Israel Studies* 1, pp. 100–126.

Ben-Yehuda, N. (1995) *The Masada Myth: Collective Memory and Myth-making in Israel.* Madison: University of Wisconsin Press.

Bock, G. (1991) "Challenging Dichotomies: Perspectives on Women's History," in K. Offen, R. R. Rierson and J. Rendall (eds) *Writing Women's History: International Perspectives.* Houndsmills, Baskingstoke, Hampshire: Macmillan.

Condell D. and Liddiard, J. (1987) *Working for Victory? Images of Women in the First World War 1914–1918.* London: Routledge and Kegan Paul.

Damousi J. and Lake, M. (1995) *Gender and War: Australians at War in the Twentieth Century.* Cambridge: Cambridge University Press.

Eck, H. (1994) "French Women under Vichy," in F. Thebaud (ed.) *A History of Women in the West, V. Toward a Cultural Identity in the Twentieth Century.* Cambridge, Mass and London: Harvard University Press.

Foot, M.R.D. and Langley, J.M. (1980) *MI9: Escape and Evasion 1939–1945.* Boston: Little Brown.

Gelber, Y. (1983) *Jewish Palestine Volunteering in the British Army During the Second World War*, vol. 3. (Heb.) Jerusalem: Yad Ben Zvi.

Gilad, Z. (1952) *The Hidden Shield: The Activities of the Underground in Palestine During the Second World War.* (Heb.) Jerusalem: Jewish Agency Pub.

Haim C. (1946) "Haviva is No More". *Hedim*, Feb. p. 1.

Hermesh, H. (1971) *Operation Amsterdam.* (Heb.) Tel Aviv: Ma'arachot.

Kadish, A. (1995) *To Arms and Farms: The Hachsharot in the Palmach.* (Heb.) Tel-Aviv: Tag.

Kuechler, S. and Melion, W. (1991) *Images of Memory: On Remembering and Representation.* Washington and London: Smithsonian.

Newsletter 8/46, of the World Union of Hashomer Hatzair, the Leadership, Nov. 28, 1945.

Paden-Eisenstark, D. (1975) "Image and Reality: Women's Status in Israel," in Ruby Rohrlich-Leavitt (ed.) *Women Cross-Culturally: Change and Challenge.* The Hague, Mouton:491–505 ff.

Palgi, J. (1946) *A Great Wind Comes.* (Heb.) Tel-Aviv: HaKibbutz HaMeuchad.

Rivlin, G., Amir, R., Stampler, S. (1995) *Parachutists of Hope.* (Heb.) Tel-Aviv: Ma'arachot.

Senesz, H. (1971) *Her Life and Diary.* London: Valentine Mitchell.

Shadmi, E. (1973) *Without Finding, Without Surrendering: Haviva Reik's Mission.* (Heb.) Tel Aviv: Moreshet.

Syrkin, M. (1947) *Blessed is the Match: The Story of Jewish Resistance.* Philadelphia: JPS.

Thebaud, F. (1994) "The Great War and the Triumph of Sexual Division," in F. Thebaud, (ed.) *A History of Women in the West, V. Toward a Cultural Identity in the Twentieth Century.* Cambridge, Mass. and London: Harvard University Press.

Weiss, J. (1996) *Love Letters to Chana Senesh.* (Heb.) Tel Aviv: HaKibbutz Hameuchad.

White, H. (1987) *The Content of the Form: Narrative Discourse and Historical Representation.* Baltimore and London: Johns Hopkins.

Zerubavel, Y.(1995) *Recovered Roots: Collective Memory and the Making of Israeli National Tradition.* Chicago and London: University of Chicago Press.

7

Primo Levi's Periodic Art:
Survival in Auschwitz and the
Meaningfulness of Everyday Life
Murray Baumgarten

Perhaps only Italy, with its long tradition of Humanism, and in Italy Turin, the capital of industrial Piedmont, where more automobiles are produced than in any other European city, a place welcoming to the Jews who settled there in the fifteenth century bringing the silkworm trade with them, and a region that emancipated the Jews in 1848, could have given birth to Primo Levi. While these elements were already present in the young man of 22 who graduated *summa cum laude* in chemistry in 1941, their unique combination endows his later writing with its characteristic shape and form.[1] As a great artist and a scientist, whose science informed his art, and as a Jew bearing witness to the ravage inscribed on body and spirit by the Nazis and Auschwitz, his work has a special interest for our modern condition. And it may be, paradoxically, that this special combination of accurate observation, rigorous analysis, clear reasoning, linguistic sensitivity, imaginative conception, multi-cultural understanding and profound feeling was one of the reasons his work had so much initial difficulty in getting published[2] – besides the great reluctance of most European and American publishers to issue books on the Holocaust in the immediate post-war period when forgetting was high on the agenda of our civilization.

These are the qualities that make his work unique and, working together, inspire a narrative art that articulates habits of resistance to the totalitarian world of the concentration camps. At the center of his writing we find reflection – thinking and seeing in both senses of the word – which he elaborates into a philosophy of living in the everyday. While it would be important to trace the philosophical thinkers connected to his views, my emphasis in this chapter is on the ways in which his art not only presents but enacts the process of resistance. His writing not only reports on his past experience in the concentration-camp universe of the Nazi war against the Jews but also engages us in the present moment of its reading to comprehend how human beings could create and operate the extermination machine called Auschwitz. Spanning past and present, his writing gives us back that process of remembering which alone makes a civilized future possible.

As we read his work – for example, what has been published in the United States in English translation as *Survival in Auschwitz, The Reawakening,* or *The Periodic Table* – we encounter not only accurate description – the how it was – but a multi-leveled analysis of why it took place. The how is past tense; the why is present tense. Thus *Se questo e un uomo,* as it was entitled in Italian and better translated in its British version as *If This Be a Man,* or *La Tregua,* called *The Reawakening* in the United States and, more accurately, *The Truce* in Great Britain – not only describes Primo Levi's experience and resistance but puts the how and why of Auschwitz to the reader. This doubled movement of the narrative (inside and outside) situates the reader in a position parallel to Primo Levi's, both as narrator of and agent in the text. We participate with the narrator in the process of discovery. That is, we too discover that the Holocaust is not simply an episode in past history but an ongoing experience demanding further inquiry, questioning and, above all, reflection.

This, after all, is what happened to Primo Levi, who survived Auschwitz and after the war returned home to Turin, and went about the business of reconstructing his life while his country and civilization were doing the same. In "Vanadium," the penultimate chapter in his autobiographical fable, *The Periodic Table* (published in Italian in 1975 and translated into English in 1984 by Raymond Rosenthal), Primo Levi recounts a series of events connected with his postwar work as manager of a paint factory in Turin. There was a problem with a shipment of resin used to make varnishes; instead of drying and hardening upon application, the varnish "after application remained indefinitely sticky, like lugubrious flypaper" (Levi 1984:212). The supplier of the resin, "a large and respectable German company," one of the segments into which, "after the war, the Allies had dismembered the omnipotent IG-Farben," and which he only identifies as W – it is still, he notes, a "large and respectable German company" that "before admitting their guilt, throws on the scales all the weight of their prestige and all their ability at wearing you down" – must be apprised of the problem in order that a resolution may be found. Primo Levi therefore writes "a well-mannered letter of protest, setting forth the terms of the problem" and in a few days receives "a long and pedantic" response that "ignored our need for immediate action, and on the essential point simply stated that the relevant tests were under way" (ibid., 212). A second letter is sent, accompanied by a request for another shipment, and urges the company "to check with particular care the resin's behavior." This letter too receives a long-winded pedantic answer, along with the suggestion that the addition of 0.1 percent of vanadium naphthenate – "an addition that until then had never been heard of in the world of varnishes" (ibid., 213) – will solve the problem. The two letters are signed by Dr Mueller, a common name in Germany, and yet, Levi writes, "I could not quiet a doubt, the kind that refuses to be pushed aside and rasps slightly within you, like termites" (ibid.), that this is the same Dr Mueller who was the civilian inspector of the chemistry laboratory Primo Levi worked in during the winter of 1944 in Buna-Auschwitz. His suspicion has been aroused by a misspelling – the h in naphthenate is missing in both letters, an error that his Auschwitz inspector had consistently made.

Many Holocaust memoirs have a heated quality bordering on the melodramatic and rely on adjectives and adverbs for their impact. By contrast *The Periodic Table* is a "cool" book, the work of a chemist "who weighs and divides, measures and judges on the basis of assured proofs, and strives to answer questions." These scientific habits carry over into this writing which finds "the right word that is commensurate, concise, and strong" to "dredge up events from my memory" and describes them "with the greatest rigor and the least clutter" (ibid:153).

What Primo Levi has stumbled into through this postwar difficulty with resin is the rare opportunity to pursue his research into "the human soul," a project triggered by his experience in Auschwitz. Chemistry and the human soul, we discover, are paired in Primo Levi's experience, in part as a result of the chemistry examination which he, the summa cum laude graduate in chemistry from the University of Turin in 1941, took in Auschwitz in the winter of 1944. Administered by one Dr Pannwitz, it led to his spending that winter in the warmth and relative security of a chemistry laboratory as well as his contact with Dr Mueller. For Primo Levi both men remain enigmatic. Since that time "I have asked myself how he [Primo Levi speaks here of Mueller but is also thinking of Pannwitz] really functioned as a man; how he filled his time, outside of the Polymerization and the Indo-Germanic conscience; above all when I was once more a free man, I wanted to meet him again, not from a spirit of revenge, but merely from a personal curiosity about the human soul" (Levi 1961:96). It is this project that has been reawakened by the vanadium naphthenate episode. This is not only a typical and representative moment in Primo Levi's writing but a revelatory one which shows us the kinds of questions he is asking about his experience in Auschwitz as well as the context which generates them. And this inquiry into the human soul will be governed by the rules of scientific evidence, a rare combination, and perhaps for that reason alone one of the most important.

Mueller, like Pannwitz, helped save Primo Levi: they were key figures among the Germans who carried out the order to produce synthetic rubber at Buna-Auschwitz, and did not flinch in the face of the Russian offensive and the probable knowledge that they had lost the war. First Primo Levi encountered Pannwitz: "he is tall, thin, blond; he has eyes, hair, and nose as all Germans ought to have them, and sits formidably behind a complicated writing-table. I, Haeftling 174517, stand in his office, which is a real office, shining, clean and ordered, and I feel that I would leave a dirty stain whatever I touched." Note how this writing brings us into the presence of that which is described and makes us a participant in the experience; perhaps it is the cool declarative sentences that produce this miracle. Primo Levi continues: "When he finished writing, he [Pannwitz] raised his eyes and looked at me."

This look sparks Levi's inquiry: "Because that look was not one between two men; and if I had known how completely to explain the nature of that look, which came as if across the glass window of an aquarium between two beings who live in different worlds, I would also have explained the essence of the great insanity of the third Germany." For Pannwitz does not look *at* but through Primo Levi; he does not recognize or acknowledge him as a member of the same species. To look at him and meet his gaze would be to encounter him as a man as he, Pannwitz, is a man – and then it would be difficult to kill him. Tolstoy described such a moment more than a hundred years earlier in *War and Peace* when Napoleon's troops during their disastrous retreat pull out Russian prisoners for execution; those whom like Pierre they look in the eye, they pass over. Not so Pannwitz:

> One felt in that moment, in an immediate manner, what we all thought and said of the Germans. The brain which governed those blue eyes and those manicured hands said: "This something in front of me belongs to a species which it is obviously opportune to suppress. In this particular case, one has to first make sure that it does not contain some utilizable element." And in my head, like seeds in an empty pumpkin: "Blue eyes and fair hair are essentially wicked. No communication possible." (Levi 1961:97).

Mueller too was a German, and, as Primo Levi learned as a result of the vanadium naphthenate encounter, also a Nazi; yet Mueller had helped him perhaps even more than Pannwitz had. Note how Levi's description helps us see not only the man but his encounter with the Jew.

> He must have been a person of some authority because everybody saluted him first. He was a tall, corpulent man of about forty, more coarse than refined in appearance. He had spoken to me only three times, and all three times with a timidity rare in that place, as if he were ashamed of something. The first time only about the work (the dosage of the Naptylamin, in fact); the second time he had asked me why I had so long a beard, to which I had replied that none of us had a razor, in fact not even a handkerchief, and that our beards were shaved officially every Monday; the third time he had given me a note, written neatly on a typewriter, which authorized me to shave also on Thursday and to be issued by the *Effektenmagazin* a pair of leather shoes and had asked me, addressing me formally, "Why do you look so perturbed?" (Levi 1984:214)

Primo Levi's response is part of his research project into this human and German soul, and it is fitting that it is first expressed in German: "I, who at that time thought in German, had said to myself, 'Der Mann hat keine Ahnung.' (This fellow hasn't got an inkling)" (ibid., 214). The puzzle, the mystery even, of Pannwitz but even more so of Mueller is captured in the German phrase, better translated into more colloquial English as, "He doesn't have a clue."

And it is not a puzzle that is dead and gone and has become a part of a historical past but a present confrontation. Primo Levi's German phrase becomes the signature of that moment. But the description does not close off the experience; the German phrase lingers in his and our memory, as the conundrum of this human being, who was in charge of a crucial unit in the Nazi war effort located in Auschwitz, and yet did not have a clue – *keine Ahnung* – about what was happening.

The phrase also echoes a central aspect of Primo Levi's experience. Unlike most Italians, Primo Levi knew some German; he had been a student of chemistry and had studied it so well as to imbibe the German in which in the first four decades of the twentieth century most serious chemical research was conducted. Faced with the shouted commands in the strange language of the concentration camps whose functional base was German, most Italian prisoners had not a clue of what was being asked of them. As a result, they were quickly judged to be useless and selected for the gas chambers. As Primo Levi comments in an interview,

> Few of us Italian Jews understood German or Polish – very few. I knew a few words of German. Under those conditions, the language barrier was fatal. Almost all the Italians died from it. Because from the very first days they

didn't understand the orders, and this wasn't allowed, wasn't tolerated. They didn't understand the orders and couldn't say so. They heard a shout, because Germans, German soldiers, always shout.

The consequences of this lack of comprehension meant that though "the order got shouted" it wasn't understood "and therefore the Italians always got there last. You'd ask for information, news, explanations from your bunk mate, and he didn't listen and didn't understand. This fact was already the first big obstacle to unity, to recognizing ourselves as comrades." The impact was to separate the Italian Jews from each other and isolate them into individuals who were then completely at the mercy of this incomprehensible system. By contrast, Primo Levi notes,

> I – I've always said I was lucky – I found I had a little bit of the German language at my command, as a chemist I'd studied it, and so I was able to establish some sort of communication with the non-Italians, and this was essential for understanding where I was living, the rules of the place. And also for perceiving the sense of unity . . . In fact, I remember that when contacts were established with some friendly French, Hungarian, and Greek prisoners, we felt that we'd taken a step upward.[3]

Building on his knowledge of German, Primo Levi was able to make his way to some extent in Auschwitz. And when he took his chemistry exam his technical scientific German came back to him, which he describes in a moving incident in *Survival in Auschwitz*, for that knowledge and skill made it possible for him to survive the bitter winter. After the war, when he was working for the paint factory, he had occasion to travel to Germany and often spoke German for business purposes. The surprise at finding an Italian speaking German always seems to have led his hosts to ask how he knew their language, whereupon his reply that he had learned German in Auschwitz significantly changed the tenor of the ensuing business negotiations.

The experience of Auschwitz even after his return to Turin remains for Primo Levi a babel of tongues. If the camps had lasted longer, Levi notes, "a new harsh language would have been born" (Cicioni: 1995: 32). In this strange mixture, certain words become the things themselves; they no longer function as parts of speech but have the weight of objects, and as such the force of a radical stripped meaning. Here is how Levi describes it at the end of *The Reawakening:*

> I reached Turin on 19 October, after thirty five days of travel; my house was still standing, all my family was alive, and no one was expecting me. I was

swollen, bearded and in rags, and had difficulty in making myself recognized. I found my friends full of life, the warmth of secure meals, the solidity of daily work, the liberating joy of recounting my story. I found a large clean bed, which in the evening (a moment of terror) yielded softly under my weight. But only after many months did I lose the habit of walking with my glance fixed to the ground, as if searching for something to eat or to pocket hastily or to sell for bread; and a dream full of horror has still not ceased to visit me, at sometimes frequent, sometimes longer, intervals.

The narrative now moves into the present tense, leaving the narrative past tense characteristic of *The Reawakening*. We move out of everyday, normal reality to reenter with this narrator the nightmare, super-reality and sur-reality of the concentration camp universe.

It is a dream within a dream, varied in detail, one in substance. I am sitting at a table with my family, or with friends, or at work, or in the green countryside; in short, in a peaceful relaxed environment, apparently without tension or affliction; yet I feel a deep and subtle anguish, the definite sensation of an impending threat. And in fact, as the dream proceeds, slowly or brutally, each time in a different way, everything collapses and disintegrates around me, the scenery, the walls, the people, while the anguish becomes more intense and more precise. Now everything has changed to chaos; I am alone in the center of a grey and turbid nothing, and now, I *know* what this thing means, and I also know that I have always known it; I am in the Lager once more, and nothing is true outside the Lager. All the rest was a brief pause, a deception of the senses, a dream; my family, nature in flower, my home. Now this inner dream, this dream of peace, is over, and in the outer dream, which continues, gelid, a well-known voice resounds: a single word, not imperious, but brief and subdued. It is the dawn command of Auschwitz, a foreign word, feared and expected: get up, "wstawach" (ibid., 193–194).

As a Jew and an Italian, an artist and a scientist, Primo Levi built bridges between the different cultures he lived in; but those bridges were not available to describe the world of the concentration camps. That world's purpose – the demolition of human beings – was perhaps beyond language, and the words in which it took place were also destroyed and turned into dumb, mute things. The early chapters of *The Reawakening* reveal the sudden and urgent need of the survivors "to become full human beings again" by using the "free words created and used by free men" which had been denied to them in Auschwitz. As Mirna Cicioni (1995:42) notes, "the entire book pulsates with the need to communicate, to create links between languages, cultures, and human beings." Primo Levi the bridge builder is making his way back to normal life by accepting and fulfilling this human need. And in counterpoint to the joy of the free use of language now available to him stands Hurbinek, the three-year-old boy, "whom nobody had taught to speak, and who dies soon after being freed, at the end of a desperate struggle to utter meaningful sounds.

> Hurbinek, who was three years old and had perhaps been born in Auschwitz and had never seen a tree; Hurbinek, who had fought like a man, to his last breath, to win his entry into the world of man, from which a bestial power had excluded him; Hurbinek, the nameless, whose tiny forearm had also been branded with the tattoo of Auschwitz; Hurbinek died in the first days of March 1945, free but not redeemed. Nothing is left of him; he bears witness through these words of mine. (Cicioni 1995:43)

It is thus both surprising and fully comprehensible that Primo Levi will comment *in German* on Mueller's unwillingness to understand the world of Auschwitz which he, as a German, has participated in constructing, in a riveting phrase: *Der Mann hat keine Ahnung.* And if Primo Levi is to make sense of this chance encounter with him in the new, free, perhaps normal world of postwar Western European culture and business relations, it will have to be in German (as well as Italian) that it is expressed. And we, his readers, will have to comprehend the world of the Lager – the word he uses so insistently – not Holocaust, not *univers concentrationnaire*, but this German word for these unspeakable places, the *Lager*, with him.

It would be worth asking, with Primo Levi, what kind of personality type functions as Mueller and Pannwitz did, conducting themselves so as "not to have a clue" about the meaning of their actions beyond the compartmentalized immediate response to a bureaucratic problem, which is solved in those terms and no others. Other writers, among them Christopher Browning and Hannah Arendt, have explored these issues as I have in other writings; what I want to focus on now is what it means that Primo Levi, *Haeftling* 174517, was carrying on such an inquiry in the middle of his unspeakable world. What kind of a man was that? And what urged him to these questions when all around him all questions had been stifled?

It is worth recalling the moment when Primo Levi first learned that questions of any kind were out of order in Auschwitz. It was part of his introduction to this new order of experience, after "the tattooing operation was finished." When Primo Levi asks a veteran of the Lager "if at least they would give us back our toothbrushes," he responds, "*Vous n'êtes pas à la maison.* And it is this refrain that we hear repeated by everyone:

"you are not at home, this is not a sanatorium, the only exit is by way of the Chimney." But this event is only the prologue to the full meaning of the Lager, enforced in the following episode.

> Driven by thirst, I eyed a fine icicle outside the window, within hand's reach. I opened the window and broke off the icicle but at once a large, heavy guard prowling outside brutally snatched it away from me. *'Warum,'* I asked him in my poor German. *'Hier ist kein warum'* (there is no why here), he replied, pushing me inside with a shove (Levi 1961:24–25).

To narrate the experience of *Hier ist kein warum* as event and action makes the recipient of its message, be it the reader or Primo Levi himself, passive; we are numbed and shocked out of the possibility of asking questions. We become one of those who await whatever fate will send their way.

In this context, Primo Levi's description of Null Achtzehn – zero eighteen – is particularly revealing, for this prisoner has even given up his name and now is identified only by the last three digits of his tattooed number – how symbolic that the first number in this series is zero – and he "passively follows orders without trying to avoid work or to acquire extra food." Given Primo Levi's – the character in this narrative – attention to detail, and his designation of prisoners and *kapos* by nicknames, the absence of a name for this prisoner "becomes a powerful lesson of how to lose one's humanity and not survive."[4] In this prisoner's acceptance of the German purpose of his destruction, Primo Levi the narrator of this book, looks towards the response of the living in "The Last One," a chapter which focuses on the hanging of the last member of the Sonderkommando revolt and the shame felt by the prisoners who march past his suspended body. There, taking on both character and narrator roles, Primo Levi notes that "to destroy a man is difficult, almost as difficult as to create one; it has not been easy, it has not been quick, but you Germans have succeeded. Here we are," he acknowledges in the voice of Haeftling 174517, "docile under your gaze; you have nothing more to fear from us; no acts of rebellion, no words of defiance, not even a look of judgement" (Cicioni 1995:29). The shame of the prisoners is that they have now all become fatalists, Mussulmen as they were called in the camps, accepting without complaint what is being done to them.

It is clear, however, that no fatalist, no Mussulman is narrating this account. While the narrator has taken on the position and perspective of Primo Levi, Haeftling 174517, accepted the system of the Lager and internalized his oppression for the moment, the reader experiences the other side of the contradiction, the will to keep on resisting. He reaches for a sense of personal dignity and identity – exactly what is being destroyed in these prisoners. In the context of the camps, dignity has been defined by Todorov as "continuing to be a subject in possession of his or her own free will, capable of making decisions followed by action" (Cicioni 1995:29). The structure of the narrative thus positions the reader and the narrator so as to make it possible both to comprehend why prisoners could become numbed and thus fall into fatalism like Null Achtzehn, *and* at the same time have the potential to become not just survivors but, as Primo Levi insists time and again, *witnesses* – for the insistent detail and sharp differentiation of individuals in this account in contrast to the haze of fatalism encourages resistance. Some other question, which encompasses that of the *Warum*, has taken hold.

The narrative has embedded this experience, which can lead in mutually opposing directions, in a set of overarching questions, at once scientific and artistic. They nest in the title of Primo Levi's books, particularly the first, so inadequately translated into American English as *Survival in Auschwitz*. Were that issue of survival the one issue at stake, the message of *Hier ist kein warum,* – there is no why here – would be followed only by recoil, acceptance and passivity – and probable death. But, throughout, all the events narrated direct us to an issue larger than the individual moment which is at the same time contained by and informs that moment. That issue is present in the Italian title of the book, *Se questo e un uomo*: If this be a man. It informs the poem Levi wrote, *Shem*a, from which he took the title of his book and which serves as its epigraph.

> You who live safe
> In your warm houses,
> You who find, returning in the evening,
> Hot food and friendly faces:
>> Consider if this is a man
>> Who works in the mud,
>> Who does not know peace,
>> Who fights for a scrap of bread,
>> Who dies because of a yes or a no.
>> Consider if this is a woman,
>> Without hair and without name
>> With no more strength to remember,
>> Her eyes empty and her womb cold
>> Like a frog in winter.
> Meditate that this came about:
> I commend these words to you.

Carve them in your heart
At home, in the street,
Going to bed, rising:
Repeat them to your children,
    Or may your house fall apart,
    May illness impede you,
    May your children turn their faces from you.

And the object of this question is whether a man can exist in the world of the Lager, which is directed to turning Jews, as well as most of its other inmates, but primarily Jews, into a species far below humans in the inverted Nazi racial evolutionary hierarchy.

We are in the presence of a powerful humanist and scientific research project: *Se questo e un uomo*: if this be a man. Nothing is irrelevant to this project; everything signifies. This is the assumption that makes it possible to turn the subhuman brute level of existence into which he and the other Jews have been forced by the Nazis to exist in Auschwitz – the prelude they thought to extermination – into a symbolic system of meaning. What Primo Levi provides us is the work of thought which brings the hope of meaningfulness into this Lager dedicated to the destruction of meaning and the extermination of the Jews. It is everywhere in his writing but nowhere more fully present than the episode entitled "Initiation," the fourth chapter of *Survival in Auschwitz*, when Steinlauf, the Austrian soldier, shows Levi how important it is to wash hands and face every morning – even in water as dirty as the hands and faces of the prisoners.

Primo Levi begins the account by confessing that "after only one week of prison, the instinct for cleanliness disappeared in me." The process of demolition, which has already begun, is interrupted by this incident. "I wander aimlessly around the washroom when I suddenly see Steinlauf, my friend aged almost fifty, with nude torso, scrub his neck and shoulders with little success (he has no soap) but great energy. Steinlauf sees me and greets me, and without preamble asks me severely why I do not wash." The question, coupled to the example of his friend's action, produces an inner questioning. Given the power of the convention of the first-person narration at work, the questions Primo Levi asks also become the reader's questions. With him we interrogate ourselves: "Why should I wash? Would I be better off than I am? Would I please someone more? Would I live a day, an hour longer?" This barrage of questions leads to an immediate, irritated response – to a set of answers that form a prologue to another set of questions. "I would probably live a shorter time, because to wash is an effort, a waste of energy and warmth." But the questions persist as the inner dialogue continues.

> Does not Steinlauf know that after half an hour with the coal sacks every difference between him and me will have disappeared? The more I think about it, the more washing one's face in our condition seems a stupid feat, even frivolous: a mechanical habit, or worse, a dismal repetition of an extinct rite. We will all die, we are all about to die: if they give me ten minutes between the reveille and work, I want to dedicate them to something else, to draw into myself, to weigh up things, or merely to look at the sky and think that I am looking at it perhaps for the last time; or even to let myself live, to indulge myself in the luxury of an idle moment.

But his friend will not leave him in the isolation of his self-justification. "Steinlauf interrupts me. He has finished washing and is now drying himself with his cloth jacket which he was holding before wrapped up between his knees and which he will now put on. And without interrupting the operation he administers me a complete lesson." What Steinlauf has done is to break through the self-absorption the Lager incites in its prisoners as part of its strategy of dividing and conquering from within as well as from without. And Primo Levi's response merges the retrospective understanding of the witness and the prospective experience of the prisoner, bridging them by commenting on Steinlauf's language.

> It grieves me now that I have forgotten his plain, outspoken words, the words of ex-sergeant Steinlauf of the Austro-Hungarian army, Iron Cross of the '14–'18 war. It grieves me because it means that I have to translate his uncertain Italian and his quiet manner of speaking of a good soldier into my language of an incredulous man. But this was the sense, not forgotten either then or later: that precisely because the Lager was a great machine to reduce us to beasts, we must not become beasts; that even in this place one can survive, and therefore one must want to survive, to tell the story, to bear witness; and that to survive we must force ourselves to save at least the skeleton, the scaffolding, the form of civilization. We are slaves, deprived of every right, exposed to every insult, condemned to certain death, but we still possess one power, and we must defend it with all our strength for it is the last – the power to refuse our consent. So we must certainly wash our faces without soap in dirty water and dry ourselves on our jackets. We must polish our shoes, not because the regulation states it, but for dignity and propriety. We must walk erect, without dragging our feet, not in homage to Prussian discipline but to remain alive, not to begin to die (Levi 1961:40, 41).

Though the passage begins with Primo Levi's grief at not remembering the exact words, it concludes with a precise, careful statement of principles. They read like the report of a careful experiment. They are principles to be inscribed on the body, mind and spirit even more thoroughly than a tattoo.

It is as a scientist, then, that Primo Levi writes. But what he writes about challenges his right to be a scientist engaged in free inquiry. How then, and under what conditions, can his research proceed? The ninth chapter of *Survival in Auschwitz*, at the very middle of the book, offers us the relevant conditions.

Primo Levi begins the chapter, "The Drowned and the Saved," not by judging but by inquiring: "What we have so far said and will say concerns the ambiguous life of the Lager. In our days many men have lived in this cruel manner, crushed against the bottom, but each for a relatively short period; so that we can perhaps ask ourselves if it is necessary or good to retain any memory of this exceptional human state" (Levi 1961:79). Where normal responses might be to respond with the desire to obliterate even the memory of the Lager, and other writers deliver apodictic judgements against it, cursing it at the very moment of its naming, Levi asks a question, and proceeds to follow it through all its implications.

> To this question we feel that we have to reply in the affirmative. We are in fact convinced that no human experience is without meaning or unworthy of analysis, and that fundamental values, even if they are not positive, can be deduced from this particular world which we are describing. We would also like to consider that the Lager was preeminently a gigantic biological and social experiment. (ibid.)

What in other writers forms the detail of the description, as they recount the events of their experience, in Primo Levi's writing is reflection. The emphasis on thinking and seeing is clear, for part of the purpose of this thinking is to recover the body-image that has been ground to bits. Given the infernal logic of the Lager, it is not surprising that no mirrors were allowed in it, and that Primo Levi can only see himself as if in a mirror when he is in the laboratory.

> Faced with the girls of the laboratory, we three feel ourselves sink into the ground from shame and embarrassment. We know what we look like: we see each other and sometimes we happen to see our reflection in a clean window. We are ridiculous and repugnant. Our cranium is bald on Monday, and covered by a short brownish mould by Saturday. We have a swollen and yellow face, marked permanently by the cuts made by the hasty barber, and often by bruises

and numbed sores; our neck is long and knobbly, like that of plucked chickens. Our clothes are incredibly dirty, stained by mud, grease, and blood; Kandel's breeches only arrive halfway down his calves, showing his big, hairy ankles; my jacket runs off my shoulders as if off a wooden clothes-hanger. We are full of fleas, and we often scratch ourselves shamelessly; we have to ask permission to go to the latrines with humiliating frequency. Our wooden shoes are insupportably noisy and plastered with alternate layers of mud and regulation grease.

What is involved here is not seeing in its simple sense but understanding – viewing the self from the standpoint of another, in a word, reflection with its doubled meanings. And this too they experience as a result of the laboratory.

Besides which, we are accustomed to our smell, but the girls are not and never miss a chance of showing it. It is not the generic smell of the badly washed, but the smell of the Haeftling, faint and sweetish, which greeted us at our arrival in the Lager and which tenaciously pervades the dormitories, kitchens, washrooms, and closets of the Lager. One acquires it at once and one never loses it: "so young and already stinking!" is our way of greeting new arrivals. (ibid., 142)

In this way his text reinforces the point that resistance in Auschwitz was not just an individual action. For Primo Levi, thinking, seeing and reflecting can only be done as part of a community. Inner speech is only possible as internalized dialogue, as Hannah Arendt reminds us; one cannot speak to oneself if there is no one else in the horizon of experience to speak with. The degradation that resulted from pitting the prisoners against each other was thus part of the systematic strategy of the Lager: not only is this the Hobbesian war of all against all, it is also the destruction of the self as agent who can continue to struggle. Given this condition, the moments of human reaching-out make it possible for life to continue.

Steinlauf's lesson is reinforced by Lorenzo, the Italian mason who provided Primo Levi with food every day for six months – and even more than that bodily nourishment.

I believe that it was really due to Lorenzo that I am alive today; and not so much for his material aid, as for his having constantly reminded me by his presence, by his natural and plain manner of being good, that there still existed a just world outside our own, something and someone still pure and whole, not corrupt, not savage, extraneous to hatred and terror; something difficult to define, a remote possibility of good, but for which it was worth striving. (ibid., 121)

These are speech-acts which reconstruct civilization; they constitute community; and make it possible for its participants to continue to resist by the daily acts of life.

It is not surprising that the need to speak about the Lager was central to Primo Levi's experience, immediately after its destruction, as well as for the rest of his life. And similarly that it was the woman who listened most closely who became his life-long partner and wife. The same impulse moved these men in the Lager, each day, like his fellow inmate, Resnyk, who "told me his story." Telling their stories, they insisted they were in the Lager but not of it. Though he has forgotten it, Primo Levi adds that it was

> a sorrowful, cruel and moving story; because so are all our stories, hundreds of thousands of stories, all different and all full of a tragic, disturbing necessity. We tell them to each other in the evening, and they take place in Norway, Italy, Algeria, the Ukraine, and are simple and incomprehensible like the stories in the Bible. But are they not themselves stories of a new Bible? (ibid., 59)

Each of these stories is different, Levi notes, and yet he also implies that they are all the same story, lurching toward the same end. Each of them is distinguished by the effort to find meaning in randomness, amid this senselessness of the Nazi mass production of Jewish suffering and death, and thus wrest at least an epitaph from the impersonality and abstractness of this grim historical process. In blending the stories together, Primo Levi's description creates a sense of the common destiny of a scattered people, echoing the biblical "emotion of multitude" (Yeats 1961:89) in which a diffused group suddenly becomes a whole motivated by similar national values and goals. His account reveals the way in which these individuals became part of the *amchu,* the muttered name, that, during these difficult times, became a secret, self-designating badge Jews used to identify themselves to each other. In this Hebrew word the possessive suffix for "your" is joined to the noun for "people" to produce a striking image. "*Your people*": the listener who hears this utterance acknowledges the speaker as one of his own community, whether or not he knows of the biblical power of this word in designating the Jews as God's (chosen) people. Hearing *amchu,* the listener recognizes the speaker's existence as a member of the professing community of Jews in a moment of mutual acknowledgment – in a moment of I/Thou recognition, rather than the I/It of the yellow star they were forced to wear.

These are the conditions that governed the chance encounter of Primo

Levi, Holocaust witness, and one Mueller, Nazi chemist with a propensity to leave out the "h" in naphthalene. The event, Primo Levi tells us,

> the return of that "pt" had thrown me into a state of violent agitation. To find myself man to man, having a reckoning with one of the "others" had been my keenest and most constant desire since I had left the concentration camp. It had been met only partly by letters from my German readers; they did not satisfy me, those honest, generalized declarations of repentance and solidarity on the part of people I had never seen, whose other face I did not know, and who probably were not implicated except emotionally. The encounter I looked forward to with so much intensity as to dream of it (in German) at night, was an encounter with one of them down there, who had disposed of us, who had not looked into our eyes, as though we didn't have eyes. Not to take my revenge: I am not the Count of Montecristo. Only to reestablish the right proportions, and to say. "Well?" If this Mueller was my Mueller, he was not the perfect antagonist, because in some way, perhaps only for a moment, he had felt pity, or just only a rudiment of professional solidarity. Perhaps even less: perhaps he had only resented the fact that the strange hybrid of colleague and instrument that after all was a chemist frequented a laboratory without the *Anstand*, the decorum, that the laboratory demands, but the others around him had not even felt this. He was not the perfect antagonist: but, as is known, perfection belongs to narrated events, not to those we live. (Levi, 1984:215)

Primo Levi wrote to ask him if he were the Mueller of Buna, enclosing a copy of the German edition of *Se questo e un uomo*. Mueller replied in a personal letter, which arrived on March 2, 1967. He admitted to being the Mueller of Buna; yes "he had read my book, recognized with emotion persons and places; he was happy to know that I had survived." He added that "he had reread, for the occasion, his notes on that period" and wanted to discuss them with me in a "hoped-for personal meeting, useful both to myself and to you, and necessary for the purpose of overcoming that terrible past ('*im Sinne der Bewältigung der so furchtbaren Vergangenheit.*')" He concluded his letter by declaring that "among all the prisoners he had met at Auschwitz, I was the one who had made the strongest and most lasting impression." Primo Levi notes that this could be flattery but it seemed that "the man expected something from me."

Now that "the undertaking had succeeded" and "the adversary was snared," Primo Levi, faced with the necessity of a reply, felt embarrassed. A colleague almost, a man who wrote like Primo Levi "on paper with a letterhead," it was "obvious that he [Mueller] wanted from me something like an absolution, because he had a past to overcome and I didn't; I wanted from him only a discount on the bill for the defective resin. The situation was interesting but atypical: it coincided only in part with that of the reprobate hauled before a judge."

Primo Levi now writes to him in Italian for in German he would have made "ridiculous mistakes." And he limits his response – though "I had many questions. Why Auschwitz? Why Pannwitz? Why the children in the gas chambers?" He asks him "only whether he accepted the judgments, implicit and explicit, of my book." (Levi 1984:217–218)

Another chapter would be needed to discuss the rest of this vanadium episode and to explore in detail his effort to understand the response of Mueller, "the work of an inept writer: rhetorical, sincere only by half, full of digressions and farfetched praise, moving, pedantic and clumsy: it defied any summary, all-encompassing judgment." (219) Primo Levi's interpretation of that eight-page letter, which contained a photograph of a man at once "grown old and at the same time ennobled by a skillful photographer," brings back to him those words "of distracted and momentary compassion" spoken in the Lager: "Why do you look so perturbed?" If Mueller had not had a clue about what was happening before – *der Mann hat keine Ahnung* – by the time he wrote the letter, things had changed. And it was for his cowardice in not acknowledging it then and now that Primo Levi judges him and his fellow Germans. Let us hope that a future historian will not judge us in similar terms.

Notes

1. "Piedmont was our true country," he tells us in "Potassium" in *The Periodic Table*, "the one in which we recognized ourselves; the mountains around Turin, visible on clear days, and within reach of a bicycle, were ours, irreplaceable, and had taught us fatigue, endurance, and a certain wisdom. In short, our roots were in Piedmont and Turin, not enormous but deep, extensive and fantastically intertwined" (Levi 1984:50–51). My thanks to Professor Ruby Rohrlich for bringing this passage to my attention.

2. Rejected by the major publishers, it was issued in 1947 in 2,500 copies by a small firm which almost immediately went out of business; it was 12 years before Einaudi published it in 1958; by 1979, 500,000 copies had been sold in Italy alone.

3. Camon 1989:23–24.
4. Cicioni 1995:36.

References

Camon, Ferdinando (1989) *Conversations with Primo Levi*. Trans. John Shepley. Marlboro, Vermont: The Marlboro Press.

Cicioni, Mirna (1995) *Primo Levi: Bridges of Knowledge*. Oxford: Berg.

Levi, Primo (1961) *Survival in Auschwitz*. Trans. Stuart Woolf. New York: MacMillan Publishing Co.

—— (1984) *The Periodic Table*. Trans. Raymond Rosenthal. New York: Schocken.

—— (1987) *The Reawakening*. Trans. Raymond Rosenthal. New York: MacMillan Publishing Co.

Yeats, William Butler (1961) *Essays & Introductions*. London: Macmillan.

8

An Uncommon Bond of Friendship:
Family and Survival in Auschwitz

Ami Neiberger[1]

The formation of "family" groups among prisoners in concentration camps was common, but historians are only beginning to understand the uncommon bonds of friendship that developed during the Holocaust. The purpose of this chapter is to describe family groups among women who survived Auschwitz, and the important role that families played in survival. The term "family" denotes a group of three or more women who tried to stay together, and identified with a shared group identity. These cohesive groups helped their members survive by pooling resources and energies, and devoted considerable effort to helping each other stay alive. This chapter draws on a variety of sources, including published and unpublished written memoirs, as well as a series of interviews conducted by the American Jewish Committee for the Holocaust Survival Project.

Several historians have commented on the need to study friendship groups among concentration camp prisoners. Sybil Milton (1984:313–314) called for a closer examination of these "little families," noting that family groups played an important role in survival. Feminist historians, including Joan Miriam Ringelheim (1985), Marlene Heinemann (1986), Andreas Lixl-Purcell (1994) and Myrna Goldenberg (1990), uncovered further evidence of women's friendship networks and discussed the need for further research.[2]

But they were not the first to observe friendship groups. Studying how people survived the camps, sociologist Elmer Luchterhand (1967) concluded that stable pairing was the most common interpersonal relationship formed by prisoners. In his study of survivors, only 8.5 percent of his sample formed few or no stable friendships inside the camps. The remainder formed a variety of stable pairs, and both small and large cohesive groups. Drawing on his interviews with survivors, Shamai Davidson (1979) described camp life as "radically social." Woven within descriptions of great suffering, Davidson unearthed stories of mutual help among prisoners and the "creation of stable social units." He wrote that the "need to help appeared to be as basic as the need for help." In particular, Davidson noted that women's groups were characterized by intense group loyalties and distinctly differentiated group identities.[3] In another study, Leo Eitinger (1994:476) observed that individuals who developed coping mechanisms which "enhanced [their] contact with a group or were based on intact or positive value systems" played an important role in determining survival and postwar recovery.

However, those who most poignantly testify to the existence of families are the survivors themselves. In her interview after the war, survivor Betty B. commented that Auschwitz was experienced not only on an individual level, but also by the community as a whole.[4] Auschwitz assaulted individuality by stripping incoming prisoners of identity signifiers, such as their names, clothing, hair and personal appearance. Combined with the loss of personal space, conditions which made even the most basic human functions torturous, a rigorous routine, and severe overcrowding, women entering Auschwitz were literally melded into a monolithic mass of persecuted humanity. Starvation, hard labor and disease reduced bodies to emaciated *Musselmännere* [the camp name for the most apathetic prisoners], awaiting imminent death. By weaving a web of relationships in a place as inhuman and barbaric as Auschwitz, families helped women survive by allowing them to rebuild their lost identities.

Sometimes uniting groups of relatives, and often assembled by circumstance, families bound together blood-related sisters, cousins, acquaintances and even unrelated strangers. When Livia Bitton Jackson arrived at Auschwitz with her mother from Hungary, they found an aunt and two cousins, and made a conscious decision to form a "family" of five (Jackson 1980:77–78). Arriving together could make conditions easier for family members. Coming to Auschwitz from Holland, Rachella M. and her sister Flora were tattooed with sequential numbers. In her interview, Rachella recalled that these numbers made it easier for them to stay together and said that she and Flora would often hold hands to keep themselves linked together in the large crowds of prisoners. They also took comfort from this simple human gesture.[5] Kitty Hart and her mother also received sequential tattoo numbers when they arrived at the camp after being shipped from a prison in Dessau, Germany. They had escaped from the Lublin ghetto and were originally from Poland (Hart 1982:62).

The high fatality rate, reshuffling of prisoners to new labor assignments and barracks, and frequent transfers to other camps made finding friends and relatives quite difficult, if not outright impossible. Searching for loved ones required ingenuity and determination, in addition to luck. Often the only free time available would be the one to two hours after evening roll-call and before curfew. Physician Gisella Perl, who worked in the Auschwitz infirmary after she was sent to the camp from Hungary, remembered treasuring her free time:

> The use of this short time was developed into an art . . . It filled our thoughts day and night and we planned every minute of it . . . First we ran to the water faucet to still our burning thirst, fighting, pushing, screaming at one another . . . we hurried to find our friends and relatives, exchange a few words of affection, and comfort one another . . . if we could only keep alive. (Perl 1984:34)

Preserving blood ties, even among distant relatives, provided a link for women to the homes and heritage they had lost. In her interview, Lydia B. recalled arriving at Auschwitz from Transylvania. Then in her late teens, Lydia formed a family group with her sister and three cousins, one of whom was a sister-in-law in her twenties who assumed a maternal role within the group.[6] Lydia B. remembered reminiscing about her home with them and credited them with saving her life by forcing her to eat food that anywhere else would have been deemed inedible.[6]

Within their family of eight Dutch women, Bloeme Evers-Emden was among the youngest. Along with Anita, she helped their "camp mothers" Lydia and Nettie with errands such as fetching water, because the others were twenty years older and their strength sometimes gave out.[7] In the same family group, Lenie de Jong-Van Naarden noted that the group came together "intuitively" and credited them with helping her survive by bolstering her spirits and sharing their food.[8] They were so devoted to each other that they maintained close friendships after the war ended.

Another survivor from Hungary who entered the camp in her teens, Lily L., described a family of five which united four relatives and included another girl from the same vicinity.[9] This was quite common. For example, Sara Zyskind's family of five formed gradually in Auschwitz. First Sara spied her friend Surtcha in another group, and managed to join her by sneaking out of line and switching groups. Jammed together in an overcrowded barracks, Sara and Surtcha befriended another girl because the *kapo* ordered everyone to sit on the floor and they sat on her. Hearing this girl weep because she was alone, Sara comforted her saying, "Surtcha and I will be your sisters. Let's try and keep together" (Zyskind 1981:196). They later added two more members to their family. Entering Auschwitz a little older than the women mentioned above, Charlotte Delbo (1968:20, 44) described a family of eight women who stayed together. Like many others, their family was characterized by stable pairing. Although the group members identified themselves as part of the larger family, they would frequently "pair off" within the group.

At times, pairing was safer for the survival of the group. Charlotte Delbo (1968:102–108) described a brutal and deadly game of "sport" by the *kapos*. Forced to carry heavy dirt while running back and forth across the compound, Delbo's family of eight survived the "sport" by splitting into pairs and supporting each other. She remembered feeling sorry for those who fell and cried out for help, but was afraid of being separated from her family members. She continued to run with them as they shared the blows distributed by the *kapos*, with stronger women in the family supporting weaker ones. Pairing also allowed individuals to form deep friendships within their families, even though social interaction was severely restricted by the rigid living conditions imposed on them by the camp routine. These partnerships could be very deep and affectionate. For example, Charlotte Delbo (1968:73–74) described her friend Viva as both her sister and her mother.

Not all family groups had five members, but cooperating within a group of five was very practical in Auschwitz. Rations were often distributed in sets of five, and several hours per day were spent lined up or marching by fives. Being able to form a row of five quickly could spare the women abuse from the *kapos,* who frequently created order by beating everyone into place. Those who could form a row of five quickly might obtain certain privileges. For example, Lily L. recalled how her "family" was able to form a row quickly at the front of a column, and credits their quick action for getting them onto a labor transport that went to a better camp in Riga and out of Auschwitz.[10]

Occasionally when the work parties marched through the camp gate going to or from their assignments outside the camp, the officials would perform a sudden selection, by standing on each side of the gate and observing each row as it marched through. Anyone who stumbled, tripped or looked ill was removed and killed. Families shielded their weaker members by strategically placing them on the inside of a row and a few paces further from the eyes of the officials. Sick inmates were carried by their family members until they reached the gate, enabling them to conserve and focus their limited strength for the inspection march through the gate (Delbo 1968:51–52, 93–94).

While a large network of friends was an advantage, pairing within a large family group allowed it to place members into different labor commandos. This enabled them to increase the variety of resources they could "organize" or steal, without forcing anyone to be alone. Noting that organizing was a calculated risk because of its danger, survivor Kitty Hart commented that organizing was the only way to survive. She described what organizing meant for a family in tangible terms: "One acquired some bread, another found a handkerchief or a pencil and some scraps of paper, another a mug of water" (Hart 1982:69–70). Kitty was employed for a while in the Kanada commando, which sorted the luggage brought to Auschwitz by the large transports of Jews shipped there for extermination and slave labor. Within her family of four girls, two sorted food, and two sorted clothing (ibid.,115). It should be noted that not all groups tried to split their workers among different labor groups. Some thought it was safer for the entire group to remain within one commando. For example, Lenie de Jong-Van Naardenf and Bloeme Evers-Emden's family of eight stayed together in a commando that moved rocks. Within the commando they split up and kept a close watch over each other.[11]

Being with persons one trusted was important in a place where physical survival was based on bread sliced as thin as paper and soup gulped from a shared tureen. Some women believed that they received more bread as a family than as individuals, because they were sometimes able to obtain an uncut loaf for the group as their ration allotment (Zyskind 1981). This allowed them autonomy in distributing the slices. Those who obtained their rations individually from the *Blockälteste* [the person in charge] or shared their rations with strangers took their chances. Sharing food was important for the identity of the family group because it confirmed the commitment of the group's members to each other. Bloeme Evers-Emden recalled that if one of them got an extra piece of bread, they would divide it into eighths and distribute it among themselves. She admitted that it might sound "absurd" to split bread into such minute portions, but dividing even the smallest resources offered a "psychological boost."[12]

Because the food itself was often nearly inedible, family members had to encourage each other to eat. Nauseated by the repugnant smell of the soup, Livia Bitton Jackson (1980:83) remembered heeding the advice of her cousins and holding her nose while gulping down her soup. Another survivor within a family of five, Lydia B., remembered picking gravel out of her food and credited her survival to her family's insistence that she eat. One of the girls in her group suffered from a weak stomach and could not keep down the food. The other four shared their bread rations with her and the slivers of potato that they found in their soup. Thanks to their efforts, the girl managed to stay alive.[13]

Even within the relatively privileged life of the women's camp orchestra, cooperation and community were keys to survival, and the orchestra functioned like a family in many aspects. Cellist Anita Lasker-Wallfisch (1988:58) said that fellow orchestra members gave her the potato pieces out of their own soup rations after she contracted jaundice and could not keep down the turnip soup. After their evacuation from Auschwitz, some members of the orchestra stayed together in Belsen and shared their food with one another (ibid., 64–66). Similarly, Gisella Perl (1984:90–91) recalled how the nine women working in the Auschwitz infirmary shared the extra food they obtained by seeing "private" patients after hours.

Families provided a sense of security in a place where the weak could easily have their food stolen from them. Nicknamed *Zugänge* [newcomer], new arrivals were often terrorized by older prisoners, many of whom had few compunctions about beating them and "organizing" their shoes, clothing and rations. Survivor Erna Low recalled the harsh conditions of the camp for newcomers, describing an environment fraught with anxiety, terror, violence and theft.[14] A teenager when she arrived in the camp from Holland with her sister, Rachella M. remembered the sense of security provided by her sister and other family members, who protected her from these assaults.[15]

Severe overcrowding in the barracks resulted in stealing and arguments among the inmates at night. In her interview, Diana G. remembered that it was common for eight to ten women to share a small sleeping platform and one blanket.[16] One survivor compared sleeping to lining up "like spoons" because it was so crowded.[17] Pessimistic about her surroundings, Betty B. recalled counseling friends not to save their bread overnight, figuring that storage in one's stomach was far safer than storage in a pocket.[18] Families could make surviving the night in the crowded bunks more comfortable. Charlotte Delbo (1982:62) described waking from a dream as, "a jumble of bodies, a melee of arms and legs . . . the leg that is moving belongs to Lulu, the arm belongs to Yvonne, the head on my chest that presses on me is Viva's head." If sleep were possible at all in a place like Auschwitz, being with people one trusted provided a sense of security at night.

Inside the barracks at night, the women helped delouse each other. They waged a constant and futile battle with vermin. While visiting a zoo several years after the war, Kitty Hart (1982:78) observed monkeys picking nits off of each other, and she flashed back to a memory of her friends in Auschwitz picking lice off each other. On rare occasions, the delousing by fellow prisoners would turn into caressing. Hart noted that often the women were too exhausted even for such simple things as delousing or sitting up in their bunks talking, but that there was a genuine human need for affection which this fulfilled.

Group pressure played a significant role in maintaining personal appearance. Appearance was extremely important because it influenced an individual's attitude, denoted status within the camp, and affected surviving a sudden selection by the SS doctors for death or a labor transport. This resulted in excessive anxiety among prisoners about how they looked, amid conditions where it was absolutely impossible to stay clean or healthy. The demands of the camp in this regard were excessively unrealistic. The prisoners would march or stand in thick mud for hours, and yet they were ordered to have clean shoes. Rampant with fleas and lice, the camp was awash in disease and many prisoners developed scabies on their bodies. Appearance anxiety escalated into panic-stricken activity immediately before a selection. One survivor recalled how prisoners would bite their lips and pinch their cheeks to make them rosier before a selection.[19] They would also critique each other's appearance and speculate among themselves over someone's chances at surviving a selection (Perl 1984:99).

Forming a family with her sister and some friends after their arrival at Auschwitz from Greece, Diana G. remembered washing in water as cold as ice and using her dress as a towel, at the insistence of her friends. In her interview, she described her family as links on a chain with the chain being only as strong as its links. The girls would often badger each other about keeping their clothing clean and faces washed.[20] The members of the camp orchestra "bullied each other" when they began to slacken in their personal hygiene, according to Anita Lasker-Wallfisch. She remembered that they were forever trying to clean mud off their shoes. She felt that "we all contributed a little to the survival of each other" (Lasker-Wallfisch 1988:87).

Because their group members encouraged them, attention to personal appearance helped individuals reassert themselves and bolstered their spirits. Sent to Auschwitz from Holland with her sister, Janny Brandes-Brilleslijper remembered being cheered by watching some French girls in her barracks. Although they had been shaved completely bald, the girls had found a comb with three prongs in it and a small piece of glass, which they used to comb their eyebrows and carefully arrange their scarves.[21] Even mental games played by the group were important. Gisella Perl (1984:58) remembered that the women in her block played the "I am a Lady Game" before they went to sleep. They would reminisce and describe a day in their lives at home, filling their stories with details.

Gisella wrote that the game helped the women sleep peacefully and restored a sense of the femininity of their past lives.

A selection resulted in mass panic and group strategizing, because the security of the group could be lost with the flick of an SS doctor's finger, separating families permanently. When Isabella Leitner's family of four faced a selection, her younger sister Rachel was very sick. In spite of her protests, they forced the girl to stand on her toes, tied a scarf on her head and pinched her cheeks so they would appear flushed and healthy. Their family stayed in Auschwitz for six months and left the camp together on a labor transport (Leitner 1978:46–47).

Because of their loyalty to each other, family members risked their own safety to help each other during selections. For example, Marika A. described how her family survived a selection together. Appearing before Dr Mengele, one of the five girls was chosen to die because she had dysentery and placed apart from the group. Because she was older than Marika and the others, Susan felt an obligation to protect them. Even though she had already passed the selection and been chosen to live, Susan slipped into the group slated for death and grabbed her younger cousin. Together they went back through the selection for a second time. Recognized by Mengele, the younger girl was not allowed to go with the others. An SS woman intervened on their behalf, and Mengele grudgingly allowed both girls to live.[22]

The daring and ingenuity highlighted in this incident were not uncommon in the aftermath of a selection which split the family group apart. Sometimes they were able to swap between groups scheduled for labor transports if the guards were not diligently watching. Separated families called to each other and arranged a hasty exchange which would keep the tallying totals accurate for the transports. Swapping prisoners between groups slated to die and live was virtually impossible, because often the identification numbers for those chosen to die were immediately written down.

These surreptitious and strictly forbidden exchanges allowed families to stay together. For example, Lydia B. and her cousin were chosen for a special labor transport out of the camp, and were separated from their family members. Some others did not want to leave the camp, so they hastily arranged a swap and were able to move their three other family members onto the transport. Because her sister was sick, and she feared that the illness would be discovered, Lydia asked the block secretary to intervene and get them into the first group scheduled to leave. A family friend from her hometown, the secretary intervened and the girls left Auschwitz together on the first transport.[23]

Many women mentioned a strong fear of separation from their family members in their memoirs and interviews. When her sister Lientje became sick and was sent to the sick barracks, Janny Brandes-Brilleslijper went with her and risked infection, believing that "the worst that could happen to me would be to lose my sister."[24] In her group, Isabella Leitner's sister Rachel rarely slept because she was terrified of being separated from her family. Rachel announced that if anything were to happen to the rest of the group and she were left alone, then she would have no desire to live without them and would go to the gas chambers. They pleaded with her to fight to live even if they were separated, but she responded that they should not ask so much of her (Leitner 1978:36). Separated from the family, Lenie de Jong-Van Naarden remembered being overjoyed when her friend Nettie survived a selection by a miraculous escape. One of the two mothers within their group of eight women, Nettie's loss would have shattered the group emotionally. Their group solidarity was very strong and Lenie noted that "without each other, we would have gone to pieces."[25]

In spite of their best efforts, some families were not able to stay together. Hospitalized with scarlet fever in the Auschwitz infirmary, Marika A. was separated from her family after the other girls were transported to another camp. In the infirmary, Marika became friends with another girl who was older, and they stayed together in Auschwitz and Belsen. Separated from her newfound sister in Belsen, Marika despaired, but took some comfort in befriending a younger girl she met there who was alone.[26] Family members who were forced to leave behind one of their members described feelings of guilt and despair over the separation. In her interview, Diana G. recounted a traumatic separation from her younger sister, Janet, then only 14 years old. Janet's severe illness prevented her from passing a selection for a labor transport. Like Lydia B.'s family, the other girls attempted to go back through the selection and to help her join them, but it was impossible. They left on the labor transport, and assumed that Janet would die alone in Auschwitz. Miraculously, Janet survived and they found her in Theresienstadt after the war.[27]

The loss of close "family" members was very traumatic for the individuals left behind. In her memoir, Kitty Hart (1982:103–104, 108–109) spoke fondly of her two "sisters," Hanka and Genia, recalling sharing food and games within their family of three. All three girls were in their teens. Hanka and Genia became ill, and while working in the infirmary with her mother, Kitty had to load Hanka and Genia into a truck which took them to the gas chamber. Had it not been for the intervention of her mother, Kitty would have climbed into the truck to join her friends. Kitty transferred to the Kanada barracks where goods stolen from the incoming prisoners were sorted, and found new "sisters." The move to Kanada removed Kitty from her memories at the infirmary, but she never described her new family members with the same depth of emotion or tight relational bond reserved for Hanka and Genia and spoke of them in a neutral and almost business-like tone (ibid.,110–115).

Clearly, families also made their members vulnerable to the pain and suffering of each other. When they arrived at Auschwitz and were ordered to strip at the Sauna, Livia Bitton Jackson (1980:137–139) remembered feeling horrified and ashamed at having to see her mother remove her clothes in front of the male guards and tried not to look at her mother's nakedness. When an SS woman later assaulted her mother for not putting on her shoes fast enough, Livia attacked the guard and suffered a severe beating. Livia's mother was powerless to protect her from the SS guards, and she looked on helplessly while her daughter was beaten, coaxing her to get up and to carry on.

The strong bonds of responsibility felt and acted upon by family members provide a mechanism for explaining camp behavior. In January 1945, Rachella M. and her sister Flora were taken on the death march out of Auschwitz. Rachella carried Flora because she was sick and dragged her along through the snow. Completely delirious, Flora ran to a guard and begged him to shoot her. Explaining that her sister was out of her mind, Rachella dragged her back into line. In a reversal of roles, Rachella told Flora that she had to fight to survive and refused to allow her to give up. Recovering her strength somewhat, Flora later stole an extra pair of boots from another prisoner for Rachella's feet, because her shoes were falling apart. On the train, Rachella and her friends had to protect Flora, who was still very weak, from the other prisoners.[28]

Rachella's and Flora's behavior can be difficult to explain rationally and morally. Risking one's life for another makes little sense in the world of Auschwitz, where the struggle for individual survival was paramount. Behavior that initially appears to prying post-Auschwitz eyes as irrational or immoral, and which could be labeled as suicidal altruism or outright insanity, can be better understood by examining the motivation for it. Some would interpret Rachella's efforts in a positive moral light because she sapped her own strength to help her sister, while interpreting Flora's actions negatively because she stole someone else's shoes. However, by understanding that the motivation for Rachella's and Flora's behavior springs from the same source, namely their sense of family obligation to each other, their risk-taking and self-sacrificing behavior begin to make sense.

The family members' dedication to each other also rekindled the individual's drive to survive. For example, Isabella Leitner (1978:35–36) wrote about her "absolute responsibility" to her three sisters to survive. "I knew also that my sisters . . . not only wanted me to get back to them – they expected me to get back. The burden to live up to that expectation was mine, and it was awesome." She wrote in her memoir that

> at times I wished I were alone, not to be asked to go constantly, on a twenty-four-hour basis, against the tide. After all, the business of Auschwitz was death . . . I am tired. Let me go . . . No, we won't. Our business is life. My darling sisters, you are asking too much. And I am asking too much of you. Yet the insanity of Auschwitz must be imbued with meaning if living is to be continued, and the only meaning to living has to be for the four of us to be where the sun shines, or the smoke blackens the sky. All of us. Together. (ibid., 36–37)

When despair overcame the individual, a family could force a member to continue on in the battle to survive. After her arrival in Auschwitz, Rachella M. suffered from dysentery, and her body quickly became emaciated. Losing her will to live, Rachella refused to eat. Embarrassing Rachella in front of the other family members, her sister Flora shook her, slapped her, shoved her own spoon into her hand and forced her to eat.[29] In another example, Charlotte Delbo (1968:83–84) became so parched with thirst that her family members believed that she had lost her sanity, and kept a close watch over her lest she get herself killed by dashing out of line toward a nearby stream. Her good friend, Viva, shared her tea with her, trying to help her satisfy her thirst.

Beyond their physical and mechanistic advantages, families allowed individuals to carve out a personal space for the expression of emotion. This was important in a place in which you felt like "you were being continually pounded by heavy hammers – on your heart, on your senses – until you were half-stunned."[30] Auschwitz crushed and belittled gestures of individual expression or kindness, but families created a sphere where members could feel emotion and express themselves. Sara Zyskind (1981:206) wrote, "Even if I had a real sister, I doubt whether I could have loved her any more than I loved each of those girls – my four sisters from Auschwitz." In a place where no one had a name, families offered a haven where names replaced tattooed identification numbers. Familiarity redeemed the individual from the persecuted masses.

Families could also assume a spiritual dimension. On Yom Kippur, Betty B. fasted with some other women in her block for the day and they prayed together and talked about their families. It was a surprising action for Betty B. to take, since she was very pessimistic about saving bread for the following day.[31] Lydia B. also fasted in her barracks with her family on Yom Kippur in Auschwitz and prayed regularly with them, and she remembered it as a positive time of reflection and encouragement.[32] In a poignant memoir passage, Isabella Leitner described praying for her sister Chicha, during a brutal punishment at *Appell* (roll call), asking God not to let her drop the rocks she was forced to hold over her head while kneeling for the duration of the roll-call, for an infraction that she did not commit. She wrote in her memoir, "God, help us to imbue her with our unified spirit, keep her arms straight, keep our souls riveted to hers, and maybe we'll all live" (Leitner 1978:44). Incidents like these enhanced group solidarity and cohesiveness.

Families allowed their members to rationalize "organizing" goods or behavior that they might have never condoned in their past lives outside the camp, in the name of assisting fellow group members. Summing this up, Kitty Hart (1982:69–70) wrote that families "helped each other and defied the rest. Outside the family there had to be bribery; within there was love and mutual help." This mental attitude of staying strong for each other helped family members justify even their own desperate measures to take care of themselves. Describing her struggle to push other people away while getting water at the faucet, Janny Brandes-Brilleslijper, wrote "the only thing you can think is, well damn it, if I can only go a bit farther so that Lientje can just get by; I'm a bit stronger than my sister . . . It was always that way: the one took care of the other."[33] Families provided their members with a place to preserve their pre-camp morality, by carving out a moral space for them. Bloeme Evers-Emden recalled that "we didn't use any foul language, we upheld a high moral standard among ourselves."[34]

In conclusion, cohesive family relationships provided an avenue for women to recover their identities and helped them survive Auschwitz by helping them pool and share resources, and providing them with a community. Building relationships with fellow prisoners allowed women to reclaim their humanity and to forge a living link to the present. Forming a family in Auschwitz was an act of resistance at the personal level, because it gave life meaning and offered support and hope.

A great deal of research remains to be done in this field. When studying interpersonal relationships, the most useful memoirs are those written by members of the same family, and the most fruitful interviews are those which focus on these groups. Of all the memoirs and interviews mentioned in this study, the only interviews which fit that requirement are the brief ones with Bloeme Evers-Emden and Lenie de Jong-Van Naarden in *The Last Seven Months of Anne Frank*. In spite of this fact, a surprising wealth of information about family groups emerged by studying published memoirs and unpublished oral testimonies about the Holocaust.

These families have not been examined in great detail for several reasons. In some cases, studies of the concentration camps have revolved around detailing structures of persecution within the camps and the mentality of the persecutors.[35] In other historical studies, the testimony of individual survivors is seen as so sacred that no synthesis of analysis is performed, not even by some of the most painstaking researchers (Shelley 1991; 1992). Those who study family groups in the camps tend to stumble onto this topic, whether it be via women's studies, sociology or some other route. Even the research presented in this chapter started out with very different intentions; it began as a master's thesis examining gender and survival strategies, which soon diverged into a study of women's memoirs from Auschwitz. With the number of survivors decreasing, time for detailed studies and focused interviews about family groups is rapidly running out.

By understanding the family groups that operated within the discrete universe known as Auschwitz, we can begin to understand one aspect of the Holocaust better. In the face of Auschwitz, the resistance of the individual to despair, isolation and death was nurtured within a community. We pay honor to the memory of the Holocaust's victims by detailing the personal aspects of their lives inside the camps, because families imbued their lives with meaning and gave them the strength to embrace life. We could bear no greater testimony to the triumph of the human spirit against adversity than to tell their story.

Notes

1. Ami Neiberger graduated with a master's degree in European history from the University of Florida in 1996. She completed her master's thesis work under the supervision of Dr Geoffrey Giles, whom she would like to thank for his assistance and guidance. She is currently working for the university in an administrative support role and plans to begin her Ph.D. in communications.

2. Katz and Ringelheim (1983); Ringelheim (1984).
3. Davidson (1992) and Davidson (1984).
4. Betty B. Interview by Judah Rubenstein. Tape recording with transcript, 1975, American Jewish Committee Holocaust Survival Project, New York Public Library Jewish Division, II: 2–105.
5. Rachella M., Interview by Shirley Tanzer, 1976, American Jewish Committee Holocaust Survival Project, New York Public Library Jewish Division, II:1-97-98.
6. Lydia B., Interview by Shirley Tanzer, Tape recording with transcript, American Jewish Committee Holocaust Survival Project, I:1–23.
7. Bloeme Evers-Emden, Interview in Lindwer (1991:124).
8. Lenie de Jong-Van Naarden, Interview in Lindwers (1991:145).
9. Lily L., Interview by Connie Lerner Adams, Tape recording with transcript, 1975,American Jewish Committee Holocaust Survival Project, New York Public Library Jewish Division, 16.
10. Lily L., Interview by Connie Lerner Adams, 16.
11. Lenie de Jong-Van Naarden, Interview in Lindwer 1991:154
12. Bloeme Evers-Emden, Interview in Lindwer 1991:130
13. Lydia B., Interview by Shirley D. Tanzer, I:2–28
14. Erna Low, I Was in Oswiecim, ME 359, Leo Baeck Institute, New York, 5.
15. Rachella M., Interview by Shirley Tanzer, II:1–94.
16. Diana G., Interview by Shirley Tanzer, Tape recording with transcript, 1975, American Jewish Committee Holocaust Survival Project, New York Public Library Jewish Division, I:2–35.
17. Ronnie Goldstein-Van Cleef, Interview in Lindwer 1991:182.
18. Betty B., Interview by Judah Rubenstein, 111:1–101
19. Bronia R., Interview by Debbi Dawn, Tape recording with transcript, 1975, American Jewish Committee Holocaust Survival Project, New York Public Division, 1–8
20. Diana G., Interview by Shirley Tanzer, I:2–35
21. Janny Brandes-Brilleslijper, Interview in Linwer 1991:58
22. Marika A. Interview by Shirley Tanzer, Tape recording with transcript, 1976, American Jewish Committee Holocaust Survival Project, New York Public Library Jewish Division, 1:2-44-45.
23. Lydia B., Interview by Shirley Tanzer, 1:2-26-28.
24. Janny Brandes-Brilleslijpere, Interview in Lindwer 1991:61.
25. Lenie de Jong-Van Naarden, Interview in Lindwer 1991:157
26. Marika A. Interview by Shirley Tanzer, 11:1–7a.
27. Diana G., Interview by Shirley Tanzer, 1:2–35.
28. Rachella M., Interview by Shirley Tanzer, 11:2-119-121.

29. Rachella M., Interview by Shirley Tanzer, 11:1–95.
30. Janny Brandes-Brilleslijper, Interview in Lindwer 1991:58
31. Betty B., Interview by Judah Rubinstein, IV : 1–138.
32. Lydia B., Interview by Shirley Tanzer, 1:2–28.
33. Janny Brandes-Brilleslijper, Interview in Lindwer 1991:64.
34. Bloeme Everes-Emden. Interview in *The Last Seven Months of Anne Frank,* edited by Willy Linwer, 124.
35. See the classic study by Des Pres (1977), and also for women's studies, see Strzelecka (1994).

References

Davidson, Shamai (1979) "Massive Psychic Traumatization and Social Support," *Journal of Psychosomatic Research*, 23:395–402.
—— (1984) "Human Reciprocity Among the Jewish Prisoners in Nazi Concentration Camps," in *The Nazi Concentration Camps. Structure and Aims. The Image of the Prisoner. The Jews in the Camps. Proceedings of the Fourth Annual Yad Vashem International Historical Conference.* Jerusalem: Yad Vashem: 555–572.
—— (1992) *Holding onto Humanity – The Message of the Holocaust Survivors: the Shamai Davidson Papers.* Ed. Israel W. Charny. New York and London: New York University Press.
Delbo, Charlotte (1968). *None of Us Will Return.* Trans. by John Githens. New York: Grove Press.
Des Pres, Terrence (1977) *The Survivor: An Anatomy of Life in the Death Camps.* New York: Pocket Books.
Eitinger, Leo (1994) "Auschwitz – A Psychological Perspective," in Yisrael Gutman and Michael Berenbaum (eds) *Anatomy of the Auschwitz Death Camp.* Bloomington and Indianapolis: Indiana University Press: 469–482.
Goldenberg, Myrna (1990) "Different Horrors, Same Hell: Women Remembering the Holocaust," in Roger S. Gottlieb (ed.) *Thinking the Unthinkable: Meanings of the Holocaust.* New York/Mahwah: Paulist Press.
Hart, Kitty (1982) *Return to Auschwitz: The Remarkable Story of a Girl Who Survived Holocaust.* New York: Atheneum.
Heinemann, Marlene (1986) *Gender and Destiny: Women Writers and the Holocaust.* Westport, Connecticut: Greenwood Press.
Jackson, Livia E. Bitton (1980) *Elli: Coming of Age in the Holocaust.* New York: New York Times Book Company.
Katz, Esther and Joan Miriam Ringelheim (eds) (1983) *Proceedings of*

the Conference Women Surviving the Holocaust. New York: Institute for Research in History.

Lasker-Wallfisch, Anita (1988) *Told By Anita: 1925–1945*. ME 360. Leo Baeck Institute, New York. London.

Leitner, Isabella (1978) *Fragments of Isabella: A Memoir of Auschwitz*. New York: Thomas Crowell Publishers.

Lindwer, Willy (ed.) (1991) *The Last Seven Months of Anne Frank*. Translated from Dutch by Alison Meersschaert. New York: Random House.

Lixl-Purcell, Andreas (1994) "Memoirs as History: Women's Memoirs and the Study of Holocaust History," *Leo Baeck Institute Yearbook* 39:227–238.

Low, Erna. *I Was in Oswiecim*. ME 359. Leo Baeck Institute, New York.

Luchterhand, Elmer (1967) "Prisoner Behavior and Social System in the Nazi Concentration Camps," *American Journal of Social Psychiatry*, 13:245–264.

Milton, Sybil (1984) "Women and the Holocaust: The Case of German and German-Jewish Women," in Renate Bridenthal, Atina Grossmann, and Marion Kaplan (eds) *When Biology Became Destiny: Women in Weimar and Nazi Germany*. New York: Monthly Review Press: 297–333.

Perl, Gisella (1984) *I Was a Doctor in Auschwitz*. Salem, New Hampshire: Ayer Company Publishers Inc.

Ringelheim, Joan (1984) "The Unethical and the Unspeakable: Women and the Holocaust," *The Simon Wiesenthal Center Annual* 1:69–87.

Ringelheim, Joan(1985) "Women and the Holocaust: A Reconsideration of Research," *Signs: Journal of Women in Culture and Society*, 10:741–761.

Shelley, Lore (ed.) (1992) *Auschwitz – The Nazi Civilization. Twenty-three Women Prisoner's Accounts. Auschwitz Camp Administration and SS Enterprises and Workshops*. New York: University Press of America.

Shelley, Lore (1991) *Criminal Experiments on Human Beings in Auschwitz and War Research Laboratories: Twenty Women Prisoners' Accounts*. San Francisco: Mellen Research University Press.

Strzelecka, Irena (1994) "Women" in Yisrael Gutman and Michael Berenbaum (eds) *Anatomy of the Auschwitz Death Camp*. Bloomington and Indianapolis: Indiana University Press.

Zyskind, Sara (1981) *Stolen Years*. Minneapolis: Lerner Publications Company.

Primary Sources (Confidential)

Betty B., Interview by Judah Rubinstein, Tape recording with transcript, 1975, American Jewish Committee Holocaust Survival Project, New York Public Library Jewish Division.

Bronia R., Interview by Debbi Dawn, Tape recording with transcript, 1975, American Jewish Committee Holocaust Survival Project, New York Public Library Jewish Division.

Diana G., Interview by Shirley Tanzer, Tape recording with transcript, 1975, American Jewish Committee Holocaust Survival Project, New York Public Library Jewish Division.

Lily L., Interview by Connie Lerner Adam, Tape recording with transcript, 1975, American Jewish Committee Holocaust Survival Project, New York Public Library Jewish Division.

Lydia B., Interview by Shirley Tanzer, Tape recording with transcript, 1975, American Jewish Committee Holocaust Survival Project, New York Public Library Jewish Division.

Marika A. Interview by Shirley Tanzer, Tape recording with transcript, 1976, American Jewish Committee Holocaust Survival Project, New York Public Library Jewish Division.

Rachella M., Interview by Shirley Tanzer, Tape recording with transcript, 1976, American Jewish Committee Holocaust Survival Project, New York Public Library Jewish Division.

Note: These special oral history interviews were conducted in the 1970s for the American Jewish Committee's Holocaust Survival Project. A large repository of transcripts from that project are available at the New York Public Library Jewish Division. To respect the confidentiality of these transcripts, last names were removed from their references and no direct quotes were used.

9

Protest and Silence: Resistance Histories in Post-War Germany: the Missing Case of Intermarried Germans

Nathan Stoltzfus

At the end of World War II intermarried Jews comprised 98 percent of the surviving German Jewish population that had not been driven into hiding.[1] These intermarried Jews survived, despite clear-cut Nazi ideology and Gestapo will, primarily because their German partners refused to abandon them. From its beginning the Nazi dictatorship had struggled, economically and psychologically, to pressure these Germans, 30,000 in 1939, into deserting their Jewish partners.[2] During the first year of the Third Reich the incidence of intermarriage among German Jews fell from 45 to 15 percent, and German leaders seemed to have good reason to hope that intermarriages would dissolve under the increasing pressures of state and society. The overwhelming majority of Germans married to Jews refused to conform, however, continuing to live with Jews in open disrespect for government ideology and laws, while bearing untold daily harassment from neighbors and colleagues, despite the exemption from these horrors that divorce (made easy for them under new German legal standards) would have granted.[3] The crux of the regime's problem was that intermarried couples united members of the "enemy" population with that of the Master Race in the venerable institution of marriage, and the Nuremberg Laws of 1935, which banned all future intermarriages, did not annul existing intermarriages for fear this could cause too much obvious dissent. Intermarried members of the "Aryan" *Volksgemeinschaft* proved that the regime, forcibly and thus publicly, would have to annul their marriages, or allow them to share the fate of "Untermenschen," the Jews. Following complaints from non-Jews on behalf of intermarried Jews who had been brutalized during the Kristallnacht Pogrom of 1938, the regime began exempting some intermarried Jews from measures to displace and concentrate German Jews. When the Final Solution of

German Jews began in October, 1941 the Nazi leadership, apprehensive of social unrest, "temporarily exempted" intermarried Jews, even though for political reasons these were the most offensive German Jews.[4]

During the following fifteen months, as intermarried couples for the most part remained together even under the new terrors, the regime repeated its decision to defer intermarried Jews from the Final Solution "temporarily." The battle of wills between intermarried Germans and the Gestapo over the fate of intermarried Jews came to a dramatic climax on February 27, 1943, as Joseph Goebbels, the Party Gauleiter of Berlin, unleashed a massive surprise action intended to make Berlin "free of Jews." The Gestapo's code name for this massive surprise arrest, often known as the "Factory Action," was the "Final Roundup of the Jews,"[5] and for thousands, this was the beginning of the end. A battalion of SS men in uniforms with machine guns, along with local Gestapo agents and Berlin street policemen, fanned out across Berlin to capture the city's remaining Jews. Every truck in the city – some 300 in all – was requisitioned for the hunt.[6] Goebbels, the Reich Minister charged with preventing public displays of dissent, hoped that the protests of intermarried Germans would be silenced by the "brute force" displayed in this arrest action.[7]

As news of the massive arrest pulsed through the city German family members of arrested Jews began gathering on Rosenstrasse in front of the Jewish Community Center where intermarried Jews were imprisoned separately, in preparation for deportation. Gathering by the hundreds these "Aryans," who were overwhelmingly women, began to call out together "Give us our husbands back." Again and again, the police scattered the women with threats to shoot them down in the streets, but each time they advanced again, resumed their solidarity and called out together.[8] Day by day the protest grew; as many as 600 or more came together at once, and as many as 6,000 had joined in by the protest's end.[9] Normally people were afraid to show dissent, but on the street they knew they were among friends. "At first it was as if I was paralyzed," recalled Johanna Löwenstein de Witt. "It was a feeling of solidarity with one another that drove us on and gave us courage."[10] Another protester recalled that she had begun her protest as an act of desperation but that as the protest continued, and as the Gestapo was unable to dispel it, she began to view the protest as a means of gaining the release of their husbands.[11]

On March 6, following a week of noisy disturbances on Rosenstrasse, Goebbels relented, and ordered the release of all intermarried Jews and their children. Hitler gave his approval. For Propaganda Minister Goebbels success, based on mass conformity, lay in making it appear as though dissent did not exist, especially in Berlin. Releasing the intermarried Jews was the best way to dispel the open protest, visible not just to Germans but to foreign diplomats, journalists and spies in the German capital.[12] To him the crowd of women calling out for Jewish family members was a "disagreeable scene."[13]

Rosenstrasse is the only incident of mass German protest against the deportation of German Jews, and as a result of it at least 1,700 to 2,000 Jews survived.[14] German "Aryans" married to Jews succeeded in rescuing thousands of Jews because of their own actions and identity, and not just due to circumstances. First, by the time of their desperate street protest, their non-compliance had already divided the Nazi leadership on how to handle intermarried Jews. Also, they had hard-earned reputations as persons willing to put their lives on the line; thus, unlike other Germans, they were guaranteed to cause the kind of social unrest the regime feared, especially following its first wartime debacle at Stalingrad just prior to the protest. Finally, they did not overplay their cards, demanding collectively just the release of their family members, and doing so in a daring, awkward street protest, rather than conspiratorially (and hopelessly) attempting to overthrow the regime as a whole with arms that would make them look to most Germans like criminals, in an area the regime was in any case greatly superior. So regardless of whether the success of intermarried German opposition in rescuing Jews is dated to Rosenstrasse or before, their non-compliance and protest produced a conflict between Nazi ideology and perceived policy options, influencing Hitler and the Gestapo to hesitate and repeatedly decide to "defer temporarily" deporting intermarried Jews – until the war ended.

Nevertheless, this powerful protest, and the contextual history of intermarriages, including the fact that 98 percent of officially registered Jews who survived Hitler were intermarried, has remained virtually unexamined and unknown. School textbooks in former East Germany as well as West Germany were silent in this regard, as were the accumulating thousands of books and articles on the resistance to Hitler. Historians too, whether from East or West, ignored or trivialized the story of intermarried Jews and Rosenstrasse, which was recorded, mostly in German, in more than two dozen newspaper articles and published personal accounts.[15] Leading historians of the Third Reich from East Germany were well aware of the protest but did not find any reason to study it. In West Germany two leading historians in the field had finally mentioned the Rosenstrasse protest by the mid-1980s, but trivialized it in one-paragraph descriptions. In his least scholarly book, Professor Wolfgang Wippermann (1982:72) of the Free University of Berlin pictured the protest as a show of courage without political significance.[16] Professor Wolfgang Benz (1989:688), now the director of the Technical University's Center on Antisemitism, dealt with Rosenstrasse in just a few sentences in his near-800-page book on Jews in Nazi Germany.[17] Benz, who inexplicably placed the story of Rosenstrasse within a chapter titled "Survival in the Underground, 1943–1945," has spoken of the protest as "local history," without significance for interpretations of the Third Reich in general.

Since 1989 and the largely nonviolent collapse of communism historians have increasingly reexamined German terror systems, shedding more light on civilian collaboration and the limits of instrumental brute force. Yet even in this light scholarly German publications in the 1990s continue to turn a blind eye to the stunning story of intermarried Germans and Rosenstrasse. Reinhard Rürup, another eminent historian from Berlin's Technical University, edited a book, published in 1995, in which a recent graduate of TU asserts that the Rosenstrasse protest was "obviously not the cause of the release of the Jews." The author continues with an emphatic declaration, in lieu of making any argument, that "interpretations that such demonstrations could have hindered the deportation plans of the RSHA certainly do not hold up within the historical context."[18] Several German encyclopedias and bibliographies of resistance published since 1984 make no mention of Rosenstrasse. The *Encyclopedia of German Resistance to the Nazi Movement*, published in English as well as German, in 1997 under the auspices of the Technical University's Center on Antisemitism, is intended to be a comprehensive overview of resistance. It is broken down into 10 essays on the main resistance groups, 63 shorter entries on various additional political groups, and 550 biographies, and yet is silent on Rosenstrasse and the astonishing impact of intermarried Germans as a whole on the Final Solution.[19]

In short, the record appears to show partiality and not just inaccuracy. Efforts to historicize and commemorate the Rosenstrasse protest have all arisen from private initiative.[20á] The silence of the German Resistance Memorial Center on Rosenstrasse is an important indicator that claiming the Rosenstrasse Protest influenced the Gestapo has been a taboo among German historians. The important and accomplished Resistance Memorial Center, located in Germany's Berlin wartime headquarters, and commissioned in 1983 to document the entire extent of German resistance, has published scores of brochures and books on a broad range of types of opposition, and yet has nothing on Rosenstrasse, not even in two of its most recent books, *Women in Resistance* and *Accommodation, Non-compliance and Resistance.* [21] When in 1995 the German scholarly journal

Geschichte und Gesellschaft published an article on Rosenstrasse, Professor Christof Dipper commented that the story "had long since been researched" (by Kurt Ball-Kaduri, who in a 1973 article on Berlin Jews of 1942 and 1943 devoted just paragraphs to Rosenstrasse and intermarriage).[22]

Why has the rescue of Jews through the non-compliance and protest of intermarried Germans gone virtually unnoticed in postwar histories and commemorations? Responding to this question in the January 1998 edition of the German monthly *Merkur*, Professor Manfred Henningsen of the University of Hawaii asked: "Is international reseach uninterested in a case which makes more difficult the deterministic explanation of the Holocaust as resulting from the anti-Semitism of ordinary Germans? Do historians and social scientists have problems with understanding primary human relationships, for example love and friendship, in their historical dimensions?"[23]

It is possible that Rosenstrasse has been ignored because it challenges accepted wisdom about an ordinary German's responsibility for Nazi crimes in several ways, and poses women as heroes. The story of intermarried Germans, culminating on Rosenstrasse, is hard to swallow for ordinary Germans since it implies that, had more ordinary Germans not abandoned German Jews socially, many more German Jews could have survived. Ordinary Germans were complicit in the Holocaust not because they participated in killing Jews or wanted to, as Professor Daniel Goldhagen has argued,[24] but because they abandoned Jews socially, leaving them vulnerable for deportation to regions where they could be murdered more easily under the pretence that they were being resettled in work camps. Also, the story of intermarried Germans and Rosenstrasse challenges the main paradigm of resistance in postwar Germany by showing, in defiance of the model in West Germany, that Germans did not have to choose between passivity and a resistance leading to martyrdom.

Women have had difficulty with having their stories told at all, in standard histories, and the notion that women would be heroes in the face of Nazi terror is even harder to fit into conventional histories. In addition, many Germans, even today, still do not think of Jews as "Germans," and are still uncomfortable with intermarriage. So intermarried Germans and their opposition in Nazi Germany has had no constituency interested and powerful enough to place it on the roster of the few, well-known acts of resistance. But it is not too late. In fact, in the search for a 'usable past' the resistance of intermarried couples is more relevant now than ever before. In the reunited Germany, and as we face the twenty-first century, the history of intermarried Germans is an especially compelling portrayal of a type of resistance that we should hasten to publicize and commemorate.

Ordinary People in Nazi Germany

The history of intermarried Germans is the principal empirical proof that the social abandonment of Jews by the Germans, as a *Volksgemeinschaft*, was a key prerequisite to the mass murder of German Jews. The regime encouraged the social isolation of Jews, but only the German people could accomplish this. Gestapo policy was to send forthwith to death camps German Jews whose non-Jewish spouses died or divorced. Those German Jews whom the regime could not isolate socially, however, generally survived. The story of intermarried Germans also illustrates the regime's sensitivity to German popular opinion and morale as well as or better than any other case.

Since the late nineteenth century, Jews had been leaders in German culture, politics, science and economics, an integral part of the national social and economic fabric. The regime tested carefully, step by step, to see how fast and to what extent it could remove such a highly visible minority from society, without causing political agitation. The Holocaust built on earlier phases of anti-Jewish measures achieved only with popular compliance and assistance. Genocide was not the only possible result of Nazi race ideology, but popular participation in racial identification, denunciations and expropriations encouraged the regime to introduce increasingly draconian policies toward the Jews.

At least since 1933, the Nazis saw intermarried Jews ("full Jews"), as well as their children ("half-Jews"), as their "certain victims."[25] But by 1942 Goebbels described intermarried Jews and their *Mischling* (part-Jewish) children as "extremely delicate questions."[26] This was the only area where extracting Jews from the German social fabric threatened to lance Goebbel's surface picture of near-perfect German unity behind Hitler's rule, a picture critical to maintaining that rule. It was the resilience of Germans in standing by their Jewish partners that made them "delicate" to Goebbels, and different from any other Jews. As in foreign conquered territories, so within Germany the regime proceeded with the annihilation of Jews first and foremost through those willing to cooperate, getting on with what it could do as quickly as it could while "temporarily" bypassing areas where non-compliance required extra resources.

Intermarried Germans rescued their partners with non-compliance and protest, arms available to any Germans that seem extremely weak in the face of Nazi terror.[27] Yet the regime did not use physical force to control or punish intermarried Germans. This can be understood as an expression of the Nazi theory of mass movement politics under charismatic dictatorship, which presupposed that its power derived from the consent of the "Aryan" people.[28] The most important German leaders jealously guarded the picture of consensus displayed in the lack of unrest and, in fact, police reports indicated that, on the whole, Germans were pleased to exchange even their civil rights for Nazi repression that promised "peace and order!"[29] Goebbels and Hitler feared that Germans, angered by forced deportations of their partners and children, would begin to question and complain. Unrest about the fate of the Jews could severely hinder the domestic social unity necessary for fighting the war. A parallel development was the increasing need for secrecy concerning the Final Solution, the revelation of which would have damaged the public morale that the regime strove to nurture, especially during war. A public discussion about the fate of the deported Jews threatened to disclose the Final Solution and thus endanger that entire effort.[30]

The importance to the regime of avoiding unrest in Germany is also indicated by Nazi policies in eastern occupied territories, where there was no fear of open, public dissent, and where intermarried Jews (and sometimes their Gentile partners as well), along with their *Mischling* children, were deported to ghettos and camps.[31] Wilhelm Stuckart, Staatssekretär in the Ministry of the Interior, claimed at his trial at Nuremberg that he had protected intermarried families, but Stuckart was too insignificant to determine Nazi policy on race. In any case, his proposal forcibly to separate intermarried couples, so that the Jewish partners could be drawn into the Final Solution, was rejected by Goebbels, who opposed it for "political reasons."[32] Also, the German Justice Minister reasoned that "a forced divorce is useless because, even if it would break the legal tie, it certainly could not break the inner ties."[33] Of course, the laws that Stuckart and his colleagues wrote could not confine Hitler in any case. At the Nuremberg Party Rally of 1935 Hitler had Stuckart's underlings drafting numerous texts until they finally had a law Hitler liked. Then Hitler asked for a Constitutional Law which would strip Jews of citizenship. Normally it would have taken months or years to develop such a significant law, but Hitler reassured them that all he wanted this time was a law corresponding with the appropriate part of *Mein Kampf*.[34] Obviously the Führer could have drafted this change to the German constitution much more efficiently by himself. But he wanted the imprimatur of respectable traditional, bourgeois institutions, so he got the ministries to draft the law, and read it before the assembled

Reichstag at Nuremberg the next day. Hitler felt his will constrained not by a handful of bureaucrats but by the German people as a whole, whose consent he considered to be the primary pillar of his power.

The complaints of the few soldiers or influential people affected by the Final Roundup could have been quietly assuaged by the quick addition of their few relatives to the *Schutzjuden* list of protected Jews. During the Final Roundup arrests, factory owners and the military also protested at the precipitous disappearance of their Jewish employees who, working for their lives, often had excellent records of production. Neither the objections of the military nor of the industrialists rescued Jews, but a public protest did.[35]

There were scattered complaints by church officials at the time of the Final Roundup, but no rallying of mass opinion in public. The German nationalism and antisemitism of key Church leaders, especially early on, legitimated and encouraged Hitler. Since January 1933 all German Catholic bishops "began declaring their appreciation of the important natural values of race and racial purity."[36] In 1935 there was no public voice of dissent from the episcopacy against the Nuremberg Laws and their infringement of the spiritual jurisdiction of the Church in the matter of marriage.[37] In 1936, the Protestant (Lutheran) Church in Berlin helped the regime identify Jews by completing a card index dating back to 1800 and reaching to 1874.[38] In mid-February 1943 the Catholic, and perhaps Protestant, parishes helped the Gestapo corroborate and update its list of intermarried Jews, in preparation for the Final Roundup.[39] The Catholic Church did fight effectively (much more than Protestants) for its own traditions and organizations, and Bishop Galen spoke out powerfully against euthanasia. Catholic activists in Oldenburg concluded that the success of their Church protests indicated that all their protests would succeed if they remained united, and in retrospect their successful protests serve to highlight their failure to protest against the Holocaust. The German episcopacy's postwar claim that it prevented the compulsory divorce of intermarried couples has some credibility. Nevertheless, the feebly raised voice of the Church in this matter – without the protest of intermarried Germans – would not have been sufficient to save intermarried Jews.[40] The key to successful Church protests, which was overlooked, was to involve or speak on behalf of many lay persons in public protests, rather than sending out letters on official stationery.

In fact, however, the Germans as a whole, and not just Church leaders, are implicated in Nazi atrocities through the social isolation of the Jews before 1939. In Nazi theory, terror was a means for controlling the fringe after the majority had acquiesced. More common in achieving the acquiescence of Germans than death and imprisonment were pressures of economy and society, jobs and status. Many Germans went well beyond what career interests or survival demanded assist the regime, however. For example, there was no general law requiring the Germans to denounce Jewish-German couples for having sexual encounters, but in July 1935, the police reported numerous denunciations, since "the public has been enlightened through the Nazi press and is now keen of hearing, keeping a watchful eye out for Jews, who go around with blond girls."[41] In 1938, Reinhard Heydrich argued successfully against establishing Jewish ghettos within Germany because "today the German population . . . forces the Jew to behave himself. The control of the Jew through the watchful eye of the whole population is better than having him by the thousands in a district where I cannot properly establish a control over his daily life through uniformed agents."[42] This was following the Kristallnacht Pogrom. When the regime made a trial deportation of German Jews in October 1940, Heydrich noted that here too the surrounding population had hardly noticed.

What could have motivated such reprehensible behavior? Daniel Goldhagen, who cites my work on the Rosenstrasse protest as an indication that Germans had power to influence the course of the Holocaust, has written that a peculiar and exterminatory German antisemitism motivated the Germans to thirst for the cold-blooded murder of the Jews.[43] But the regime strove for the entire duration of the genocide to conduct it in secrecy. Regardless of whether this policy succeeded, it remained official policy and the official explanation, girded with euphemisms, was always that Jews were being resettled in work camps. The regime relied on secrecy in part because it did not trust the Germans to accept genocide.

The history of intermarriage indicates that self-interest, as well as ideology and terror, led to the critical social isolation of Jews, but not to a desire for genocide. It points out that National Socialism conflated the motivations of antisemitism and self-interest, a motivation that is apparent across a wide spectrum of German responses to Nazi Jewish policies, from passivity to mild collaboration, to denunciations, to perpetration. Under the circumstances of war and dictatorship in particular, individuals were concerned overwhelmingly with their own fates. In Nazi Germany antisemitism was rewarded and friendliness to Jews punished. The Nazi Party came to have such extensive control over institutions and norms that self-interest, as far as many Germans could perceive, came to coincide with antisemitism. Latent antisemitism surfaced, and acts of antisemitism also served as a means of self-protection and self-promotion. How many

Germans would have risked their lives, or even their jobs, in order to put their antisemitism into action? We do not know, because the regime rewarded rather than punished antisemitism, as Goldhagen writes.[45] Yet Goldhagen neglects the role of Goebbels in the organization of those incidents which were made to appear like widespread popular acts. The Propaganda Minister portrayed Jews as the main rabble-rousers, even while stimulating incidents of public unrest at swimming pools, movie theaters and weddings of mixed couples, particularly during the months leading up to the Nuremberg Laws. Even the police, as well as the Justice Minister, surmised that the incidents of public antisemitism in 1935 were instigated by Goebbels, not the public.[46] Goebbels sponsored the April 1, 1933 boycott of Jews in part to convince the law-making ministries that the Germans were generally antisemitic; he was behind the Kristallnacht pogrom, rather than the wrath of the people's soul, as he claimed.[47]

This by no means exonerates the Germans of the Third Reich. The Nazi regime built on popular acquiescence and acclaim, and translated its race ideology into genocide in interaction with the German people. With the help of denunciations, social bonds between Jews and Germans were dissolved, and it became possible to enforce racial policies.[48] Although the Nazi leadership later pursued its racism to the extreme of genocide that it did not trust the public to accept, support encouraged the regime to tighten anti-Jewish measures to the point of publicly dispossessing and expelling German Jews. At this point the state could better hide from popular opinion.

Thus Germans in general during 1933–1945 can be said to bear responsibility as persons who did not rightly perceive their own degree of responsibility and influence relative to their own government. A grim lesson of the period is that politics are terribly important. Germans of Nazi Germany do bear responsibility not only for allowing but for encouraging the antisemitism of a regime so sensitive to popular morale and opinion that it compromised its most basic premise, racial purity, in order to prevent a major scene of popular unrest at Rosenstrasse. The rescue of intermarried Jews by their marriage partners who refused to divorce suggests that the regime's ideology might not have developed as it did had the German people not isolated the Jews socially, the prerequisite for deportation and mass murder. As the prestige of the Führer expanded to encompass each of his great new achievements, the regime grew confident that, with such broad general support, the public would also support its anti-Jewish policies, or at least not oppose them. This flies in the face of the standard resistance paradigm, which holds that ordinary Germans could do nothing to limit the exercise of power by the

Nazi dictatorship, a model that does not account for the role of German mass support in the rise of Nazism.

Between Passivity and Martyrdom

Had Germans married to Jews cooperated with the regime, and had they not aggressively protested against the imminent deportation of their Jewish partners, these intermarried Jews would have been among the murdered. Intermarried Germans who had not divorced by 1943 had repeatedly demonstrated a capacity to oppose the regime to save their families. Their track record had put the regime on its guard from early on, and lent their street protest influence when it happened. By 1943, however, it was too late for other Germans to convince the regime that a significant sector of the general population strongly opposed the deportation of Jews. The claim that Germans could not have protested effectively cannot exonerate those Germans who did not protest because they had already proven that they supported the regime, and this in turn buoyed the regime's confidence for continuing, harsher policy expressions of its racist ideology.

Like most Germans of the 1930s, most of the military conspirators of July 1944 – the main symbols of German resistance – also supported Hitler. For decades after the war the military conspirators were idealized into portraits of resisters who had put aside all personal interests to sacrifice themselves for political ideals. Because of their ideals, leading to an attempt to overthrow the entire regime, they represented the *Widerstand* ideal of resistance (which of course Rosenstrasse does not). Yet since the 1970s and 1980s distinguished historians have pointed out that the spotless depiction of the truly heroic military conspirators matches the definition of *Widerstand* resistance better than reality itself; the motives as well as the achievements of those who attempted to kill Hitler in July 1944 were flawed. In response, in the interest of maintaining the status of the military conspirators as resisters, histories now tend to take account of the human foibles and the entire history of the conspirators.[49] As Hitler's desperate ventures turned to shocking crimes and military defeats, the conspirators plotted his death, even though, by 1944, it was virtually impossible to overthrow the regime from inside. No single group of Germans was entirely responsible for the rise of Nazism, which suggests that it was in fact unrealistic for an elitist German institution acting clandestinely to overthrow the popularly based power *in toto*. The military conspirators knew they were courting martyrdom, but to hold them up as *the* German resistance is to present resistance as a choice between martyrdom and passivity, a false dichotomy and a counter-productive one; black-and-white portraits of resistance, like those prevalent in Germany, do not challenge very many persons to act in defense of democracy.

The Rosenstrasse protest, however, did not demand "all or nothing," and succeeded to a lesser extent, by less dramatic, if not less dangerous, means. (What more dangerous act could German civilians have dared than a face-to-face confrontation with the Gestapo over "racial purification," the fundamental Nazi principle?) These intermarried Germans knew they were putting their lives on the line at Rosenstrasse, but they had worked up to this courageous confrontation. During the ten years leading up to the protest, intermarried Germans openly offended the entire spirit of the regime and on occasion disobeyed its laws, to remain married. For ten years these couples had survived with each other as the certainty of survival diminished step by step, year by year. Friends dropped away, jobs disappeared, living space dwindled, starvation loomed, persecution bore down, as Victor Klemperer's recently published diaries illustrate. Of course they were motivated to defend only their families, but they were not selfish. Selfishness for intermarried Germans might have included denouncing Jews or seeking favors with the Nazi Party in other ways. Minimally it would have included divorce and complete removal from the fate of Jewish family members. Some of these couples divorced after the war, indicating the possibility that the German partner had stayed with the Jewish partner for the sake of saving a life.

The political defiance of intermarried couples throws light on previously overlooked aspects of the ways in which the regime exercised power, and in turn, ways in which it felt its power was limited. Comparative cases of Church and family protest indicate that civilian (non-Jewish) Germans could circumscribe the regime's efforts to gain total power. Civilians successfully opposed the regime in defense of traditions, customs and family. These cases also indicate that mass public protest was the most powerful form of civilian opposition. Goebbels could control the press, but public protests openly communicated that the seamless popular unity he claimed existed only in propaganda.

Racial Hygiene programs, so basic to Nazism, raised protests when they divided families and murdered victims. As German protests against euthanasia became "unignorable," the regime was forced to resolve the tension between racial hygiene and social quiescence. In the case of euthanasia as well as in that of intermarriage, the regime resolved this problem in favor of popular morale. Although the potential number of Germans victimized by euthanasia was much greater than those potentially victimized as relatives of intermarried couples, the opposition of inter-married Germans was successful because it represented the crucial, unavoidable junction between Nazism's intended victims and members of the "Aryan" master race. Families stood up for their victimized members, even though the war, as regime leaders calculated, facilitated genocide, and despite the fact that many Germans were radicalized along with the regime during the course of the war.

Hitler's Halt Decree of August 1941 did not completely stop euthanasia but it did stop public protests. The gassings were replaced by a decentral-ized effort, much more limited, and more difficult to blame on the regime. In nineteen months, from January 1940 to August 1941, euthanasia had claimed some 70,000 victims, but in the final forty-four months of the greatly reduced euthanasia program, 30,000 more died. Many of the victims of the new scaled-back cautionary "wild euthanasia" had no German families, and thus no voice to protest for them. They were orphans, or forced laborers from the East.[50]

Thus we see that civilian opposition, in certain forms, was strong enough to prevent the government from ruling in totality, even late in the war. Catholic opposition peaked with the euthanasia issue in 1941, but the opposition of Germans married to Jews indicates that the regime remained responsive to public protest at least through early 1943. The historian Ian Kershaw has argued that these limited, single-policy successes of resisters hardly mattered since they did not hinder the overall effectiveness of the regime to govern. "If the meaning of 'resistance' is not to be wholly diluted," Kershaw argues, "it seems sensible to restrict it to active participation in organized attempts to work against the regime with the conscious aim of undermining it or planning for the moment of its demise."[51]

By Kershaw's standards, no Germans hindered the regime's capacity to rule. And yet no Germans curtailed the regime more, or more signifi-cantly, than intermarried Germans. Due to their civil disobedience, and the threat to public morale that forcing them to cooperate might have developed, intermarried Germans blocked the regime from achieving its most basic goals, offset its drive for "racial purity," and saved thousands. The opposition of intermarried Germans is so significant because it placed a (minuscule) limitation on the aspect most notorious about the regime, genocide.

The non-compliance of intermarried Germans, by the time the deporta-tions of Jews in Germany began, had influenced Hitler to hesitate. Hitler did not like to be publicly associated with divisive matters. Rather than making public pronouncements on intermarried Jews, he gave vague and contradictory orders on whether to include them in the deportations, from behind the scenes, and to his confidants only. Despite attempts by high Party and SS officials to include intermarried Jews and *Mischlinge* in the deportations, Hitler acted "temporarily to defer" them from the Final Solution in 1941 and 1942.[52] Perhaps by 1942 he had begun to think that deporting intermarried Jews should wait until after the war.[53] But true to his style, the Führer awaited the right moment for including them, the moment when he sensed that this could be done without weakening morale,[54] and thus in 1943 his position regarding intermarried Jews wavered.

Had their German relatives not protested, the Jews imprisoned at Rosenstrasse would have been deported in early March 1943, and Hitler would have been happy to be rid of them. Yet Goebbels reported that Hitler understood the response to the "psychological" conditions of unrest that caused him to release the intermarried Jews.[55] Three months later, however, Hitler gave a very different signal to Himmler. While meeting with Himmler at Obersalzburg, the Führer agreed with Himmler that the Jewish Problem would have to be resolved radically, regardless of the unrest it caused.[56] At the time of this meeting, in June 1943, Jews in mixed marriages were the only group of officially registered Jews remaining in Germany. Despite Hitler's pronouncement, intermarried Germans rescued their partners from certain death – and they posed a challenge to those who stood by or actively assisted the regime as it found its way toward committing the greatest crime in history.

In the cold calculations of the Nazi leadership, crushing the protest wasn't worth it. In the decade since 1933 these protesters, by refusing to cooperate with the regime on racial matters, had divided the leadership on how to deal with mixed couples. The Nazi destruction of European Jews would have entwined German intermarried Jews without the least further ado, had it not been for their married partners who, through non-compliance, created a special policy issue on the fate of mixed-marriage Jews. Power plays among Nazi agencies were rife, but power plays surrounding decision-making on intermarried Jews and *Mischlinge* do not so much explain the survival of these Jews as point to the regime's fear of unrest. There would have been no hesitation and no conflict among officials, had intermarried Germans cooperated fully with Nazi racial aims. Nazi leaders knew that these Germans, unlike just about any others, could not be got rid of without raising the specter of intense German dissent to Nazi rule. And of course these civilians did not try to challenge the regime on its own terms – armed force – nor did they act conspiratorially, but publicly. They succeeded because they were willing to be martyred, but in succeeding they showed that martyrdom was not the only alternative to passivity.

Cause Without Constituency?

Paradigms, once established, are extremely hard to change, and Rosenstrasse clashes with establishment resistance paradigms. One explanation for the silence in postwar Germany regarding intermarried Germans who defied the Gestapo's attempt to draw their partners into the Holocaust derives from their identities: these rare Germans did not defy the Gestapo to win laurels and they have not had a political constituency to put their story forward as a symbol of resistance. As a symbol of resistance, the July conspiracy, as it re-legitimated German rearmament, has had the backing of German as well as Americans in high politics. Like the *Kreisauer Kreis*, it has also had surviving family members from the venerable German nobility to keep its story in the public eye. Family members were also key to the record of the White Rose resistance. Communist resistance, well-represented at the German Resistance Memorial Center despite the considerable controversy it has stirred, has had an entire state, in the German Democratic Republic, to represent it. When the German Resistance Memorial Center in Berlin decided to honor Communist actions as resistance, it did so in the face of the opposition of many, including surviving relatives of the truly heroic military conspirators. Charlotte Israel Freundenthal, a protester on Rosenstrasse, had long felt like an unsung hero, but when she attempted to write her autobiography she broke off in February 1943, overwhelmed by her feelings about that epic event. Protesters were effective only as a group, not as persons with special status or privileges, and they did not collectively push their story forward after the war.

Why is there no constituency for the single mass German protest against deportation of Jews? It not only does not fit the established paradigm of resistance but also clashes with continuing paradigms of marriage, and the picture of Nazi rule as a whole. It is also misunderstood. Recently an American broke into tears of anger at first hearing of this street protest by intermarried Germans. The story was nonsense, she said, since there were no kind-hearted Nazis. Of course kind-heartedness was not the motive for the Gestapo to release intermarried Jews. Yet some also respond to the story by claiming that we cannot treat intermarried Germans as either resisters or rescuers, since we do not know who or what was the agent that protected intermarried Jews. In other words, maybe the Nazis, as at least one Gestapo man claimed self-servingly in a postwar trial, chose to allow intermarried Jews to live out of respect for persons, rather than as a tactical response to a perceived threat to their power. Given the ways in which intermarried couples were particularly loathsome to Hitler and National Socialism, how can one suppose that Nazi leaders, without outside pressure, made a series of decisions to "temporarily defer" deportation of intermarried Jews?

Until recently, revolution and certainly effective resistance to Nazism have been connected in the minds of almost everyone with the use of violence – and of course the protest of intermarried Germans would have been to no avail had it not been for the context of massively violent intervention by the Allies. Yet within this context, protest succeeded, and was particularly influential because it was open for the *Volksgemeinschaft* to notice. If the protesters had attempted to act conspiratorially and use guns at any point the result would certainly have been a massacre. In fact the protesters might well have been shot in any case, by a decision that went another way, by a trigger-happy Gestapo officer, and so forth, and it is hard to believe that the unruly women on Rosenstrasse would not have been better commemorated after the war, if they had lost, and been martyred. Women's histories, in any case, are less likely to be told, especially as politically influential history, and particularly within the context of a ruthless dictatorship.

Another reason why the Rosenstrasse protesters have no political constituency today is perhaps due to the fact that intermarriage still makes people uncomfortable. Intermarriage does not neatly separate Jews and Gentiles, and many Germans today – at least up until the collapse of the Berlin wall and the subsequent large influxes of Jews from Eastern Europe into Germany – still do not think of Jews as "German." Of course it is also true that leaders of organized, religious Jewish communities tend to discourage intermarriage. The well-discussed concern about the preservation of the Jewish community in the face of the inroads of intermarriage has led to some ambivalence concerning the fact that virtually the only German Jews who survived were intermarried; the only Jews who earned protest had married out.[57] Not only Jews but also Germans, as well as other non-Jews, have a tendency to talk about the "Germans" and the "Jews" as if these were wholly separate, a separation disturbed by the idea of intermarriage, a category acceptable to institutions if, when the couple has a child, it decides to belong to either one religious institution or the other. In Germany, in fact, the term "intermarriage" derived from the Churches (and the Nazis used the term while radically altering the meaning to refer to two "races" rather than two religions within one marriage).

In the early twentieth century, intermarried Germans were individualistic and self-defining. As social and institutional pressures grew, intermarried couples learned to rely on themselves and each other to an unusual extent for their sense of meaning and identity. Is this a model pointing toward the future?

Another Paradigm for Another Century?

In the Germany of the 1920s and 1930s, given the advances of the broad masses into the processes of politics in Europe during the preceding century, it was already too late not to expect conscious consent of those whom a government, even a dictatorship, pretended to govern. Hitler and the Nazi Party recognized that in the twentieth century, the new age of the masses, no government could survive long "without the consensus, whether forced or passive, of a broad social stratum."[58] In this century the processes of increasing mass participation in politics had been extended through the spread of ideas, participatory politics, economic opportunities and other factors. This does not assure us that democracy is here to stay, however, as Robert Kaplan writes in asking whether democracy and its moment in history will fade.[59] In the 1990s, from the former East Germany to the countries of the former Soviet Union, the paramount challenge for democracy generally, and German unification specifically, is the growth of individual courage and sense of social responsibility that is the backbone of civil society, and a functioning free market economy.

Despite the chorus of western voices calling for the growth of civil society within Eastern Europe since the fall of the Berlin Wall, Germany continues to commemorate an attempted *coup d'état* by an elitist institution as the main symbol of resistance to its most hideous dictatorship, under Hitler. Of course it is notoriously difficult to find any resisters to Hitler's fascism and the search for a "usable past" can never justify making it look otherwise. Yet one key to telling history like it really was, while also recognizing intermarried Germans, is to acknowledge the ambiguity of resistance. The military conspirators had mixed motives and limited credibility; if they wanted to make a statement with martyrdom they succeeded, but as a symbol of resistance they are flawed, just as are the Rosenstrasse women, who protested only to protect their own families. Both groups illustrate Václav Havel's observation that the line between resistance and collaboration runs through each individual, rather than between groups of persons.[60] If both the July conspirators and the Rosenstrasse protesters are recognized as partial resisters, then we can

Nathan Stoltzfus

draw from both cases without laying claim to a greater amount of resistance overall, and illustrate civil courage, independent of elite institutions, of the kind called for in defending democracy in today's Europe.

For Germans, the intermarried Germans of Rosenstrasse remain a two-edged sword. Yes, there were ordinary Germans who made a difference – but why were there so few? Georg Zivier, a Jew married to a German and an eyewitness to the protest on Rosenstrasse, wrote in December 1945 that it was "a small torch that might have flared into a fire of general resistance," if the public had taken note.[61] It is not too late to take note. Commemoration of Rosenstrasse could provoke thought about what gave these intermarried Germans the courage to confront the Gestapo, even if their actions were neither *Widerstand* nor altruism. They were ordinary but not "normal" Germans and we could learn from them.

Notes

1. Statistics of the Central Organization of Jews in Germany (Reichsvereinigung der Juden in Deutschland) show that as of September 1944 there were 13,217 officially registered Jews in Germany. All but 230 lived in intermarriage. BA, Potsdam, R.8150, 32. This does not indicate that some intermarried Jews were not murdered; some were.
2. Hilberg (1945:169). In 1939 there were still about 30,000 intermarried couples in the German Reich and its Czech protectorate area. Almost one in ten Jews was married to a non-Jew.
3. Ursula Büttner estimates the number of divorces throughout Germany based on statistics from Hamburg and Baden-Würtemberg. Büttner (1988:57).
4. Trial against Otto Bovensiepen et al. IJs9/65 (hereafter cited as Bovensiepen Trial), Supporting Document 96. The five sets of deportation directives (concerning which categories should be sent to which camps) issued between October 1941 and February 1943 ordered *Mischlinge* and intermarried Jews to be "vorläufig zurückgestellt" from the deportations..
5. Walter Stock, the former head of the Judenreferat of the Berlin Gestapo, referred exclusively to the mass arrest action later popularly known as the "*Fabrikation*," as "Judenschlußaktion" or derivatives

of this, including "Abschluß der Juden Aktion" or "Schlußaktion gegen die Juden."

6. Statement of Else Hannach (who escaped Germany in July 1944), 26 and 31 July 1943, Bovensiepen Trial, Supporting Document 30.

7. His diary shows that Goebbels talked with Sepp Dietrich about using Hitler's SS division, the SS Leibstandarte Adolf Hitler, to help in the first two days of the Final Roundup, and the SS also arrested intermarried Jews and *Mischlinge*. Goebbels, Diary entry for February 2, 1943, Bundesarchiv NL118/95.

8. Annie Radlauer interview (collaborated in her testimony to the court in the Bovensiepen Trial), 12 March 1985; 29 May 1985. See also the indictment of Otto Bovensiepen, LBI, Anklageschrift in der Strafsache gegen Otto Bovensiepoen et al. (1969), Microfilm Reel 239, pp. 207–217. LBI, Wiener Library microfilms (AR 7187/Reel 600) contains eyewitness statements and a list of women participants in the protest, some of whom also reported that the protesters called out together.

9. In the East German Communist Party newspaper Inge Unikower wrote that "foreign news sources reported at the time 400 to 600 . . . including London Radio." Although she titled the article "Silent Protest," Unikower reported that protesters called out "Give us our husbands back. We want to have our husbands again." Inge Unikower, "Stummer Protest," *Neues Deutschland* (No. 46, 14 November 1964), 2.

10. The solidarity of the protesters was registered and reiterated not just through physical togetherness but through their common voice, "give us our husbands back." "At first it was as if I was paralyzed," recalled Johanna Löwenstein de Witt. "It was a feeling of of solidarity with one another that drove us on and gave us courage," Brandt (1984:126).

11. Interview with Elsa Holzer, 16 July 1987, 16 August 1989.

12. Interview with Leopold Gutterer, 16 July 1987.

13. Lochner (1948: entry for March 6, 1943, 276). Street protests were a form of politics so powerful that the Nazis guarded it jealously. In May 1933 a law ("For the Maintenance of Public Quiet and Security") banned public demonstrations without prior police permission. "Verordnung zur Aufrechterhaltung der öffentlichen Ruhe und Sicherheit vom 20 Mai 1933," excerpted in BA Potsdam, 50.01 (PROMI), 63, pp. 2 ff. In December 1934, to quell further fears of non-Nazi crowds, the dictatorship banned even all public gatherings other than "ancient, traditional . . . processions and

pilgrimages. "Pr. GSta., Rep. 90 P, 12. Given his view that demonstrations were effective weapons in the struggles of power politics, Goebbels considered the law that banned mass, public gatherings, in May 1933 an important cornerstone of the Nazi takeover and consolidation of power.

14. An inmate at Rosenstrasse estimated that there were 2,000 imprisoned there (Statement of Ferdinand Wolff, 4 May 1951, Trial against Walter Stock, Landgericht Berlin, Pkls 3/52, hereafter cited as Stock Trial) while a police officer who spent one night there estimated only 1,000. Statement of former street policeman Anton von Kryshak, Bovensiepen Trial, 1968. Hauptscharführer Karl Krell, the unemployed baker turned Gestapo agent for Berlin's Jewish Desk, claimed at his "de-Nazification trial" after the war that he had ordered the release of 2,000 intermarried Jews. Statement of Karl Krell, 4 SpLs 16/47 Bielefeld, BA, Koblenz.

15. The story of the Rosenstrasse protest and the release of Jews following it is mentioned very briefly in dozens of newspapers and books, mostly German. The indictment of Otto Bovensiepen gives a summary of the *Schlußaktion* and Rosenstrasse protest, based on testimony to the court in this trial from victims as well as from Gestapo men and their support staff, LBI Anklageschrift in der Strafsache gegen Otto Bowensiepen et al. (1969) Microfilm Reel 239, pp. 207–217. LBI, Wiener Library microfilms (AR 7187/Reel 600) contains eyewitness statements and a list of women participants in the protest.

16. Wippermann (1982:72)

17. Benz (1989:688).

18. Rürup (1995:253,266). Astonishingly the author cites my work as evidence for his claims.

19. Benz and Pehle (1997); Cartarius (1984); Ruck (1995).

20. For the last few years there has been a memorial to the protesters on Berlin's Rosenstrasse – a sculpture undertaken on personal, not official, initiative by Ingeborg Hunsinger.

21. Wickert (1995); Schmiechen-Ackermann (1997). This is hardly an oversight, since I have written a number of letters on this matter to the Gedenkstätte Deutscher Widerstand beginning in 1989.

22. Stoltzfus (1995).

23. Henningsen (1998).

24. Goldhagen (1996).

25. Losener (1961:268). See also Büttner (1988:12) for further evidence that Party leaders wished to eliminate *Mischlinge*. On the regime's

Mischlinge policies in general, see Noakes (1989:291–354); Grenville (1986:91–121); Adam (1972); Adam (1976).

26. Reuth (1963; entry for March 7, 1942). Far from protecting their Jewish spouses, intermarried Germans were incapable of understanding the basic tenet of National Socialism and should share the fate of those with whom they chose to associate, Goebbels wrote. Goebbels, like Hitler, referred to problems of public morale as "psychological problems" – problems of aligning public morale with official policies through "sophisticated" propaganda.

27. Certainly intermarried Germans possessed a totally different degree of motivation for protecting the Jews they stood up for than other Germans had for attempting to protect Jews in general. Also, intermarried Germans had personal everyday experience with Jews, and most did not readily fall victim to propaganda's abstract evil depictions. It was through intermarriage that Germans had developed feelings for Jews, Himmler complained near the end of the war. Report by Himmler, 1944, Berlin Document Center, File 0.2409 11.

28. Neumann (1963:98) In *Mein Kampf* Hitler wrote that popular support is the primary foundation of political power. "The first foundation for the creation of authority is always provided by popularity." With this support in hand, political leadership must then employ force, "the second foundation of all authority," to stabilize its power. Political power established through popularity and stabilized with force, however, would never be enduring until it was supported by social traditions, that final cornerstone of power. A popular authority, stabilized by police force and aligned with popular traditions "may be regarded as unshakable" (Hitler 1939:764, 765). This concept of power was an elaboration of an opinion characteristic of the Nazi Party. Even if National Socialism's theory of mass movement politics perhaps forced the regime to make unnecessary concessions for the sake of public morale, there is no doubt that this Nazi theory was more important for establishing and maintaining Nazi power than it was in limiting the regime. With this approach, the regime elicited far more support than unrest. Most Germans supported the regime, so that it had become accustomed to acquiescence.

29. Kershaw (1987:52, 53).

30. Raul Hilberg (1985:430) concluded that "The Jews in mixed marriage were finally made exempt because in the last analysis, it was felt that their deportation might jeopardize the whole destruction process. It simply did not pay to sacrifice the secrecy of the whole operation for the sake of deporting 28,000 Jews, some of whom were so old

that they would probably die naturally before the operation was over." Ursula Büttner (1988:14) has written that the Nazis exempted Jews in intermarriages from the deportations because this would cause social unrest.

31. U. S. Holocaust Memorial Museum Archives, Washington, D.C. Orders of the Reichskommissar for the Eastern Occupied Territories concerning the "treatment of Jewish Mischehe," Riga, October 7, 1942.

32. Compulsory divorce was not a delicate enough instrument for dealing with the wide variations represented in the thousands of German intermarriages, according to the calculations of the Propaganda Ministry. ND NG-2586-H.

33. Schlegelberger to Bormann, April 5, 1942, ND 4055-PS. Schlegelberger's proposed solution for both maintaining the peace and purifying the race was to deport both partners to Theresienstadt. Goebbels suspected, however, that this too might cause protests from German relatives of these couples. West Germany. Interview with Leopold Gutterer, 17 August, 1986.

34. Lösener (1961:275, 276).

35. According to the Jewish Orderly Max Reschke, charged with overseeing the Jewish staff of workers at the Grosse Hamburger Strasse, entrepreneurs and factory foremen appeared at the collection center to show that they had the authorization to employ individual Jews. The Gestapo received "work letters showing military authorizations . . . From military industrial factories, private firms, and also from the military itself came protests, all with the aim of getting their Jewish workers released again," Reschke reported. "Dobberke [the Gestapo man in charge of the main pre-deportation detention center in Berlin] took all the work books and the protests into account. They didn't do a bit of good."

36. Reports of regional administrators and the Gestapo along with Hitler's dinner conversations and other records amply indicate the church's popularity and the political pitfalls the leadership perceived in proceeding against the Catholic Church. Catholic Church leaders condemned resistance to the state, exhorting obedience and warning against seditious activity, which discouraged "any spirit of opposition" (Lewy 1964:309, 313, 314).

37. Some prelates welcomed the laws, and implied that from the Church's point of view there could be no objection to legal discrimination against Jews. (Lewy 1964:274–275, 281–282).

38. Aly and Roth (1984:70, 71).

39. On February 17, the Relief Help Office of the Catholic Bishop of
    Berlin wrote to Catholic parishes throughout Berlin, requiring each
    parish to identify its intermarried couples, their children, and in some
    cases, their place of work. Most parishes replied by February 27,
    and a few replied during early March. The resulting lists, which were
    given either to the Jewish Community or directly to the Gestapo,
    contain hundreds and hundreds of names and addresses, identified
    in separate categories of "Privileged Intermarriages" and "Non-
    privileged Intermarriages," and "Catholic Non-Aryan, or "Non-
    Aryan-Catholic Heads of Households." Library, Jewish Community,
    Berlin (Fasanenstr.). This is an unmarked folder from the Berlin
    Jewish Community, titled "Lists Due to the Forced-Deportations."
    The lists are carefully marked with checks, slashes and crosses.
    The correspondence on hand is between Catholic offices, but the
    Protestant Church, under official orders, was almost certainly also
    doing work to identify and locate all Berlin Jews who had converted
    to Protestantism.
40. Lewy (1964:289). One German episcopate, Archbishop Bertram, did
    specifically request German Justice and Interior ministries to with-
    draw proposals for compulsory divorce of intermarriages, but he did
    so well after Himmler and Goebbels had already decided, in early–
    mid-1942, that there should be no such law (Goebbels argued that it
    would cause unrest and Himmler said it would only bind the regime's
    hands and limit its options). It is ironic that some argue that the
    Church was the force responsible for protecting intermarried Jews,
    while also maintaining that the Church could not have made any
    difference to Nazi Jewish policy even if it had protested. The success
    of any thorough state program of determining who was Jewish and
    who Aryan depended on Church cooperation, for example, since
    the churches possessed the only records of births and marriages in
    Germany before 1874. The churches made their records available,
    implying that their members should complete the forms the regime
    requested on race.
41. By the summer of 1935 these Nazi Party-instigated disturbances grew
    so large that observers described them as demonstrations. IML,
    Lagebericht (Allgemeine Übersicht über die Ereignisse im Monat
    Juli 1935), St3/673.
42. Minutes of the meeting of officials following the Kristallnacht Pogrom,
    Nuremberg Trial Documents, PS-1816, quoted in Hilberg (1985:168).
43. Goldhagen (1996:207). Goldhagen, who cites my work (using numbers
    not from my work) on the Rosenstrasse protest, is not convincing

when he argues that protests against euthanasia and not against the Holocaust betrays general antisemitism in Germany. Of course there was a protest against the genocide of Jews, the Rosenstrasse protest – when and only to the extent that it disrupted families. Likewise, protests against euthanasia were also precipitated by family members of euthanasia's victims. Thus family ties (extended self-interest), not ideology, were the major cause of fearful rumors and protests against both euthanasia and Holocaust. Protests against euthanasia arose initially – and von Galen's later public denouncements built on these – due to divided families. These protests arose from families the regime divided into two parts – victims of National Socialism, and exalted members of the victimizing National Socialist community.

44. The emphasis on self- and family-interest as the basis for cooperation (as well as opposition) in Nazi Germany does not discount the importance of antisemitism. Antisemitism was the intellectual backdrop for the Holocaust, and to National Socialism. Jews represented not just a dangerous "race" but the most dangerous of all races, and when Germany invaded Poland and the Soviet Union Jews were the primary, if not the only, target of the army's mass murder of civilians.

45. Ibid., 97

46. IML, St3/673, 54–56; BA Potsdam, 30.01 (RJM) Nr. 1389, 176

47. The Germans looked on the pogrom passively, and their silence allowed Goebbels to declare it a result of the righteous indignation in the collective German soul, and of the regime, the direct agent of the people. German Press, 12 November, 1938.

48. Gellately (1990:5) has shown that the regime needed the everyday cooperation of the people in order to enforce its racial policies. "There has been a tendency to suppose that the 'police state' relied on an extraordinarily large police force, which in turn could count on the collaboration of an army of paid agents and spies."

49. Hamerow (1997) eulogizing, criticizing, synthesizing.

50. Schmuhl (1990), No. 4, 412, 13; and Burleigh (1990:13). Under the modified euthanasia program, "the goal to strive for is to make indistinguishable, in all but a few exceptions, death by Euthanasia and natural death." Quoted in Schmuhl (1987:223)

51. Kershaw (1985:779–798).

52. On August 13, 1941, in a final meeting before the beginning of the genocide of German Jews, officials from the Party Chancellery, the SD in the Reichsicherheitshauptamt (RSHA), and the office of Racial Politics agreed to expand the definition of Jews in occupied territories to include *Mischlinge*. Lösener (1961:297). See also Longerich

(1991:220, 221). But immediately thereafter, at the time he was meeting with Goebbels, Hitler rejected the Party Chancellery's plan to count *Mischlinge* as Jews. Lösener heard of Hitler's decision on August 16 (Lösener: (1961:304). The Gestapo then received instructions to "temporarily defer" all German *Mischlinge* and all intermarried Jews from the Final Solution deportations, which began in mid-October 1941.

53. Some have suggested that Hitler had decided already by 1942 to defer the deportation of intermarried Jews until after the war. They base this on a file of fragments from the Justice Ministry known as the Schlegelberger Minute" (which is discussed further below). In part, this minute states that "Reichminister Lammers reported that the Führer had repeatedly told him he "wished to have the Solution of the Jewish question deferred until after the war." Thus the contention that Hitler had at this point already decided to defer deporting intermarried Jews until after the war rests on interpreting the phrase "Jewish question" in this case to mean only "intermarried-Jewish question." BA "Behandlung der Juden," R 22/52. If the Schlegelberger Minute does refer only to intermarried Jews, it indicates how painstaking is the research on the matter, given the subtle use of language. The term "Jews" here is interpreted to mean only the "intermarried Jews," and elsewhere in Nazi documents intermarried Jews are classified under the category of *Mischlinge*, or, alternately, all intermarried Jews are referred to as "privileged," when formally only a part of them had this designation.

54. Regarding intermarried Jews, Hitler was following his habit of waiting for his intuition to inform him of the opportune moment for taking action. "You must understand that I always go as far as I dare and never further," he said. "It is vital to have a sixth sense which tells you broadly what you can and cannot do." Noakes and Pridham (1992:550).

55. Lochner (1948:288 ff., entry for March 9, 1943, and interview with Gutterer, 17 August, 1986; 10 December, 1989).

56. NA, TR - 175/R 94/2615097. In Himmler's words, Hitler said that "the evacuation of Jews was to be radically carried out in the next three to four months, despite the still developing unrest." This is a small part of a larger memorandum, much of which concerns the East. Hitler's statement, however, should be interpreted as general policy for Europe. The practice of referring to the deportation of intermarried Jews or *Mischlinge* reflects the vocabulary of Eichmann, who said that he would "radically resolve" the question of German

Mischlinge. Statement of Adolf Kurtz, 28 June 1961, Israel Police Document (144), quoting Eichmann's response to two prelates who inquired about Eichmann's intentions regarding intermarried Jews.

57. One Israeli acquaintance told me that a religious Jew would avoid research into intermarriage of the Third Reich (and Rosenstrasse), while a secularized Jew would likely avoid study of the Third Reich altogether. Of course the heart-rending story of Rosenstrasse is hardly a triumph for intermarriage either. For Germans who married Jews did not do this primarily because they wanted a Jewish partner, nor did they protest to save their partners from the camps because they were Jewish, but primarily because they were family.

58. Steinert (1977: 1).

59. Kaplan (1997).

60. Havel (1997).

61. Zivier (1945).

References

Adam. Uwe (1976) "An Overall Plan for Anti-Jewish Legislation in the Third Reich," *Yad Vashem Studies* 11.

Aly, Götz, and Roth, Karl Heinz (1984) *Die Restlose Erfassung*. Berlin: Rotbuch Verlag.

Benz, Wolfgang, and Walter Pehle (eds) (1997) *Encyclopedia of German Resistance to the Nazi Movement* (trans. Lance Garmer). New York, N.Y.: Continuum.

Brandt, Leon (1984) *Menschen ohne Schatten. Juden zwischen Untergang und Untergrund, 1938 bis 1945*. Berlin: Oberbaum Verlag.

Burleigh, Michael (1990) "Euthanasia and the Third Reich," *History Workshop Journal*, February: 13

Büttner, Ursula (1988) *Die Not der Juden teilen. Christlich-jüdische Familien im Dritten Reich*. Hamburg: Forschungsstelle für die Geschichte des Nationalsozialismus.

Cartarium, Ulrich (1984) *Bibliographie "Widerstand"*. Munich: K.G. Saur.

Gellately, Robert (1990) *The Gestapo and German Society: Enforcing Racial Policy, 1933–1945*. Oxford: Oxford University Press.

Goldhagen, Daniel Jonah (1996) *Hitler's Willing Executioners*. New York, N.Y.: Alfred A. Knopf.

Grenville, John A.S. (1986) "Die 'Endlösung' und die 'Judenmischlinge' im Dritten Reich," in Ursula Büttner (ed.) *Das Unrechtsregime: Internationale Forschung über den Nationalsozialismus*. Hamburg: Hans Christian Verlag.

Hamerow, Theodore S. (1997) *On the Road to the Wolf's Lair: German Resistance to Hitler.* Cambridge, Ma.: Belknap Press.

Havel, Václav (1997) *The Art of the Impossible: Politics as Morality in Practice.* Trans. Paul Wilson. New York: Alfred A. Knopf.

Henningsen, Manfred (1998) "Deutscher Widerstand für Deutsche Juden: zu den Büchern von Victor Klemperer und Nathan Stoltzfus," *Merkur,* January.

Hilberg, Raul (1985) *Destruction of the European Jews.* New York and London: Holmes and Meier.

Hitler, Adolf (1939*) Mein Kampf.* Eds. John Chamberlain and Sidney B. Fay. New York, N.Y.: Reynald and Hitchcock.

Kaplan, Robert D. (1997) "Was Democracy Just a Moment?," *The Atlantic Monthly.*

Kershaw, Ian. (1985) "'Widerstand ohne Volk': Dissens und Widerstand im Dritten Reich," in Jürgen Schmädeke and Peter Steinbach (eds) *Der Widerstand gegen den Nationalsozialismus.* Munich: Piper.

—— (1987) *The "Hitler Myth": Image and Reality in the Third Reich.* Oxford and New York: Oxford University Press.

Levy, Guenter (1964) *The Catholic Church and Nazi Germany.* London: Weidenfeld & Nicolson.

Lochner, Louis (ed.) (1943) *The Goebbels Diaries, 1942-1943.* New York, N.Y.: Doubleday & Co. Inc.

Longerich, Peter (1992) *Hitlers Stellvertreter: Führung der Partei under Kontrolle des Staatsapparates durch den Stab Hess und die Partei - Kanzlei Bormann.* Munich: K.G. Saur.

Lösener, Bernhard (1961) "Als Rassereferent im Reichsministerium des Innern," *Vierteljahreshefte fur Zeitgeschichte* 9.

Neumann, Franz (1963) *Behemoth: The Structure and Practice of National Socialism.* New York, N.Y.: Octagon Books.

Noakes, Jeremy (1989) "Nazi Policy toward German-Jewish Mischlinge," *Yearbook Leo Baeck Institute* 34:291–354

Noakes, Jeremy, and Pridham, Geoffrey (eds) (1992) *Nazism: A History in Documents and Eyewitness Accounts, 1919–1945.* New York: Schocken.

Reuth, Ralf Georg (ed.) (1963) *Joseph Goebbels Tagebücher, vol. 4: 1940–1942.* Munich and Zurich: Serie Piper.

Ruck, Michael (1995) *Bibliographie zum Nationalsozialismus.* Cologne: Bund Verlag.

Rürup, Reinhard (ed.) (1995) *Jüdische Geschichte in Berlin: Essays and Studien.* Berlin: Edition Hentrich.

Schmiechen-Ackermann, Detlef (ed.) (1997) *Anpassung.Verweigerung.*

Widerstand: Soziale Milieus, politische Kultur und der Widerstand gegem den Nationalsozialismus in Deutschland im regionalen Vergleich. Berlin: Gedenkstätte Deutscher Widerstand.

Schmuhl, Hans-Walter (1987) *Rassenhygiene, Nationalsozialismus, Euthanasie: von der Verhütung zur Vernichtung "Lebensunwerten Lebens" 1890–1945*. Göttingen: Vandenhoeck & Ruprecht.

—— (1990) "Die Selbstverständlichkeit des Tötens: Psychiater im Nationalsozialismus," *Geschichte und Gesellschaft* 16.

Steinert, Marlis (1977) *Hitler's War and the Germans: Public Mood and Attitude during the Second World War* Ed. and trans. T.E.J. de Witt. Athens, Ohio: Ohio University Press.

Stoltzfus, Nathan (1995) "Widerstand des Herzens: Der Protest in der Rosenstrasse und die deutsch-jüdische Mischehe," *Geschichte und Gesellschaft*, 21.

Wickert, Christl (ed.) (1995) *Frauen gegen die Diktatur – Widerstand und Verfolgung im nationalsozialistischen Deutschland 1933–1945*. Berlin: Gedenkstätte Deutscher Widerstand.

Wippermann, Wolfgang (1982) *Steinerne Zeugen: Stätten der Judenverfolgung in Berlin*. Berlin: Hentrich.

Zivier, Georg (1945) "Aufstand der Frauen," *Sie*, December.

-10-

French Women in the Resistance:
Rescuing Jews
Margaret Collins Weitz

[E]xcluded Jews found a place in their native land which neither denied nor rejected them. This fragile French Resistance was theirs also. To share its hope, they accepted momentarily the silences and doubts, faithful to themselves, women and men [representative] of their history and their time.[1] (Laborie 995:259)

This chapter documents the presence of women in the French Resistance, a commitment they frequently made as a direct response to the persecution of the Jews both by the Nazis and by the Vichy government of Marshal Pétain. Until recently, women have been largely absent from the memory of the French Resistance (1940–1945); a central issue, since postwar France has been largely built upon the memory of the Resistance. Women's absence from postwar Resistance historiography can be attributed in part to the problems inherent in defining *resistance*, and to the nature of women's contribution – largely extensions of their everyday activities, such as offering "hospitality" to Jews fleeing persecution. Thus far emphasis has focused principally on military undertakings, although the Maquis (clandestine paramilitary groups) and the French Forces of the Interior (FFI) did not play an important role until late in the Occupation (1940–1944).

Why has so little been written about French women's role in resisting the persecution of Jews in the Holocaust? As suggested, resistance activities were frequently differentiated by gender. For men, resistance included sabotage and armed encounters, while for most women, resistance undertakings assumed forms related to their everyday activities, and were thus marginalized. In addition to sheltering the pursued, French women did most of the clandestine clerical work, including typing underground tracts and papers, which came to include efforts to alert the largely passive French public about the Vichy government's antisemitic program, as well as that of the Nazis. In order to assess and better understand the nature of French resistance and efforts aimed at saving Jews, some historical background is required. The historical context is augmented by first-hand testimony from those involved, including interviews selected from a corpus of over eighty I conducted in the 1980s which were utilized for *Sisters in the Resistance: How Women Fought to Free France, 1940–1945* (1995).

Little happened in France during the "phony war," the period from the declaration of war on September 3, 1939 to the German blitzkrieg of May 1940 which overran Holland and Belgium and then proceeded to invade France. On June 14, 1940 Paris was declared an open city and surrendered without resistance. The French government joined the massive exodus preceding the invading forces and reassembled in the port city of Bordeaux. Marshal Philippe Pétain was named head of a new French government. To the anguished population his name inspired hope: he was the victor of the Battle of Verdun of World War I. Even though the troops were still fighting, Pétain went on national radio on June 17 to announce that he was asking the Germans for an end to the hostilities. The following day, Charles de Gaulle spoke to the French people from London via the BBC, assuring them that "the flame of French resistance must not die, and will not die." Few heard his speech: even fewer responded.

Pétain and his entourage moved to the spa town of Vichy in midsummer 1940 where he presided over the demise of the Third Republic. The National Assembly voted itself out of existence – without debate – and granted Pétain full powers. The Franco-German armistice, which had gone into effect on June 25, contained the fateful word *collaborate*. In September 1940 most of France was divided into two major zones: the occupied zone, encompassing the northern three-fifths of the country; and the unoccupied or so-called 'free' zone in the south, which included Vichy.

Prominent resistance figure Lucie Aubrac recounts the population's confusion of the time.

> In the early days of the Occupation few French were willing to undertake risks and join the Resistance. Unlike, say Holland or Denmark, France had a national government collaborating with the German occupiers. In France the situation was ambiguous, compounded by French patriotism and nationalism. Marshal Pétain, the head of the government, was a man over eighty and a hero of the preceding war. The French respect age and authority. (Interview, May 1985)

Small groups began to meet to discuss the situation and determine how best to continue the struggle. By and large, the aims and nature of their efforts were determined by location. Those in the occupied zone had to deal with the German presence. In the absence of uncensored information, those in the north attributed Vichy's increasingly disconcerting measures (principally the antisemitic statutes) to German pressure. Late in the war some still accepted the myth of the "grand old man" playing a double game and doing his best to shield and save France. In reality, as historian Robert Paxton (1972:46) shows, Vichy "sought neutrality, an early peace, and a final settlement on gentle terms with Germany." The postwar myth of Vichy's passivity was just that – myth. Scholar Tony Judt (1972:1018) describes Pétain as embodying "the incompetence of the French High Command, the deep-rooted antisemitism of his class and caste, [and] the instinctive desire of many of the French to wait out the war."

Pétain started to implement a National Revolution. Seduced by Pétain's reputation, reactionaries and opportunists sought revenge against those they charged with France's defeat: leftists, Communists, trade-unionists, civil-libertarians, Freemasons – and Jews. Freed from the constraints of an assembly, Pétain instituted a series of statutes and decrees aimed at strengthening and purifying the French state. Efforts to purify the French state focused on the Jews, traditional scapegoats. Michael Marrus and Robert Paxton convincingly demonstrate that Vichy inaugurated its own antisemitic policies *before* any German text regarding the Jews in France had been published, and *without* having received direct orders from the Germans; the only West European country to do so. Vichy fostered the illusion that it could thus assert its authority and pre-empt German legislation.

The Vichy regime immediately set up a commission to review every case of French citizenship granted since 1927. In the process, more than 15,000 people had their citizenship revoked, including over 6,000 Jews who now automatically became foreigners, hence vulnerable to persecution. A July 1940 decree forbade Jews – even native-born ones – from holding positions in France's extensive national administration. Barely two months after the armistice a statute was promulgated defining Jews by *race* that included a more restrictive definition than that formulated by the Nazis. This statute, and those passed in the following year, virtually excluded Jews from the professions. Among those who found Vichy's antisemitic measures unacceptable was Violette Morin, a student at the University of Toulouse in southwest France.

My family was Catholic and devoted to republican traditions and values. There were few foreigners where I lived so I was somewhat insular and naive about the country's policies regarding strangers. Then I went to Paris for university studies and worked with the Vigilance Committee of Antifascist Intellectuals (CVIA). When hostilities broke out I transferred to the University of Toulouse to continue my studies. Now aware of the so-called "Jewish problem," I was outraged to learn that several of my favorite teachers had been relieved of their teaching responsibilities. Why? Because they were Jews. This I found unacceptable. An irrepressible feeling of revolt seized me. I looked for some way to combat those who imposed such decrees and joined a resistance group. (Interview, June 1983)

The October 3, 1940 decree permitted internment of foreign Jews or assignment to forced residence. The previous year, when war was declared, those viewed as "foreign enemies" – a threat to France's security – were interned. To this group were now added the large number of foreign refugees without legal status. In *Camps de la honte* (Camps of shame), Anne Grynberg (1991) states that by 1949 there were approximately 40,000 Jews in the southern zone camps.

Various humanitarian groups trying to help detainees in French camps (two-thirds of whom were Jewish) set up an umbrella organization, known as the Nîmes Committee, in November 1940. One of the groups was CIMADE (Intermovement Committee for Evacuees), under the direction of dynamic young Madeleine Barot. CIMADE had been set up by Protestant organizations in September 1939 to help those evacuated from Alsace and Lorraine. A small group of committed Christians (composed largely of young women since their male colleagues had been mobilized) worked during France's "phony war" to help refugees. CIMADE concentrated on helping foreign Jews made vulnerable by Vichy's antisemitic legislation. Both Protestants and Jews were minority groups that had suffered persecution in earlier centuries in Catholic France. Now, under Pétain, France was again militantly Catholic. Barot and her colleague, nurse Jeanne Merle d'Aubigné, installed themselves in the French camp at Gurs, near the Spanish border. Gradually other groups – Quakers, Swiss and several Jewish organizations – managed to send representatives to the camp. As more internment camps were set up inside France, other teams were sent to help.

Barot's work expanded when a small number of detainees were allowed to live outside the overcrowded camp as residents under surveillance; provided housing could be found for them. The group's last major project was to try to halt the deportation of Jews in France to eastern Europe for extermination. Madeleine Barot and her colleagues directed "God's Underground." They hid many Jews, mainly children. While some Jews succeeded in living hidden in France throughout the war, whenever possible, they were sent to Switzerland, although the Swiss did not always welcome them. The volunteers who accompanied them to the border were at peril. They had to deal with dogs and fusillades; if captured they risked torture, deportation and death.

Polish-born Sabina Zlatin served with the French Red Cross as a nurse during the fighting of 1939–1940. When she learned of the shocking conditions in the camp at Agde (in south central France), Zlatin volunteered to work there. Appointed social assistant for the internees at Agde, she hoped to improve living conditions.

Zlatin worked with a group of clergy. They succeeded in having the 12,000 internees at Agde transferred to the Rivesaltes camp, in the Pyrénées region. Conditions there were marginally better. Now Zlatin's concern was focused on the many children among the 25,000, largely Jewish detainees at Rivesaltes. There were many deaths; disease was widespread. With some difficulty she secured permission to free 100 children (mostly Jewish) under twelve years of age each month. Generally the children were taken to a vacant nearby sanatorium Zlatin had rented so the children could be treated before being placed with families.

When the Germans occupied all of France in November 1942, Zlatin continued to care for the children in the Rivesaltes camp, even though German sentries now joined the French guards overseeing them. Then, in spring 1943, local authorities asked her to take seventeen Jewish children, "forgotten" by officials, to the Alps region. They found what seemed like a safe home in the mountainous region of Izieu, east of Lyon. They were joined by her husband, a woman doctor, several helpers, and other children – at times up to eighty. Sabina Zlatin and her husband sold personal effects to help finance operating expenses for the children's home. For a while things appeared to be going well. Then a Maquis, a clandestine paramilitary group, was set up in the region during the winter of 1943–1944. Zlatin was afraid the Maquis would attract German attention so she went to look for another place. On Holy Thursday 1944, while she was away examining possible locations, the Germans arrived and captured everyone but a male helper, who escaped. None of the forty-four children returned: presumably they went directly to the crematoriums. Zlatin herself was warned in time. Later it was learned that the group had been denounced by a refugee from the annexed province of Lorraine. The fate of these children of Izieu led to the 1984 extradition of the infamous Klaus Barbie, nicknamed the "Butcher of Lyon." His telegram stating that he had "cleaned out" the Jewish children's home was a major piece of evidence at his trial. Even though all the children she thought saved were lost, and her husband was missing, Zlatin continued resistance work in Paris and the surrounding region. She was wounded in an unsuccessful attack on a prison, but survived nonetheless (Testimony, February 1947).

The well-known feminist, historian, and sociologist Evelyne Sullerot opposed the occupiers and the Vichy regime while still a teenager. Sullerot attributes her involvement to her family milieu. Her parents were both Christian and Socialist. Her mother held strong political convictions and was very upset that she could not vote. (French women received that right in 1944.) Sullerot's father was a minister in the French Calvinist Church who became a psychiatrist, directing a Protestant clinic for those with "nervous" disorders. Protestant pastors, the evangelicals, were very active in Germany trying to combat Nazism. Before the war they formed a network that helped Jews flee Germany. When young, Sullerot saw and heard these German Jews who stayed at her home; she also read books about Nazism and the persecution of Jews. At sixteen she was imprisoned briefly for anti-Vichy activities (including listening to the BBC).

> In 1943 my mother died, aged forty-four. My father stayed in the clinic near Compiègne (north-east of Paris), and I was left alone in our apartment to care for my younger brother and sister. Through childhood friends I became involved in a resistance network. I did liaison, transporting grenades and plastic explosives. As a young girl in charge of two younger children, I was not suspected. But then I became seriously ill so we joined my father at the clinic in the forest.
>
> There were twelve patients there, along with eleven Jews we were hiding. We needed to find food for everybody. It was a *tour de force*. We had two sheep and a cow. But there were always problems. We had no fertilizer, insecticides or machines. You would find the cow bloated, the rabbits dead. We spent a great deal of time caring for the livestock. We had to grow vegetables. Each day we had to pick off insects, like the potato bugs.
>
> Because of the Jews we had hidden, we could not hire just anyone to help us. Some of the Jews were not always careful. Others were, for they realized we risked our lives for them. When the Germans came, from time to time, we put the Jews in straitjackets and told them to shriek and howl. Since the Germans were afraid of mental illnesses, they did not stay long. At the Liberation those we had hidden were astonished to discover who were the *real* mental patients and who were not. (Sullerot interview, June 1983)

With unusual efficiency, and utilizing the latest technology, Vichy set up a coded card index of French Jews and their property. For the first time in seventy years, data on ethnic background were required of French citizens. The extremely detailed information gathered in these surveys was of major importance in facilitating the later Nazi decision to implement the Final Solution in France. Only 2,800 of the more than 75,000 Jews deported from France returned. But a quarter of a million survived, according to historian Susan Zuccotti. She attributes this in part to the help of committed French people, and to the silence or benign neglect of the majority of the French population. (Zuccotti 1993:288)

* * *

The question is frequently raised. Why did the French Resistance, and French resisters who were Jewish, not focus earlier and more aggressively on the rescue of Jews? As might be anticipated, the answer is complex. One obvious explanation was the delay in finally realizing the Nazis' goal of exterminating all Jews. Early accounts were dismissed as fantasies; too horrible to merit credence. Another factor was that a considerable number of native-born French Jews were assimilated. Others, while acknowledging their Jewish identity and marking major holy days, did not go to temple regularly (just as many French Catholics do not attend Sunday Mass on a regular basis), nor join Jewish groups. Initially French Jews did not see themselves at particular risk.

Jews signed on with different resistance movements and groups, both Communist and non-Communist. Their individual, rather than collective, decisions were consistent with the republican tradition of seeing themselves as French citizens first and foremost. Joining the Resistance as individuals counteracted enemy efforts to designate them as a specific minority group. The prewar view held that the French Republic did not recognize minorities. In whatever group, being Jews made these volunteer resisters doubly vulnerable if captured. On the other hand, some believed that as Jews they had more reason to resist. Jewish women volunteered as "soldiers of the night" in greater proportion to their overall representation among the French population at that time. These women did not try to keep a low profile or spend the dark years of the Occupation in hiding in the hopes of surviving. Yvette Bernard Farnoux is an example of one such woman.

When petite, blonde Yvette received unwelcome attention from German soldiers stationed in Paris, she found an excellent way to discourage them. She told them that she was syphilitic – in German. Yvette was born into an Alsatian-Jewish family that left Alsace rather than become German when the province was annexed after the Franco-Prussian War. Her father served in World War I as an officer in a French antitank unit. When war broke out again, she was nineteen and had completed the *baccalauréat* school-finishing degree. Yvette would have liked to pursue medical studies, but few Jewish students were accepted so she went to a private school that trained social workers. She was completely opposed to working in the German-occupied zone. When she received her diploma, the school's director, Jeanne Sivadon (an early resister), gave her the Lyon address of the Unemployment Commission headed by resistance heroine and martyr Berty Albrecht. Berty asked her to contact a group of prisoners, who, unbeknownst to Yvette, were resistance members. It was a difficult assignment, a test, but she succeeded. Berty asked her if she would be willing to do social work for these people.

> That is how I started doing resistance work. I was young and unattached. Generally married women were not as free. They had to get their husband's permission [under France's paternalistic legal code]. And there were women with children, like my sister, who could not join as readily. Frankly, I do not know if I would have joined if I had had children then.
>
> I broke off contact with my family and went underground, taking the name Claude. Under the orders of Berty Albrecht, my job was to help her care for the prisoners and develop what became the social services for the movement Combat [which Albrecht helped co-found with Henri Frenay]. This entailed talking with the lawyers, the chaplains, the prisoners, the families. Often when people were arrested, their families had few resources. The Resistance gave them what little it could, but that was all they had. Family or friends who normally might have helped were not always there. Sometimes our contacts with these families were very difficult since they did not always know that the father or son had joined the Resistance. Other families knew and approved.
>
> By and large, the chaplains were fabulous. For example, I remember a priest who did everything he possibly could to help me. Once he even gave me keys to the prison. He passed all sorts of papers and documents in and out of the prison and helped us arrange escapes. We had to hide the escapees while waiting for a plane to pick them up and take them to London. For some we had to find hospital beds and medical supplies. Women were better suited for this work. They were more secure, less suspect. Women know how to solve these problems. They were not that different from the problems women have to deal with all the time.

One day Farnoux noticed a handsome young man going into the office of Jacqueline Bernard, another of Berty's assistants. "Too bad," she thought, "it must be her fiancé." No, it was not Jacqueline's fiancé, but her brother Jean-Guy Bernard, Frenay's assistant.

It was love at first sight. We started to live together, that is, when we could manage it. Those were happy days. Our common goal was to rid France of the Germans. Then Berty was arrested [May 1942] and I was asked to head our social services. Our biggest job was with the prisoners. They needed food above all. Supplies varied greatly. There were times when I spent entire weeks scouring the countryside trying to get food. We resistance members needed provisions as well. We had nothing, absolutely nothing. I asked friends to give a little something. Stores often were closed, and there was no time to stand in line. On occasion we were forced to use the black market.

We had no training for this kind of work. Initially we did not know what we were dealing with, and what we should be doing. Here luck played an important part – along with trial and error. We were truly amateurs, but we learned. I started in 1941 and was arrested in 1944. When you consider what was happening in France during that period, three years was a long time. Gradually we built up the support services until they met our needs. Then the work becomes more or less habit and you are not as careful. That is when arrests occur. In the concentration camps, the Germans reserved a special category for those of us who had been in the Resistance [as opposed to political, racial, or forced labor deportees].

In summer 1943 I discovered I was pregnant. Since both of us had gone underground, and had no legal identity, this was a real problem. Having an abortion in those days was very difficult [the Vichy government made it a crime against the state, punishable by death]. In any event, we were both opposed to the idea. I think it was the notion of perpetuating oneself – in spite of everything – when you are living so dangerously. At least that is what I think now, although I am not quite certain about how I viewed it at the time. Fortunately Jean-Guy's family was wealthy and could support the child if something happened to us. We knew they would welcome the baby. We got married in a small village when my pregnancy was quite advanced. In those days you did not have a child unless you were married. With difficulty we found a village, Margency in Seine-et-Oise, where we were married without having the banns published [as required]. Six of us took the train from Paris to this little village. The ceremony lasted thirty seconds, the time it took to sign the papers. The entire wedding party was clandestine.

In the fall of 1943 the Germans stepped up their pursuit of resistance agents. Farnoux continued her clandestine activities, using her maternity girdle to conceal documents, funds, even guns. Jean-Guy was now in charge of sabotage plans for both the railway and mail and telephone system of the Lyon region. His picture was on wanted posters. When his secretary was arrested in January 1944, Yvette and Jean-Guy went to find a place in occupied Paris (a major problem), where they could continue their work. Three weeks went by without incident so the couple assumed the secretary had not "talked" (if captured, you were to remain silent for at least 48 hours), and felt out of danger. They moved into an apartment that had been made available to the group. Instead, after holding out for three weeks, the secretary gave the Germans that address thinking it was now safe to do so. The couple were arrested on a Sunday they had decided to "give to themselves." When the doorbell rang they could have fled by back windows, but no one had been arrested on a Sunday evening – before.

I was told that unless I talked, they would kill my baby as soon as it was born – unless, of course, they decided to give it to a German family to raise – so I decided to commit suicide with a razor blade I had hidden in my coat hem. I was not afraid of torture or death, but I could not bear the idea of the Germans taking my child. I was seven and a half months pregnant. In the dark, I cut my left wrist deeply. The next morning I was bathed in blood – but still conscious. They dragged Jean-Guy into my cell, thinking that the sight of me would make him talk. Of course he didn't. Before taking him out they beat him in front of me. That was the last time I saw him. A German nurse stitched my wrist without anesthesia, but I was in such a state I didn't even feel it. Several weeks after my arrest, and alone in my cell, I gave birth to a stillborn daughter. You simply cannot imagine what that was like.

My sister-in-law, Jacqueline Bernard, managed to arrange my escape from prison five days later. Since the house I was to hide in turned out to be under surveillance we went to another place. Jacqueline was convinced that this place was being watched as well so she went to find an ambulance for me as I was still very weak. When the Germans arrived the next morning, I was not there. Suspicious myself about this latest "safe" house, I decided to leave at dawn. How I managed to walk those five miles, I do not know. A car stopped and offered me a lift. The driver was the adopted daughter of the woman whose house I had just left, whom I had just met the previous evening. She gave me a lift – to the police station. I was put in prison, in Vendôme. This girl was the mistress of the notorious, so-called Rudi von Mérode, a Frenchman working for the Gestapo. She betrayed both her adopted mother and me.

In the prison cell no one wanted to make room for Yvette except a prostitute who insisted she be given the best place on the straw; she also cleaned her infected wounds. Then Yvette was taken to Gestapo head-quarters in Paris for more interrogations, and, just a few days before D-Day, deported to Auschwitz. They put her with a group of eastern Jews who spoke Yiddish, which she did not understand. After ten months there she was marched with other prisoners to Ravensbrück (the camp to which most French women in the Resistance were deported).

After her return from the camps Yvette resumed social work. She founded Revivre (Back-to-life) to take care of orphans of the Resistance

– the children of those who had been executed, killed in military encounters, or died in the camps. When liberated by the Russians from the camp in Germany, she met the man who was to become her husband, also a freed deportee. She remarried and had three children They are grandparents. But she cannot shake off the anguish caused by what she endured. Once while in New York someone noticed the number tattooed on her arm and asked Yvette if she had been in a concentration camp because she was Jewish. Yes, she replied, she was Jewish, but she was deported because she was involved in the Resistance. This, she emphasizes, is a very important point: Jews who might have lived out the war in hiding took a double risk when they joined the Resistance. However, in another way, they could understand why they had been deported (Interview April 1986).

Specifically Jewish resistance has become the subject of more study in recent years. Lucien Lazare (1996:31) defines Jewish resistance as organized efforts not only to sustain the morale of the Jewish population, but also "to ensure their physical survival by distributing means of subsistence, often clandestinely, by rescuing Jews from internment and deportation, and, finally, by carrying out military operations." This overall definition notwithstanding, the groups themselves were quite disparate, as were their priorities. For example, Jewish Communist groups privileged political action, rather than rescue efforts. The history of Jewish resistance is far from complete, in part because of the death of many involved.

As more and more anti-Jewish decrees were published, some Jews formed their own Resistance group, the Organisation Juive de Combat (OJC). The Jewish scouting group (Éclaireurs Israélites Français) undertook escorting children along escape routes. Marianne Cohn was a member of this group. On her last mission the young woman succeeded in leading twenty-eight Jewish children, aged three to sixteen, as far as the French side of the Swiss border. There they were arrested by German border guards. Eleven of the group were taken into custody. Cohn had a chance to escape but refused to leave the children and was subsequently killed (Weitz 1995:172–73).

The testimony of noted historian Annie Kriegel illustrates the situation of many French Jewish families and the problems inherent in undertaking resistance.

> Our family was modest, liberal, and open. Although not religious, we acknowledged ourselves as Jews. We did not observe the sabbath or the high holy days. My first political shock came in 1934, when I was just eight. I have never forgotten it. My mother was with a group of mothers waiting for their

children outside school. They were crying as they listened to a dirty, unshaven man. I came over and learned he was a newly arrived German Jew. He was telling everyone about the situation in Germany.

The night Marshal Pétain announced that he was seeking an armistice (June 17, 1940) the family was grouped around the radio listening to him. For the first time in her life Kriegel saw her father cry. When asked why he was crying he answered "My children, France is defeated." He stopped for a moment and then added: "And, my children, we are Jews." The priority of his preoccupations was very significant, she observes. Coming from a line of Alsace-Lorraine Jews, he was a fervent, intransigent patriot who saw himself first as a Frenchman. Moreover, he was a veteran who had been decorated with the war cross and the military medal. He was a devoted father, always concerned about paying his taxes on time, always anxious to show that he was a law-abiding citizen. His first concern was for France. His second concern, inevitably, was the realization that from that time on he had a new burden; that of dealing with a situation where henceforth his principal identity would be that of a Jew.

At first life in occupied Paris appeared comparatively normal. Then all Jews had to register for a census. They never considered *not* obeying. Her father would never have considered disobeying the law. For that matter, everyone knew they were Jewish. So they registered. Kriegel notes that no group warned Jews *not* to register. Then the vise gradually tightened. The first stage was the roundup of a thousand prominent Jews in December 1941. One of her uncles was in that group. He and most of the others never returned from deportation. That roundup proved conclusively that the Nazis were going to destroy the Jews, whatever their origin. Up till then – not to their credit or foresightedness it must be said – French Jews thought they would be treated differently from foreign Jews. That day they realized that they shared a common destiny. This important lesson influenced the French Jewish community in the postwar years. They recognized that they shared a common destiny whatever their background. To Kriegel, this explains the generous welcome extended to the Jews from France's former colonies.

Life became progressively more difficult for the Kriegel family. In the spring of 1942 (after the decision at the Wannsee conference to proceed with the Final Solution) additional far-reaching administrative measures and restrictions against the Jews were passed. After her uncle's arrest, Kriegel's father decided not to sleep in their apartment and spent nights in the home of the family's household helper. Once he narrowly escaped arrest when the concierge told the police – who were checking identifications in the building – that there was no one home.

On July 16, 1942, almost 13,000 French Jews living in Paris were collected in the infamous Vel d'Hiv roundup. Young Annie Kriegel witnessed that roundup. She notes the help of a woman whose identity she never learned, one of many women – like the family helper who let Kriegel's father sleep at her place, and the concierge who told the police her father was not home – whose resistance contribution in rescuing Jews has not been recognized.

We had been warned about the roundup. And when I say 'we,' I mean most Jews. White Russians working at the Prefecture told their Jewish compatriots, who in turn alerted others. That day I was taking the oral examination for the *bac* [*baccalauréat*] at the Sorbonne. Mother appeared unexpectedly. She told me that rumors about a roundup, scheduled for that evening, were circulating in the neighborhood. She warned me not to return home. Instead, I was to try and find someone to take me in. Several people I approached could not take me in, for one reason or another. Someone suggested I go to a house that was said to be taking in Jews. So I went to an unpretentious house in our Marais district where a woman answered the door and led me into a large room with perhaps fifty or more people. There was a heavy silence, like that in a dentist's office. I never learned who this woman was; what her affiliation was; or why she took in all those Jews.

I found a spot in a corner and tried to sleep, although I was very frightened. Young girls then were not as emancipated as they are today. When I woke at dawn I looked out the window. Things appeared calm so I decided to return to our house. On the way there I saw French policemen carrying suitcases followed by entire families. I kept on and then suddenly heard screams; screams like those one hears in hospital delivery rooms. It was all the human pain of both life and death. In a garage they were separating men and women before loading them into the buses. I sat down on a bench and thought about what I should do. There, on that bench, I left my childhood.

Her father decided the family had to escape to the unoccupied zone. Two weeks later they crossed the demarcation line under extremely difficult conditions. It was her teacher at Grenoble, where they settled, who put her in touch with the organization she joined, a Communist youth group, because she saw the young girl's organizational talents. This was the Resistance branch for the young people in MOI (Main-d'Œuvre Immigrée); a French Communist Party organization for foreign workers, many of whom were Jewish.

Kriegel explained how, not yet sixteen, she was able to join this group. Generally speaking, the Gaullist movements accepted recruits young, but not *that* young, and their recruits were generally male. The only organization willing to accept adolescents for active Resistance work was the Young Communists, the JC-MOI. Moreover, she was Jewish, which made her involvement almost "commonplace," she holds (Interview, June 1983).

The accounts of both Jewish women like Yvette Bernard Farnoux, Annie Kriegel and Sabina Zlatin, and non-Jewish women like Madeleine Barot and Evelyne Sullerot, none of whom were involved in specifically Jewish resistance groups, help one better to understand and appreciate how courageous French women resisted the persecution of the Jews.

Note

1. Unless otherwise indicated, all translations are by the author.

References

Clandestins de Dieu, CIMADE 1939–45. Jeanne Merle d'Aubigné, Violette Mouchon, and Emile C. Fabre (eds) Paris: Le Signe Fayard, 1968.

Grynberg, Anne (1991) *Camps de la honte: Les internés juifs français, 1939–1944*. Paris: La Découverte.

Jacques, André (1989) *Madeleine Barot*. Paris: Editions du Cerf.

Judt, Tony (1990) "The War Between the French," *The London Times Supplement*, Sept. 28–Oct. 4.

Kriegel, Annie (1984) *Réflexions sur les questions juives*. Paris: Hachette.

Laborie, Pierre (1995) "La Résistance et le sort des Juifs 1940–1942," in Jean-Marie Guillon and Pierre Laborie (eds) *Mémoire et Histoire: la Résistance*. Toulouse: Privat.

Lazare, Lucien (1996) *Rescue as Resistance: How Jewish Organizations Fought the Holocaust in France*. Trans. Jeffrey M. Green. New York: Columbia University Press.

Marrus, Michael and Robert Paxton (1981) *Vichy France and the Jews*. New York: Basic Books. (The French edition, *Vichy et les juifs*, contains the texts of all the anti-Jewish legislation.)

Michel, Henri (1970) *La guerre de l'ombre*. Paris: Grasset.

Paxton, Robert (1972) *Vichy France: Old Guard and New Order 1940–44*. New York: Knopf.

Poznanski, Renée (1977) *Juifs en France pendant la Seconde Guerre Mondiale*. Paris: Hachette.

Pougatch, Isaac (1971) *Un Bâtisseur: Robert Gamzon*. Paris: FSJU .

Weitz, Margaret Collins (1995) *Sisters in the Resistance: How Women Fought to Free France, 1940–1945*. New York: John Wiley.

Zlatin, Sabina (1947) Unpublished testimony of February 4, from the Marie Granet archives given to the author.

—— (1992) *Mémoires de la "Dame d'Izieu"*. Paris: Gallimard.

Zuccotti, Suzanne (1993) *The Holocaust, the French and the Jews*. New York: Basic Books.

–11–

"A Great Moral Victory":
Spanish Protection of Jews on the
Eastern Front, 1941–1944
Wayne Bowen

From 1941 to 1943, over 40,000 Spaniards served on the Eastern Front in the *División Azul* (Blue Division), a unit of volunteers in the German *Wehrmacht*. While the Nazis saw the arrival of the Blue Division as a sign that their racist world-view was gaining converts, the soldiers of the Blue Division saw their own presence differently. Although incorporated into the *Wehrmacht* and sworn to obey Adolf Hitler, the soldiers of the Blue Division did not follow the mandates of Nazi racial policy. On the Eastern Front and in the hospitals of the unit, the soldiers and medical personnel of the *División Azul* befriended and protected Jews from the Holocaust and Russian civilians from the worst excesses of the Germans' racial war until the withdrawal of the Division in late 1943. Spaniards joined to take part in "a crusade of the European order against Asiatic barbarism" and a "popular mobilization to fight against Soviet Communism along with Germany." They saw themselves not as racial warriors defending the purity of Europe against the Jews, but as enemies of Communist ideology. When the Spanish press wrote of a "brotherhood of blood in the common fight for Western civilization," the "blood" to which they referred was that shed by Germans and Spaniards during the Spanish Civil War, not any Nazi-inspired notions of Aryan supremacy or Slavic racial inferiority. [1]

German and Spanish military documents demonstrate conflicts between Nazis and Spaniards over the conduct of the war, but it is in the oral history of Spanish veterans of the Blue Division that the full story develops. On the Eastern Front, Spanish soldiers fraternized with civilians of all ethnic and religious backgrounds, against strict *Wehrmacht* orders. They shared food, living quarters and even romance with the local population, much to the anger of the German High Command. In these memories of scorching summers and frozen winters in Russia, collaborative resistance to Hitler's war of annihilation emerges.

How was this possible, that a unit under German command could flout Nazi policies of extermination? First, the soldiers of the Blue Division were under the jurisdiction of Spanish, rather than German, martial law. Second, Spanish commanders were very proud and protective of their legal island, and insisted to their soldiers the importance of behaving according to international law. Third, they saw their presence on the Eastern Front as part of a crusade against Communism, rather than as a war against Jews and Slavs. Finally, Spaniards of the Blue Division increasingly identified with the native Russians in their zone of operations. Given their joint disdain for the brutality of both Stalinism and Nazism, the two communities, Spanish soldiers and Russian civilians, cooperated and collaborated for mutual protection and survival.

The *División Azul*, officially known as the *División Española de Voluntarios*, was a volunteer unit of Spaniards within the German army, created at the initiative of the Spanish government in the days following the German invasion of the Soviet Union on 22 June 1941.[2] Spanish volunteers enlisted in the Blue Division primarily to fight Communism, however, rather than as unadulterated supporters of Nazism or the Third Reich. Many soldiers of the Blue Division did feel gratitude to Germany for its assistance to the Nationalist forces during the Spanish Civil War, but far stronger was their visceral hatred for what the Soviet Union had visited upon them and their families during the recent conflict, when Stalin provided military and political support to the Second Republic through the Spanish Communist Party.[3] The 18,000 men of the Blue Division left Spain in mid-July 1941, passing through occupied France on their way to their initial phase of instruction in Germany.

After several weeks of training at the *Wehrmacht* military base in Grafenwöhr, Bavaria, the soldiers of the unit were sent east by rail as far as Suwatki, in occupied Poland. Because of a shortage of rail assets, from there the Spaniards had to march to their positions near Novgorod, in northern Russia. Along their route of march, which took them through German-ruled Poland and the Soviet Union, the Spanish soldiers had their first serious encounters, not only with Polish, Belorussian, Lithuanian and Russian civilians, but also with the horrors of Nazi racial policies.[4]

Despite the harshness of their daily marches, during which the *divisionarios* would trudge as many as 40 kilometers, the Spaniards found time and energy during evening's rest to make contact with local civilians. Almost immediately the Spanish troops warmed to the Poles in Suwatki and other towns, even attending Roman Catholic Masses in Polish churches.[5] More troubling for the Spaniards, however, was what awaited them in another Polish city: Grodno. This urban center, which had been home to over 25,000 Jews out of a total population of 60,000 before the war came to Poland, had been reduced to rubble during the Soviet retreat, with less than 10,000 residents remaining in the late summer of 1941. It was in Grodno that the soldiers of the Blue Division encountered Jews for the first time, as well as their first Jewish ghetto, and the murderous Nazi policies which made these restricted zones centers of poverty, famine, disease and death.[6]

In Grodno, the Spanish soldiers tried to treat Polish Jews as they had Polish Gentiles, but German policy made this difficult. The physical separation of the ghetto from the rest of the city, as well as the under-standable reluctance of Grodno's Jews to consort with soldiers of the German army, Spaniards or not, made social relations difficult between Spaniards and Poles. During the few days their unit remained encamped near Grodno, however, Spanish soldiers made every effort to make the acquaintance of young women, Jews among them. Even when warned away by the Jews themselves, who knew the Nazi rules on fraternization, the Spaniards insisted on disregarding the yellow stars of David worn by that sector of the population. Some Spanish soldiers even got into shouting matches with Germans near the Jewish ghetto over the proper treatment of Jews, not wanting to abide the hard labor and starvation regimens imposed on the Jews, even the very young and old, by the Nazi occupation.[7]

> We were [in Grodno] two or three days. It had a very friendly population . . .
> We could make ourselves understood in French. [Grodno had] a pretty large
> Jewish community. There was an incident between a German and a Jewish
> man. A German attacked and insulted an old Jew in German, so we yelled
> back insults [at the German] in Spanish. Yes, he was a Jew, but he was just an
> old man.[8]

Despite rules which prohibited Spanish and German soldiers from speaking to Jews, some Spaniards spent their evenings in private homes, dancing with the daughters of Jewish families and bringing joy to the grim surroundings while defying Nazi racial policies at the same time. For the Spanish soldiers, the girls they danced with were young women who happened to be Jewish. The greatest consideration for the Spaniards was whether or not the girls were pretty and friendly, not what religion their families practiced.[9] During subsequent contact with these communities in Eastern Europe, Spanish troops did what they could to help, by giving food, clothing, and cigarettes to perpetually underfed and poorly dressed Jewish slave laborers:[10] "and to us, the only friendly visitors to the ghetto, came the grateful sympathy of the Jews. 'I am a Jew. It is forbidden to speak to me,' the Jewish girls would say to us, trying to warn us; but very soon we infringed, with great cordiality, on the severe rules of the occupying Army."[11] What did these Spanish troops know of the Nazi plans, then well advanced, to exterminate every Jew of Europe? According to one soldier, the Spaniards only saw some of the early phases of these terrible policies.

> Things were very bad. The Germans had [the Jews] under restrictions from Hendaye [the Hispano-French border] to northern Europe, prohibiting them from leaving their zones. They had a five-pointed star that they had to put on their backs, which said "*Jude.*" They could not enter into any business except on certain days. They had them very oppressed. It was shameful. When we arrived in Witebsk, in our motorized convoy, we found half of the town closed off completely. Nobody could leave or enter. And in that place the Jews died.[12]

After over six weeks and over 1,400 kilometers of marching, in mid-October 1941 the Blue Division reached its battlefield positions around Grigorovo and Novgorod, Russia, near Lake Ilmen. Almost immediately, the Spanish soldiers established warm bonds with the local population. Unlike the Germans they replaced on the front lines, who had expelled Russian families from their homes, the Spanish troops lived amicably in the small villages and towns along the front. The soldiers of the division, unlike German troops, never considered themselves to be at war against the Russians, but only against Communism and Stalin's dictatorship. A fine distinction, perhaps, but one which was carried out in practice. Russian women often lived with Spanish troops, cooking, cleaning and providing companionship in exchange for protection from the Germans.[13] Under pressure from the *Wehrmacht*, the *Estado Mayor* (General Staff) of the Blue Division issued orders forbidding contacts with Russian civilians, Jews and Polish women. As one decree made clear, Jews on the Eastern Front deserved the worst.

> The fight against Bolshevism must proceed energetically and without any consideration for the Jews, who are its principal sustainers. Consequently, the High Command of the [German] Army has ordered the cessation of all collaboration of the same with the civilian Jewish population, which openly or covertly is the enemy of our cause, as well as all employment of Jews in auxiliary services for the army. The passes which accredit them as working for military purposes cannot be extended in any case by subordinate authorities.

The only exception is the employment of Jews in special columns of workers, but these must be directly under German control.[14]

This order makes clear several things. First, that Spanish troops were employing Jews in the Blue Division's zone of operations. Second, they were providing them with special passes (the *Ausweise*) to make this possible. Finally, the Germans were aware of this situation and wanted to prevent its continuation. Lieutenant-Colonel Luis Zanon, the Spanish officer who signed the order, was probably following through on a directive from German Field Marshal Wilhelm Keitel, chief of the High Command of the Armed Forces, who over a month earlier had issued an analogous command to the armed forces.[15] This and similar regulations were, however, cheerfully ignored by the Spanish troops, if the constant flow of similar instructions reveals anything.[16] Despite the language barrier, Spaniards and Russians established a *modus vivendi* of mutual support, using a mix of German and Russian words, along with energetic gestures and pantomime, to communicate with the civilian population.[17]

The Blue Division, while clearly a military asset to the thin German front, did not fit well into the Nazi vision of the East. Not only did these Latins fight as well as any German unit, the Spaniards refused to adopt the Nazi attitude and behavior toward Slavs. The soldiers of the Blue Division did not treat Polish and Russian Jews and Gentiles like subhuman animals, fit only for slave labor or death. Instead, they ate, lived, laughed, danced and shared shelter with them, crimes in the Third Reich, but standard behavior in Hitler's only Spanish division.[18] Perhaps many Spaniards suspected that they themselves had Jewish ancestors in their family trees, a likely prospect given the assimilation of Sephardic Jews in Spanish communities before 1492.[19]

Although the soldiers of the *División Azul* served in the *Wehrmacht*, the relations between the Spanish troops of the Blue Division and Russian civilians were unlike those between Nazi warriors and Soviet citizens. As the testimony of Spaniards, Germans and Russians indicates, the arrangements between *divisionarios* and the inhabitants of the territory they occupied were both intimate and illegal.[20] This proved to be a constant source of annoyance to the German Corps and Army commanders. From 1 to 10 June 1943, the commanders of the regiments and battalions of the *División Azul* wrote letters to the divisional commander, General Emilio Esteban-Infantes, insisting that none of their soldiers had relationships with the civilian female population or were cohabiting with Russian women.[21] These letters were obviously deceptive, written to deceive the *Wehrmacht*, as hundreds of Spanish soldiers had been adopted by Russian families, sharing living quarters, food, protection and more intimate arrangements with the civilian population.[22] As the General himself later remarked, there was between Russians and Spaniards "a current of sympathy . . . that surprised the Germans".[23]

Despite German disapproval and official, albeit unenforced, prohibitions from the divisional command, the Spanish soldiers continued their friendly relations with the civilians in their zone.[24] During the bitterly cold winters, Russian peasants and Spaniards shared dances, *teploe moloko* (warm milk), *isbas* (wood cottages) and jokes about the Germans. Against German army regulations, the Spaniards shared their food with Russians, traded excess uniforms and equipment for warmer clothing, and by their mere presence protected their villages from both Soviet and Nazi forces. Spanish military doctors even provided medical care to local civilians when the burden of military casualties decreased to a manageable level.[25] At times, Spanish soldiers had to be chastised by their officers for being too trusting and casual with the local population, even giving civilians rides in their military vehicles and leaving their military equipment, including weapons, documents and maps unguarded.[26] Soldiers of the Blue Division, despite serving in the German army, were governed by Spanish martial law and under those regulations, fraternization was not a crime. Spanish officers, from the commanding general down, made it clear to their soldiers that they would not tolerate any criminal behavior against civilians, and were prepared to punish those unwilling to comport themselves according to Spanish martial law.[27] At times, Spanish soldiers even came to blows with elements of the *Wehrmacht* units over German mistreatment of Russian civilians. The Spaniards could not understand that the Nazi war against the Soviet Union was a brutal racial war, not merely an ideological campaign against Soviet Communism.[28]

While they fought for the New Order on the front lines and in the divisional rear area, the Spaniards behaved unlike soldiers of the *Waffen-SS* and *Wehrmacht*. The command of the division insisted on obedience to established standards of international law. Even though the Blue Division was in the German Army, these orders were possible because, under the terms of Franco's dispatch of the unit, only Spanish martial law applied to its soldiers.[29] The troops received instruction on the proper treatment of prisoners, civilians and other matters. Reprisals, hostage-taking and exactions from civilians, common practice in the *Wehrmacht* and *Waffen-SS*, were forbidden except at the express order of the divisional commander or his superiors. While these regulations did not exactly mirror those of the Geneva and Hague conventions, on the Eastern Front they reflected that Spanish conduct toward civilians was more humane than that of either the German or Soviet forces.[30] Later additions to these rules of engagement permitted Spanish soldiers to evacuate and burn villages proved to be supporting Communist partisans, but only with the authorization of the German Army Corps commander. In a departure from previous rules, the new policy directed Spanish soldiers to shoot civilians straying from designated evacuation routes.[31] There is no evidence that Spanish soldiers ever exercised this option, although along the route to the front, and once deployed in their final positions, they did witness Nazi persecution of Jews in the occupied territories, including forced labor, ghettoization and hanging.[32] In Riga, where the division stored some of its supplies, Spanish soldiers occasionally came into conflict with Nazi policies, as one veteran noted.

> Once, when we came from the front lines, we went to Riga, the capital of Latvia, to pick up food supplies – huge crates of food. A Latvian appeared, incredibly strong, and offered to help. While he was carrying one of the crates, a German officer appeared and said: "This cannot be, because he is a Jew." And I said, "And why should I care if he is a Jew?" We almost came to blows with the German officer, but we were soldiers [and obeyed]. We picked up the crates ourselves and carried them. That was February of 1942.[33]

There was one black mark in the unit's relationship with Jews in Russia. A few issues of the divisional newspaper, the *Hoja de Campaña*, contained antisemitic articles by Mario Xosa, a soldier of the unit. These editorials denounced "The Wandering Jew," blamed the Jews for the French Revolution and strongly praised the 1492 expulsion of the Jews from Spain.[34] Xosa also denounced the Jews' alleged attempts to control the Americas, indicating that the resistance of the United States to Spanish involvement in Latin America was a thinly veiled disguise masking Jewish attempts to control the Americas. To Xosa, "America for the Yankees" really meant "America for the Jews."[35] The writings of this soldier were not representative of the personal and ideological inclinations of the Blue Division, the behavior of which illustrated its true character.

The hospitals of the Blue Division represented the best and worst of Spanish action on the Eastern Front. The hospitals in Berlin, Vilnius, Hof, Riga and Königsberg continued to support the Nazi war against the Soviet Union and to receive numerous visits by representatives of the Nazi Party and *Wehrmacht*, enjoying "the spirit of brotherhood that our two nations maintain in the fight for civilization."[36] This was not their only business, however. Spanish medical staff and patients also continued to employ and shelter educated Poles, Lithuanians, Russians and Jews from the Nazis. While the Germans did not shrink from using Eastern European civilians as unskilled laborers, Spanish hospitals incorporated Polish doctors, Lithuanian and Jewish nurses, and Russian prisoners of both sexes into their medical staffs, working together in conditions of "mutual respect," but in direct and blatant violation of Nazi racial policies.[37] The hospital in Riga boasted a full complement of Spanish medical staff and the most advanced equipment of German medicine. Local Latvian personnel, including nurses, tailors and groundskeepers, worked alongside their Iberian and German counterparts. Relations among the three ethnic groups ran smoothly, to the point that during the summer of 1942 a Spanish soccer team, made up of convalescing soldiers and medical staff, played against German and Latvian teams.

The vast majority of Jews in Riga, who before 1941 had numbered 35,000 out of 360,000 in the Latvian capital, were unable to share in these comradely games, however. Those who had survived the mass shootings and deportations of 1941 remained in Latvia as slave labor, their numbers successively whittled away by forced starvation, overwork and further shipments to death camps. The Latvian capital even received shipments of German Jews, whose numbers increased even more the horrible conditions in the Riga ghetto.[38] The Spanish staff was aware of these atrocities, but could do little. The knowledge of these crimes was a painful experience for the young Spanish nurses working in the hospital, who did what they could to protect the few Jewish nurses who worked in the hospital, disguised as Latvians by their Spanish supervisors, but these were far outnumbered by those falling victim to the Holocaust in Riga.[39] By the end of December 1941, over 25,000 Jews had been shot in and around Riga, most notoriously in the Rumbuli Forest massacres of November 30 and December 8. While these numbers would subsequently rise with the arrival of German Jews, by January 1942 only 2,500 Jews remained in the Riga ghetto.[40] While Spaniards assigned to the hospital in Riga did not realize the extent of these murders, they were generally aware that something nefarious was happening. Because of the long hours and many casualties passing through the hospital, the Spanish medical staff were extremely busy and focused on their own losses from the war. They could not help but see the conditions of the Jewish community in the same city. As one Spanish nurse remarked about the Nazi treatment of Jews in Riga,

> All of that caused me a great deal of pain. It really destroyed me. Riga was to us very much like San Sebastian [Spain]. It was hard to see the poor Jews there, with the yellow star on their backs. We didn't know about the killings

of Jews, although we had heard rumors, but we did ask why the Jews had to wear the yellow star. The Germans could never give us a good answer.[41]

At the campaign hospital of the Blue Division in Vilnius, Spaniards, Poles, Lithuanians and Jews worked together in relative harmony, out of the direct supervision of the German army. The Spanish hospital at Vilnius, which opened February 5, 1942, was the only one of the five main hospitals to be a freestanding institution, without important numbers of German staff members or an affiliation with a larger *Wehrmacht* military hospital. This independence allowed the Spanish staff to conduct itself away from Nazi oversight and racial policies.[42] While the Jewish hospital workers, mostly young women, were relegated in nearly all cases to subaltern positions, they understandably preferred to work for the Spaniards, who protected them from Nazi "special treatment." The Spanish administration did what it could to protect their Jewish assistants, as remembered by a wounded soldier who spent several months at the hospital in Vilnius.

> The male and female Jews who worked in our hospital in great numbers went through some difficult moments. I remember that because of the murder of three Germans, perpetrated in the outskirts of Vilnius, they made the Jewish population pay for the deaths many times over. It seems as if they [the hospital] received concrete orders to reduce to an absolute minimum these [Jewish] subalterns, indicating that those who were not indispensable should be sent to who knew where, where they would be concentrated together. All of the Jews of the Spanish Hospital were classified as indispensable and not a single one was evacuated, augmenting with this gesture the devotion and affection that they [the Jews] felt for us.[43]

The most important Jewish staffers were allowed to sleep in the basement of the hospital near the heating units, while the others went home every night to the ghetto, often escorted as far as possible by Spanish soldiers.[44] Whenever feasible, the Spanish medical staff tried to use the full talents of their Jewish workers, allowing them almost complete professional and personal liberty within the confines of the hospital. For example, the head of the Jewish staff and the director of the pharmacy at the hospital in Vilnius was a degreed Jewish pharmacist, who spoke German, Polish, Yiddish, Russian and Spanish.[45] The few Jews who worked in this hospital were exceptions, as almost the entire Jewish community of Vilnius had been murdered by the end of 1941. Out of a prewar Jewish population of over 35,000, the population of the Vilnius ghetto was down to 12,000 by the end of December 1941.[46]

As the Blue Division entered its second year of existence, however, international politics was moving forward. In the fall of 1943, under Allied pressure, Francisco Franco agreed to withdraw the Blue Division from the Eastern Front, a decision which would bring Spain more in line with a sincerely neutral diplomatic position. In October 1943, under the premise of needing a rest from the front lines, the unit withdrew from its trenches southeast of Leningrad and prepared to be repatriated back to Spain. Although welcomed by many soldiers of the Spanish division, this sudden departure was unexpected and grim news for those under the protection of the Spaniards: Russian civilians in the Spanish divisional zone, and Jewish workers in the unit's hospitals. When the Spaniards withdrew from Antropschina, Russia, the Orthodox High Priest of the region gave them a letter of thanks on behalf of the entire community, thanking them for their good behavior and humanitarian treatment of civilians, an unthinkable gesture had it been proffered to a unit of the *Waffen-SS*.[47]

A smaller unit of just over 2,000 soldiers, the *Legión Española de Voluntarios*, or Blue Legion, remained on the Eastern Front, but its life was short, only from December 1943 to March 1944, and without dramatic results. With the departure of the Blue Division, all unit hospitals closed, except for Riga, which received the remaining casualties from the others. The Legion, after a brief period of reorganization and training in November and December, returned to the front in January 1944. Less than two months later, it too received a repatriation order, much to the dismay of the local population in its area of operations. As a gesture of thanks for the unit's generosity and comportment, a group of Soviet prisoners working for the Spaniards even presented a letter of thanks and an Orthodox icon to the Legion's commander.[48] By the first week of May 1944, the final Spanish medical personnel of the Riga hospital crossed the Pyrénées, ending official Spanish military involvement in World War II. Henceforth, the former soldiers, nurses and doctors of the Blue Division would watch the war from the safety of Spain.[49]

As the final elements of the Blue Legion were being repatriated in early 1944, Spanish diplomats continued their struggle to rescue others from Nazi-occupied Europe. Throughout the summer and fall of 1944, Spain's diplomats used what little influence they had left in the Third Reich to rescue Jews, as they had been doing since the beginning of the conflict. With the strong efforts of the Spanish Foreign Ministry, Spain's ambassadors in Berlin, Bucharest, Budapest and other capitals managed to save thousands of Jews by the end of the war.[50] While the Spanish government could have acted more energetically in this regard, even

"England and the United States did not regard the rescue of Jews as an important issue of the war" until too late to accomplish much.[51]

What became of the Jews, Poles, Latvians, Lithuanians and Russians who had been protected by the soldiers and medical personnel of the Blue Division? Given the Nazis' murderous policies against Jews, as well as the Soviet Union's understandable, but nonetheless brutal approach toward those who had collaborated with the Axis, it is hard to be optimistic. Even though the unit had protected hundreds of Jews and Soviet civilians during its time on the Eastern Front, the withdrawal of the Blue Division was probably a death sentence for those who had served it or been helped by its soldiers. As far as the Jewish ghettos in Riga and Vilnius, their liquidations preceded the withdrawal of the Blue Division. Most of the Jews in the Vilna ghetto were executed in August and September 1943, while the final 4,000 Jews in the Riga ghetto were shot or evacuated to Auschwitz or other death camps.[52]

This evidence demonstrates that, even in the hellish conditions of the Eastern Front, where barbarism was commonplace and compassion the exception, not all succumbed to the imperatives of brutality. Nazi racism was offensive to the Spanish Catholics of the Blue Division, who believed that conversion was the solution to "the Jewish question," which never became part of Falangist ideology. In their conduct on the Eastern Front, Spaniards rejected antisemitism by word and deed. The soldiers of the *División Azul*, whether Falangists, monarchists or apolitical, shared food, shelter and humor with groups the Nazi considered *Untermenschen* (subhumans).

In the end, the Spaniards on the Eastern Front did not treat Jews or Slavs with any special regard or special disfavor. Spanish medical personnel protected Lithuanian Catholics and Lithuanian Jews with equal compassion, while the soldiers of the Blue Division accorded humane treatment to Soviet prisoners of war, Russian civilians and Lithuanian Jews alike. Given the "special treatment" offered by the Germans, however, Spanish behavior was more than enough to save lives and enhance the image of the few Iberians on the Eastern Front. As one Spanish soldier remarked, "For me, a Jew is a human being, just of a different religion."[53]

Unfortunately, while Spaniards did defy Nazi racial policies in Russia, winning "a great moral victory, [saving] the lives of many women, children, young people and the elderly, who were condemned to die from inattention, totally forgotten and abandoned to their fates" in the process, the results of this were as short-lived as the Spanish presence in the German army.[54] For all of its merits, the Blue Division was only one unit among hundreds on the Eastern Front. Even if the division had not been withdrawn in 1943, and the Legion in 1944, the short respites it won for a handful of Jews could not endure. The Nazi death machine rolled on, killing Jews almost until the final shots were fired by the last defenders of Hitler's empire in 1945.[55] Only the defeat of the German armed forces by the Allies finally ended the horrors of the Holocaust, far too late to save the 6 million Jews who perished in Nazi death camps, ghettos and killing fields.

Notes

1. *Arriba*, 3 July, 7 December 1941; 1 and 25 January 1942.
2. *Servicio Histórico Militar*, Ávila, *Armario* 29, *Legajo* 44,*Carpet*a 44, *Pagina* 73 (hereafter SHM 29/44/7/73).
3. Interview with Leopoldo Esposito Chozas, Madrid, July 14, 1997.
4. The division was called "Blue" for the shirts of the thousands of the Falangist university students and party members who joined the unit in a wave of anticommunist enthusiasm in June and July 1941.
5. Interviews with Juan Chicharro y Lamamié de Clairac, Madrid, July 10, 1997, and Leopoldo Esposito Chozas, Madrid, July 14, 1997.
6. The definitive work on the Blue Division is Kleinfeld and Tambs (1979).
7. Castelo Villaoz (1984:56).
8. Gómez Tello (1945:43–44)
9. Interview with Miguel Salvador Gironés, Alicante, March 24, 1994. Martínez Esparza (1943:145–148).
10. Interwiew with Miguel Salvador Gironés, Alicante, March 24, 1994.
11. Interview with Juan Chicharro y Lamamié de Clairac, Madrid, July 10, 1997. Eugenio Blanco 1954:57. Sala Iñigo 1988: 95, 101.
12. *Blau División*, January 1966, excerpt from the diary of Miguel Lorenzo de Nema, March 21, 1943.
13. Eugenio Blanco (1954:57).
14. Interview with Juan Chicharro y Lamamié de Clairac, Madrid, July 10, 1997.
15. *Blau División*, April 1981 and November, 1993.
16. SHM, 28/28/5 General Instruction 2010, October 28, 1941, Lt.Col. Luis Zanon, *Estado Mayor*, DEV, "Los judiós de las zonas ocupadas."
17. Reitlinger (1961:215–216).

18. SHM, 28/7/15. Memo, September 2, 1942, German Commander, Hof, to Spanish Military Delegation; SHM, 28/5/4/74 and 141. Order, OKW (High Command of the German Armed Forces), undated, prohibiting Spaniards from giving or selling Wehrmacht uniforms to Russian civilians or prisoners-of-war. SHM, 28/28/18/3. General Instruction 2016, 4 May 1942, Lt. Col. Luis Zanon, *Estado Mayor*, forbade all fraternization, especially with Russian women. It further prohibited dancing, conversations about anything related to military subjects, photos from being taken with or by civilians and visiting civilians at home, SHM, 27/29/1/10 Order, 10 July 1942, *Jefe del Estado Mayor*, SHM 28/29/10/27. 30 December 1942 *Jefe del Estado Mayor*, ban on all business dealings with civilians; SHM, 28/29/11/7. Order, February 1, 1943, Jefe del Estado Mayor, restating ban on relations with Russian women. On the violations of these rules, see Sala Iñigo Aquella Russia, 90, 114, 151, 104; Díaz de Villegas 1967: 80–81 Castelo Villaoz (1984:61, 63) .
19. *Blau División*, April 1981.
20. After searches of Spanish and German military records, hours of interviews with veterans and extensive reading on the Blue division and Blue Squadron, this author has found no evidence of war crimes by the soldiers or pilots of these Spanish units.
21. SHM 28/30/12/3–9.
22. The general admitted these relationships in his own book on the Blue Division (1956:140). A few Spaniards even married Russian women, although these unions did not survive the withdrawal of the Blue Division. Von Studnitz (1964:100).
23. Esteban-Infantes (1956:139).
24. SHM, 28/29/11/17. "Secret" Order, February 1, 1932, from the Divisional Chief of Staff to subordinate unit commanders, banning relations between their soldiers and Russian women.
25. Manuel Salvador Gronés, "Recuerdos de Rusia," *Blau División,* February 1957 and interviews with Felipe Fernández Gil, January 30, 1994, Cáceres, Spain, Miguel Salvador Gironés, Alicante, March 24, 1994, and Félix Barahona Sáinz, Madrid, July 11, 1997.
26. SHM 28/45/8/4. General Instruction 4016, April 6, 1942, Lt. Col. Luis Zanon, *Estado Mayor*, DEV .
27. *Fundación División Azul.* Divisional Order September 3, 1941, by Gen.Agustín Muñoz Grandes, prohibiting attacks against civilians or their property, looting and other crimes against civilians, with a maximum penalty of death. Diáz de Villegas (1967:159–160), and photographs between pages 80–81. Interviews with Juan Chicharro

y Lamamié de Clairac, Madrid, July 10, 1997, and Leopoldo Esposito Chozas, Madrid, July 14, 1997.

28. Interview with Juan Chicharro y Lamamié de Clairac, Madrid, July 10, 1997. Even in Berlin, Spaniards tried to intervene on behalf of Jews. In one case, a Spanish officer agreed to marry a German Jewish girl in a failed attempt to extend Spanish protection to her. Hilberg 1992:156–158).

29. Díaz de Villegas (1967:159–160). Gen. Muñoz Grandes even refused to let Spaniards in German hospitals be subject to German military law. SHM 28/5/8/5. Telegram November 12, 1942, from the German High Command (OKH) to Muñoz Grandes. Scribbled in the margin is the note: "El General no la autoriza" (The General does not authorize this).

30. SHM 28/4/5. Order, August 4, 1941. *Estado Mayor, DEV*, General Instruction 3005. "Explicación de Normas jurídicas internas y de derecho international."

31. SHM, 28/34/11/9–10. General Instruction 3031, March 27, 1942, by Lt. Col. Luis Zanon, Jefe del Estado Mayor, 2nd section, *DEV*. "Lucha contra los partisanos."

32. Gómez Tello (1945:43-44). Sala Iñigo (1988: 954, 101–102, 115–116).

33. Interview with Juan Chicharro y Lamamié de Clairac, Madrid, July 10, 1997. According to Chicharro, after the war the Jewish man later became a Latvian boxing champion, but this author has been unable to verify this.

34. Hoja de Campagña, April 21, 1943. "El Judío Errante,' by Mario Xosa.

35. Hoja de Campagña, May 16, 1943. Other examples of antisemitic writing or illustration is the Hoja de Campagña. 3, 17 and 31 October, 1943 and 21 November 1943. It should be noted that the newspaper was published with the collaboration of a Wehrmacht *Propaganda Kompanie (PK)*

36. 29/46/18/44-42. Report, 8 January 11932, by Inspector of Hospitals, División Española de Voluntarios.

37. SHM, 29/46/19/2-36. Annual report, 31 December 1942, by Hospital Director in Vilnius, Medical Captain Sanchez Mesa. Interview with Félix Barahona Sáinz, Madrid, July 11, 1997.

38. Bauer (1982:200). Friedlander (1995:289),. Browning 1992:44)

39. Interview with María de Castro Aguirre, Madrid, July 10, 1997; Cogollos Vicens (1985:136–148).

40. Reitlinger (1961:217–218); Noakes and Pridham (1990:1093–1094)

41. Interview with María de Castro Aguirre, July 10, 1997.
42. Manuel Salvador Gironés, "Cosas de por allá," *Blau División*, April 1962, April 1965, May 1969 and November 1972. Alvarez Esteban (1947:377). SHM, 29/46/19/2-36. Annual report, December 31, 1942 by Hospital Director in Vilnius, Medical Captain Sanchez Mesa.
43. *Blau División*, April 1962.
44. Manuel Salvador Gironés, "Cosas de por allá," *Blau División,* April 1962, May 1965, April 1967, February and March 1973 and January, February and July 1974.
45. Manuel Salvador Gironés, "Cosas de por allá," *Blau División,* December 1967.
46. Reitlinger (1961:216).
47. Esteban-Infantes (1956:141).
48. Letter of Gratitude, March 4, 1944, from Russian prisoners to Colonel Antonio García Navarro. Accompanying the letter was an Orthodox wood icon of the Virgin and Child. The original letter, engraved in wood, and the icon are in the museum of the *Fundación División Azul*, Madrid.
49. In late April 1944, Russian civilians begged Félix Barahona Sáinz, the last Spanish military doctor stationed in Riga, not to leave their city. Interview with Félix Barahona Sáinz, Madrid, July 11, 1997.
50. On this effort, see Archivo de Ministro de Asuntos Exteriores, Madrid, Archivo Renovador, Leggio RD1372, Expediente 2 and Legajo R23093, Expediente 10,. Various documents, 1943–44. During the war, Spanish diplomats managed to save 40,000–50,000 Jews, mostly of Sephardic origin. According to most scholars, no Sephardic refugees were turned away at the Spanish border for being Jewish. Ysart 1973; Ayni 1982, Ospina 1987, and Lipschitz 1984.
51. Avni (1982:12 and 199).
52. Reitlinger (1961:289–291).
53. Interview with Juan Chicharro y Lamamié de Clairac, Madrid, July 10, 1997.
54. Pérez Caballero (1986:12).
55. During the past decade, groups of veterans have returned to their Russian fields of combat and have been received extremely well by the civilian population, some of whom were children or young adults when the Blue Division occupied their region. Interview and video screening, May 7, 1994, with Ramón Pérez-Eizaguirre and Fernando Vadillo Valdeolmos, Guadalajara, Spain; interviews with Miguel Salvador Gironés, Alicante March 24, 1994, Juan Chicharro

y Lamamié de Clairac, Madrid, July 10, 1997, and Leopoldo Esposito
Chozas, Madrid, July 14, 1997.

References

Alvarez Esteban, José. (1947) *Agonia de Europa*. Madrid: Estades.
Avni, Haim (1982) *Spain, the Jews and Franco*. Trans. Emanuel Shimoni.
Philadelphia Jewish Publication Society of America.
Bauer, Yehuda (1982) *A History of the Holocaust*. New York: Franklin
Watts.
Browning, Christopher (1992) *Ordinary Men: Reserve Police Battalion
101 and the Final Solution in Poland*. New York: HarperCollins.
Castelo Villaoz, Pablo (1984) *Aguas frias del Wolchow*. Madrid: Ediciones
Dyrsa.
Cogollos Vicens, José (1985) *¿Por qué? y ¿Para qué?* Valencia, Spain:
Imprenta Nacher.
Díaz de Villegas, José (1967) *La División Azul en línea*. Barcelona:
Ediciones Acervo.
Esteban-Infantes, Emilio (1956) *La División Azul: Donde Asia empieza*.
Barcelona: Editorial AHR.
Eugenio Blanco, Juan (1954) *Rusia no es cuestion de un dia*. Madrid:
Publicaciones Españolas.
Friedlander, Henry (1995) *The Origins of Nazi Genocide: From Euthanasia
to the Final Solution*. Chapel Hill: University of North Carolina Press.
Gómez Tello, J.L. (1945) *Canción de invierno en el este: Crónicas de la
División Azul*. Barcelona: Luis de Caralt.
Hilberg, Raul (1992) *Perpetrators, Victims, Bystanders: The Jewish
Catastrophe, 1933–1945*. New York: HarperCollins.
Kleinfeld, Gerald and Lewis Tambs (1979) *Hitler's Spanish Legion:
The Blue Division in Russia*. Carbondale and Edwardsville, Illinois:
Southern Illinois University Press.
Lipschitz, Chaim U. (1984) *Franco, Spain, the Jews, and the Holocaust*.
New York: Ktav Publishing House.
Marquina, Antonio and Gloria Inés Ospinal (1987) *España y los judíos
en el siglo XX: La acción exterior*. Madrid: Espasa-Calpe.
Martínez Esparza, José (1943) *Con la Division Azul en Rusia*. Madrid:
Ediciones Ejército.
Mayer, Arno (1988) *Why Did the Heavens not Darken? The "Final
Solution" in History*. New York: Pantheon Books.
Noakes, Jeremy and Geoffrey Pridham (1992) *Nazism: A History in*

Documents and Eyewitness Accounts 1919–1945. vol. II. New York: Schocken Books.

Pérez Caballereo, Ramón (1986) *Vivencias y Recuerdos: Russia 1941–1943.* Madrid: Novograph.

Reitlinger, Gerald (1961) *The Final Solution: The Attempt to Exterminate the Jews of Europe 1939–1945.* New York: A. S. Barnes & Co.

Sala Iñigo, Juan. (1988) *Aquella Rusia.* Zaragoza: Mira.

Studnitz, Hans-George von (1964) *While Berlin Burns.* London: Weidenfield and Nicolson.

Ysari, Federico (1973) *España y los judíos en la Segunda Guerra Mundial.* Barcelona: DOPESA.

Archives

Servicio Histórico Militar, Ávila. Archivo de la Guerra de Liberación, División Española de Voluntarios.

Archivo de Ministro de Asuntos Exteriores, Madrid. Archivo Renovador.

Fundacion División Azul, Madrid.Archive and Museum.

Cybrary of the Holocaust.

Interviews

Félix Barahona Sáinz, Madrid, July 11, 1997.

María de Castro Aguirre, Madrid, July 10, 1997.

Juan Chicharro y Lamamié de Clairac, Madrid, July 10, 1997.

Leopoldo Esposito Chozas, Madrid, July 14, 1997.

Felipe Fernández Gil, Cáceres, Spain, January 30, 1994.

Ramón Pérez-Eizaguirre and Fernando Vadillo, Guadalajara, Spain, May 7, 1994.

Miguel Salvador Gironés, Alicante, Spain, March 24, 1994.

Valdeolmus, Ferdinando Vadillo, May 7, 1994

Periodicals

Arriba (Madrid)
Blau División (Alicante)
Hoja de Campaña (Riga-Reval)

–12–

Foundations of Resistance in German-Occupied Denmark
Myrna Goodman

Introduction

Analysts of the Holocaust have generally concentrated their research on
the historical and political circumstances, structural arrangements, and
ideologies that contributed to the victimization that typifies the experience
of the European Jews during World War II. But there were also instances
when individuals and groups actively opposed the implementation of the
measures designed to isolate a nation's Jewish population and deport them
to the ghettos and concentration and extermination camps. The most
common form of support for Jews was performed by isolated individuals,
constrained by an environment of rigid German control and under great
personal risk. As such, much of the research on rescuers focuses on the
behavior, motivations, and moral character of individuals. The underlying
motivation for much of that research is a desire to understand the processes
that lead to the development of moral character, altruism and prosocial
behavior in individuals.[1] An unintentional result has been the consolidation of actions on behalf of the European Jews without regard for the
networks of support for them (Fein 1990).

Threats of discrimination and/or the implementation of measures
against the Jews of Europe did provoke open resistance to the Nazis and
were often a stimulus to both covert and public collective action on their
behalf. In some instances, individuals were subsequently drawn into work
with organized resistance movements, in others, the action was the work
of already formed resistance groups. In February 1941, Dutch workers
launched a general strike to protest against the deportation of 425 Jews.
The National Organization for Assistance to Divers (LO) hid 24,000 Jews,
16,000 of whom were never captured by the Germans (Baron 1992:
312–313). Zuccotti (1993:232) has shown that Jews fleeing deportation

received assistance not only in the village of Le Chambon, but also in several villages in the Cévennes region as well .

The rescue of the Danish Jews is the most dramatic example of social defense of Jews during the war. The successful rescue was usually attributed to the relatively benign German administration (Marrus and Paxton 1989:193), but three additional factors are also deemed important: (1) the small number of Danish Jews;[2] (2) the geographical proximity of neutral Sweden;[3] and (3) the relatively late date.[4] Certainly the Nazis' initial lack of resolve in the matter of the Danish Jews, the character of the German occupation, and the closeness of a country which offered refuge to them were necessary conditions in their survival. Those factors do not, however, sufficiently explain why the vast majority of Danes so closely identified the preservation of the Danish way of life with the safety and protection of the Jews in Denmark (Arendt 1965:171; Davidowicz 1975:358; Jergstrup 1986:262; Yahil 1969; 1989:190) or how Danes were able to mobilize the resources necessary to carry out their successful evacuation to Sweden.

We are drawn to the Danish case because of its unique outcome, but it is the process that is of interest to us. The rescue of the Danish Jews is informative because it is a definitive example of collective action "inspired by values that go beyond self-interest . . . [and are] . . . socially rooted" (Walton 1992:319).

The spontaneous character of the rescue operation left little room for advanced planning and the social actors involved were required to call upon underlying and taken-for-granted social repertoires to inform and facilitate their rescue work. Because of the danger involved and the tasks that needed to be performed, rescue workers were dependent upon the trust of individuals. The rescue could not have been accomplished without the consent of a majority of the people in the areas where the Jews lived, were hidden and placed on fishing boats. There are two other factors which contributed to the successful operation. Prior to the action against the Jews, a significant proportion of the population began to link the autonomy of the country with the preservation of its fundamental ideals. The underground press, which was run by a wide spectrum of political and social groups, continually framed Danish patriotism in the context of the life of the Danish nation. Because virtually every Dane knew that a fundamental difference between the Danes and the Germans was embodied in their different view of the right of Jews to be treated like all other Danes, any threat to the Jews became threat to the entire nation. This pervasive climate of support assured rescue workers would be able to mobilize ideological support for their project and also guaranteed that they would have the monetary and material resources necessary to carry out their mission.

Often accounts of the rescue of the Danish Jews attribute its success to the entire Danish nation.[5] Thousands of people contributed to the successful operation, but Kirchhoff (1995:474) points out that most of the Jews in Denmark lived in Copenhagen and that there were only an estimated 600–700 transports to Sweden. The rescue operation, therefore, could not have directly involved "the whole nation."[6] But time after time, that which was needed was given. So many ordinary citizens lent help, whether it was money, temporary shelter for a night or two, or the name of another person who might offer assistance. Even those who turned away and didn't help, but did not report suspicious activity to the authorities, were complicit in the operation.

Social ties have a direct positive effect on participation in collective action (Oliver 1984). Strong social ties were firmly embedded in every aspect of Danish society and directly connected people who wanted to act with each other. For many Danes, the *razzia* against the Jews in Denmark provided a direct incentive to join the resistance movement.

The character and goals of the German occupation in each country must be taken into account in any analysis of collective action on behalf of the Jews. The more control the Germans exercised over day-to-day life, the more difficult it was to maintain customary social and political structures. But even in Poland, where German control was the most severe, social, political and economic disintegration were not complete (Gross 1979). In Denmark, where German control did not disrupt the structures of everyday social and personal life, the people's "troubles" were relatively minor. Left free to associate in public but bound by the government and the King to peaceful and correct demeanor, they spent three years preparing for active resistance to the Nazis.

In this chapter I examine the Danish rescue in light of two crucial factors in the successful mobilization of people and resources for the operation: the origins of the strong political and social solidarity in the general population and the ideological discourse that framed and shaped the context of support for the Jews in Denmark. I explore how, in the context of long-standing public and private solidarity with the ideals of Danish democracy and the changing political opportunities, a diverse and extensive network of average citizens, political activists, business and religious leaders, and members of the organized Danish resistance movement mobilized active, effective support for the Jews in Denmark.

Historical Overview

Following the German invasion of Denmark on April 9, 1940, the Danish government, realizing it was powerless in the face of a much stronger German army, surrendered without significant armed resistance. The Danes negotiated an agreement with the Germans which, despite a sizable German military presence, allowed the government to remain autonomous. The King was allowed to remain as the head of state and the Danish police and armed forces remained intact. The government publicly announced that although they had signed a pact with the Germans, "they had not bound themselves to follow the lines of German ideology" (Gudme 1942:165). Protection of the Danish Jews was a high priority from the first days of the occupation and the German authorities were well aware that actions against the Jews could disrupt the initial agreements they had negotiated. The German Plenipotentiary in Denmark sent the following cable to his superiors six days after the occupation:

> The Danish authorities are apprehensive as to whether we will, for all that, show too much interest in the internal situation and take steps against Jewish, refugees, and extreme leftist groups, and create a special police organ to this end. If we do anything more in this respect than is strictly necessary, this will cause paralysis of, or serious disturbances in, political and economic life. The importance of the problem should not therefore be underestimated. (Yahil 1969:42)

Attitudes toward the Jews were characterized by the absence of any meaningful Danish antisemitism; government officials and the general public resisted every German attempt to isolate the Danish Jews. Danish politicians asserted that the rights of the Jews in Denmark were inviolate. Pressured by officials in Berlin to initiate actions against the Jews, German officials warned that: "any tampering with Danish Jews' civil rights would result in a violent reaction on the part of the Danes that could do much harm to the otherwise peaceful relations between the two countries" (Flender 1963:28).

The policy of support for the Jews living on Danish soil began well before World War II. Despite a lack of antisemitic sentiment in Denmark, Danish authorities took proactive steps to prevent the spread of Nazi racial doctrines. Until 1939, these measures were mainly informational, but following the excesses of Kristallnacht in Germany, the Danes amended their Criminal Law of 1939 to include the following provision: "[A]nyone who by virtue of false rumors or slander incited hatred against any section of the Danish population by reason of its religion, origin, or citizenship would be subject to fine or imprisonment" (Yahil 1969:497).

The Danish Nazi Party (DNDSAP) was small and remained largely uninfluential. Its membership was concentrated in South Schleswig amongst a population that included 50,000 minority Germans. The DNDSAP received 5 percent of the vote in the national elections of 1939. Monthly enrollment of new members peaked in 1940 and declined progressively after the German occupation. The parliamentary elections in March of 1943 produced only three seats for the party (Hohne 1970:497) and reflected only 2.1 percent of the total vote (Kirchhoff 1995:466).

Like most of Scandinavia, Denmark was generally immune to the development of strong Fascist movements during the 1920s and 1930s. "With a heritage of religious and cultural homogeneity going . . . back to the Reformation, . . . its minorities . . . [were] . . . fairly integrated" (Lindstrom 1985:59). While nationalism was widespread in Denmark and became even stronger under the German occupation, it was the wrong type to be of much use in the formation of fascist movements. Danish nationalism was a composite of Pietism, puritanism, and populism, sentiments that were antithetical to Fascism. Additionally, the cleavages between urban and rural interests and the splits between left and right which marked the growth of Fascism in other parts of Europe never materialized in Denmark (Lindstrom 1985:178–186).

There were also those who collaborated with the Germans throughout the occupation. Their numbers were far less proportionately than in other occupied nations, but they still posed a potential hazard to the rescuers. Speaking about a neighbor whose small factory was producing parts for the Germans, Mimi Milstein explains how intimidation was used to control collaborators:

> We saw 4 bomb-blowups, just around the corner from where we lived. This was done to a collaborator . . . , once to his dwelling (left of our place) and trice [sic] to his little radio component factory (right of our place). Each time was carefully timed so nobody got hurt, maximum damage was caused, and production was halted until lots of time and money was invested in rebuilding. (Milstein 1995)

Although social sanctions against collaborators were not complete, they were effective: fewer than 2 percent of the fleeing Jews were apprehended by the Germans (Fein 1979:150–151).

For three years Danish politicians engaged in a pragmatic policy of accommodation and negotiation to prevent open confrontation with the

Germans on issues of contention between them. The entire period from the invasion until the declaration of martial law in August 1943 was marked by governmental policies of compromise, purposeful side-stepping, evasion, delaying action and passive resistance on the part of the general public (Jones 1970:168–169). The underlying motivation behind this course of action was to keep as "much control in Danish hands as possible, even if that meant the Danish Parliament had to make repressive and probably unconstitutional laws and Danish Courts had to impose harsh sentences on resisters" (Fitzmaurice 1981:19).[7]

German policy toward the Danes was moderated in an effort to maintain peaceful relations with them. Denmark was making substantial contributions to the German war economy. Danish farmers were supplying enormous amounts of food to the Germans and Danish factories produced diesel engines, airplane parts and armored vehicles vital to the German war effort (Flender 1963:29).

The Danish Jews, mindful of their precarious position, adopted a policy of circumspect behavior: restrained and cautious. Nonetheless, they were lulled into relative normalcy by the benign conditions of the German occupation and the unconditional support they received from the Danish government.[8] Danish political independence proved to be illusory, however. Many of the policies the government adopted to placate the Germans and moderate their control abridged the Danes' civil rights. The general population became increasingly disenchanted and impatient with government officials as they made more and more concessions to the Germans on economic matters, freedom of speech and foreign policy.

Increased German encroachment on Danish sovereignty and systematic exploitation of the Danish economy resulted in a concomitant increase in popular unrest. The increasing food shortages, optimism over the changing fortunes of war, and growing revulsion over reports of Nazi atrocities in Eastern Europe reported in the underground press (Flender 1963: 204) also contributed to a shift in public opinion; an increasing number of people were willing to challenge German authority openly.

The incidence of sabotage increased dramatically during 1943 and widespread conflict erupted during August. The August crisis was provoked when, among other factors, general strikes erupted in several major cities and dock workers in Copenhagen defiantly went out on strike. The German administration responded by suspending the Danish constitution, declaring martial law and placing the King under house arrest.

Escalating German control also included the initiation of the deportation process. Enraged by Danish insubordination, Hitler ordered the deportation of the Danish Jewish community (Yahil 1990:575).[9] German officials scheduled actions against the Jews for the night of October 1, 1943 (Hilberg 1967:341), but Danish politicians who had contacts in the German Foreign Office were warned in September. Word spread to Copenhagen and Zealand, where most Jews lived. The atmosphere was full of "rumors of the imposition of 'Norwegian' and 'Polish' conditions, terror and persecution of the Jews" (Kirchhoff 1995:467). The warnings were such that Jews with political connections went into hiding during mid-September.

On the morning after the German action, it was apparent that the operation had been a failure. Only 481 Jews were captured (Kirchhoff 1995:468)[10] and the remainder of the Jews in Denmark were in hiding. During October 1943, an extensive network of individuals and organizations emerged spontaneously (Jergstrup 1986:266) and an estimated 7,056 Jews (Haestrup 1983:196) were transported to neutral Sweden in Danish fishing ships.

Not all the Jews in Denmark were able to reach safety in Sweden. "There were those who did not receive any warning, those who ignored the warning, those who physically or practically were unable to reach safety, and those who were caught during their flight" (Haestrup 1983: 196). The original German plan called for deporting the Danish Jews to Auschwitz, but because of persistent inquiries by Danish officials about them, the Nazis deported them to Theresienstadt concentration camp instead. Representatives of the Danish Red Cross,[11] the Women's League for Peace and Freedom and government officials coordinated relief efforts for the deportees. Their persistent negotiations resulted in shipments of clothing, food and medicines to them (Haestrup 1983: 227–235), "something that was quite unheard of in the history of the Holocaust" (Kirchhoff 1995:474). The majority of the deportees survived; they were among the first internees repatriated in the last month of the war.

The care and concern evidenced for the Danish internees in Theresienstadt is an accurate reflection of the level of support for Jews in Denmark and is fully in keeping with the relatively favorable circumstances that mark Jewish settlement in Denmark, which dates from the early seventeenth century. The Danish Jewish experience reflects a consistent pattern of relative tolerance over the course of 300 years.

The Jewish Danes [12]

In 1622, in order to promote commerce in his kingdom, King Christian IV invited a group of Dutch Jewish merchants to settle in Denmark. The small community lived in a benign atmosphere, but their legal status remained marginal until they were granted citizenship in 1814 (P. Friedman 1978:419). With the adoption of the Danish constitution of 1849, Jews were granted complete civil equality. While the granting of full civil equality had the manifest function of eliminating any remaining discriminatory practices and granted Danish Jews the same rights as all other Danish citizens, its latent function was the "Danefication" of the Jewish community. By the end of the nineteenth century the distinctions between Jews and Danes had largely disappeared (Jergstrup 1986:262).

At the time of the German invasion, there were just under 8,000 Jews in Denmark and of those, 1,500 were half-Jews. The total also included a number of Jews who settled in Denmark early in the twentieth century after fleeing Russian persecution (Bamberger 1983:114–117). The Eastern European immigrants were generally less assimilated and less affluent than members of the "old " Jewish community.[13] In addition, 1,400 young Jewish refugees were training on Danish farms in preparation for their eventual emigration to Palestine (Lampe 1957:67).

During the 1930s, Denmark had a mixed record of aiding refugees from Germany. Immigration was severely restricted, even following the excesses of Kristallnacht in 1938, but Danish women's organizations were successful in increasing the number of German Jewish children allowed to attend summer camp in Denmark; several of them were trapped in Denmark following the occupation. Through the efforts of the Jewish community and with the assistance of government officials, the number of young Jewish agricultural trainees was increased just prior to the outbreak of the war (Haestrup 1983:78–115). In general, however, the Danish record in the matter of allowing the immigration of Jews fleeing German persecution is as dismal as that of most countries in Europe.[14]

The high rate of intermarriage, assimilation and social integration among the majority of Jewish Danes was a crucial factor in their eventual rescue. Unlike the Jews of Eastern Europe and those in many Western European nations, they had a widespread network of non-Jewish Danish friends and relatives; those linkages greatly facilitated their rescue (Flender 1963:207).

The Foundations of Resistance

Prior to the start of the war, the Danish government pursued its customary but increasingly unrealistic foreign policy of neutrality. While Danish relations with Germany were marked with caution, they were also influenced by a traditional antipathy to the Germans which had its origins in the loss of the provinces of Schleswig and Holstein to them in the war of 1864 (Gudme 1942:6). That antagonism was deeply rooted in the evolution of modern Danish society.

Three important institutions of Danish civil society also had a profound effect on Danish culture. The cultural practices and traditions embedded in the Danish Folk High School system, Danish Lutheran Church, and the economic cooperative movement contributed to the underlying ideological foundations of modern Denmark. The synergy produced by the connections between these three institutions produced a modern Denmark characterized by a pervasive respect for democracy and freedom, and the foundations they set in place played a crucial role in shaping the meanings Danes gave to the threat against the Jews.

The Folk High School System

The non-state-supported voluntary Folk High School system is a distinctly Danish social institution. Responsible for producing an unusually high level of adult education, the schools also played a vital role in institution-alizing citizen participation in the democratic process; folk high school students were influential actors in the development of the democratic values and norms that characterize the institutions of modern Danish society. The schools provided ideological support for the economic cooperative movement and had a powerful effect on Danish respect for the democratic process (Manniche 1939:11).

Founded in 1844, primarily for adult farmers in agricultural commun-ities, the schools profoundly influenced the development of modern Danish society. "Without them present-day Denmark would have been impossible. Every institution bears their imprint, as does the entire peasant population. They are woven into the life . . . [and] into the democracy of the country" (Howe 1936:125). Under their influence, Danish farmers adopted the politically liberal views that characterized their efforts to gain equality with other groups during the years that shaped the modern Danish nation.

The schools were a response to changes in the social and economic structures of Danish society during the late eighteenth and early nineteenth centuries. Their philosophy of education was influenced by the spirit of the Enlightenment and progressive reformers who believed expanded education would improve the material and spiritual lives of farmers and peasants and bring Denmark into the modern world.

The ideology of the Folk High School movement has its origins in the philosophy of the nineteenth-century cultural historian, theologian, and poet N. F. S. Grundtvig. His concept of education and reverence for

freedom pervades all modern Danish institutions and his influence in
shaping modern Denmark cannot be underestimated: "His emphasis on
folk high schools that would combine practical and theoretical knowledge
with an ethical sense of personal responsibility and concern for the
fate of others provided an institutional basis for the modernization of
Denmark" (Wolfe 1989:177–178).

Grundtvig was a Lutheran theologian with sectarian leanings. He
wanted to establish an educational system that would give the Danish
peasant the ability and the opportunity to express himself (Jones 1970:68),
inculcating *folkelighed* or "spirit of the people" in the Danes. He believed
the folk high schools should provide a general education for its own sake,
divorced from the rigid examination-ridden grammar schools. He wished
to encourage Danish patriotic sentiments combined with a liberal Christian
outlook (Jones 1970:69). His primary interest was to encourage individual
freedom in ordinary people so that they could speak comfortably in the
nascent political assemblies of modernizing Denmark and do so "on an
equal footing with educated people" (Thanning 1972:86).

Grundtvig formulated much of his philosophy during the accelerated
Danish–German political discord over which nation should have rightful
possession of Schleswig and Holstein. Denmark's eventual loss of
Schleswig led to a national movement to consolidate and redefine the
essence of a humbled Danish nation. A national debate began at that time
to define the qualities and characteristics that were uniquely Danish.

The first schools were founded by Grundtvig's followers. Many
"graduates" became members of the national parliament, the *Folketing,*
became associated with the Grundtvigian leftist movement, and eventually
joined the Social Democratic labor party. They also influenced the
development of the economic cooperative movement. Although students
at the folk high schools were primarily farmers and their experience was
different from that of the workers in towns, those differences were largely
occupational. The cleavages between urban and rural interests and
the splits between left and right which marked the growth of Fascism
in other parts of Europe never materialized in Denmark (Lindstrom
1985:178–186).

Underlying culture as well as geopolitical differences contributed to
the differences between Denmark and Germany. While Germany had
adopted Roman Law, with its notion that the people exist for the sake of
the state, Grundtvig was a proponent of the Nordic tradition that freedom
is a "matter of relationships between different people" (Thanning
1972:92), not solely a relationship between the state and the individual.
Grundtvig's discourse is inherently libertarian (Østergård 1992:22).

A primary goal of Grundtvig's philosophy was to synthesize the concepts of Danish patriotism, Nordic culture and liberal general education to produce a modern Danish peasantry/citizenry. The folk high school movement influenced the definition of Danish nationalism and political culture and profoundly affected the strong social solidarity that characterized twentieth-century Denmark. The liberalism of the Danish folk high schoolers was an essential influence in shaping the political liberalism of the entire populace.

The Danish Lutheran Church

The Danish Lutheran Church viewed Jews and Christians as members of a common religious family, "people related by sacred history" (Fein 1979:115). The Danish Church responded quickly, directly and publicly to threats against the Jews both before the war and during the occupation. The Bishops of Copenhagen and Zealand denounced the persecution of the Jews in Germany after Kristallnacht in 1938 and instructed their pastors to pray for the Jews. They also called for prayers to protect the Danes from the "poisonous pestilence of anti-Semitism, hatred of the Jews and persecution of the Jews" (Fein 1979:115).

The position of the Danish Lutheran Church is striking when contrasted with the lack of moral authority exhibited by the German Lutheran Church and its failure to speak out against Nazi antisemitic policies. The differences in responses to persecution of the Jews can be found in the historical and ideological foundations of Lutheranism. From its beginnings, the Lutheran Church was dependent on the patronage of the territorial princes of northern Europe:

> For Luther the political authorities are divinely instituted; to rebel against them is to act contrary to the will of God. Government must be obeyed even when it is unjust or capricious . . . The wicked prince, no less than the good one, exercises a God-given power, and it is God, not man who will sit in judgment of the prince (MacDonald 1986:52).

A key difference in the response of the Danish Lutheran clergy and the German Lutheran Church lies in who constituted the legitimate authority in each state. Hitler carefully maneuvered the Lutheran Church into accepting the legitimacy of his leadership. In Denmark, however, the King and the government, whose support of the Jews in Denmark was resolute, represented the properly constituted authorities. In resisting the Germans, the Danish Church: "found its historical traditions and its ethical responsibilities . . . in complete harmony" (MacDonald 1986:52–53).

Myrna Goodman

The Danish Economic Cooperative System

The modern Danish state developed as its modern economy unfolded. In the "silent revolution" of the late eighteenth century, agrarian reforms in Denmark resulted in the break-up of the large estates and the redistribution of land to small farmers. The increase in agricultural production led to prosperity in the provincial towns and to a steady rise in the standard of living of both the peasants and the middle classes (Yahil 1969:7).

In the late nineteenth century, world wheat prices fell abruptly because American and Australian produce flooded the market (Friedman 1978: 545–586). To adapt to this change in commodity markets, Danish farmers increased their output of butter and cheese, which they exported to England. Cooperative production societies arose to distribute the risk associated with marketing perishable commodities. The cooperatives shared in the continued success of the Danish dairy industry (Manniche 1970:71) and economic cooperatives were highly developed at the time of the German occupation. In 1939 "[o]f the 205,000 farmers in Denmark over 190,000 . . . [were] . . . members of one or more co-operative associations" (Manniche 1939:11). The network of cooperatives was ubiquitous:

> The farmer buys his necessities at his cooperative retail store. He borrows money and places his savings in a cooperative bank; his fertilizers, fodder, seeds, etc., are obtained from cooperative buying and import associations; his cement comes from the cooperative cement factory, and his electricity from a cooperative power plant. He delivers his milk to the cooperative dairy, his pigs to the cooperative slaughterhouse, his eggs to the Danish Cooperative Egg Export Co., and his cattle to the Danish Cattle Export Cooperative. It is usual for a farmer to be a member of at least half a dozen cooperative societies covering the entire range of his economic needs. (Howe 1936:62)

Cooperatives also emerged in urban areas. Miller (1968:17) shows that the labor movement was closely associated with "urban consumer cooperatives, bakeries, fuel purchase associations and building enterprises." The cooperative movement spread to diverse urban industries: workers' cooperative housing associations (apartment construction), barber shops, life insurance, breweries, milk supply societies, and banks (Manniche 1970:160–163).

The cooperative societies brought important economic advantages to Denmark's farmers and workers, and also facilitated training in the art of self-government, encouraging participatory democracy. Former students at the folk high schools spread Grundtvig's philosophy to the cooperatives, which were living laboratories of democracy. "The formal organisation model was as a rule extensively democratic" (Thyssen 1983:393).

The group processes inherent in the cooperative movement and the ideology of the folk high school movement produced a high level of group solidarity in twentieth-century Denmark. The universal character of the cooperative movements also contributed to consistent patterns of cooperation throughout Danish society. Danes learned that cooperation was the best overall strategy for achieving their goals (Axelrod 1984:137).

The Evolution of Resistance

Many Danes considered the weak showing of armed resistance to the invading Germans a national disgrace, but most set aside their objections to the government's decision to surrender (Jones 1970:169–170) and presented a unified Danish position to the Germans. There was, however, a strong undercurrent of resentment in the population and while most people went about their everyday lives, many individuals, especially young people, took every opportunity to show contempt for the Germans (Holbeck 1996).

Until August 1943, resistance was primarily passive and marked by open contempt for the Germans. Danes challenged German authority in a manner just short of direct insubordination, a characteristic Danish humor pervading their acts:

> German soldiers did not manage to make any sort of contact with the Danish people. The Danes simply did not see them. They stared through them as if they were made of air; they walked right through the ranks of marching columns, and if a German asked the way he got no answer. That was the beginning of the "cold shoulder" which later developed into a fine-and-varied-art. (Gudme 1942:34)

Eric Holbeck (1996) reports that people who understood German would often stare at German soldiers who were trying to communicate with them, shrug their shoulders to indicate they did not understand and then move on. This behavior became known as the "cold shoulder." In displays of symbolic nationalism, Danes began the custom of wearing badges in their button holes engraved with: portraits of the King, the Danish flag, the British Flag, the colors of the RA F, or simply the letters DKS (*Den kolde skulder* or "the cold shoulder"), SDU (*Smid dem ud* or "chuck them out"), or KLUMP ("long live the King; out with the mob") (Gudme 1942:34).

During times of ambiguity and social uncertainty participation in public rituals can reinforce prior connections or establish new bonds between individuals and the "moral communities on which . . . [they] depend" (Wuthnow 1987:117–123). In the early days of the occupation, public displays of the "cold shoulder" and the use of outward markings allowed Danes openly to reaffirm their solidarity with each other. There were also public displays of solidarity at large gatherings; *Alsang* or song festivals were held and Danes gathered to sing patriotic and religious songs. The Germans present at an *Alsang* for students in January 1943 were not pleased when a request that the audience sing the two anthems dearest to the hearts of Danes resulted in the singing of the Danish national anthem followed, not by "Deutschland Über Alles," but by Hatikvah, the Zionist anthem (Levin 1968:393).

Danes also began actively reaffirming their loyalty to the principles of Danish nationalism. There was renewed interest in studying the history of modern Denmark and "Grundtvigism with its special mixture of patriotism and Christianity, took on new significance" (Jones 1970:171). As early as three days after the occupation, preexisting civic and cultural groups began to discuss the best methods for preserving and fortifying the Danish national identity at their regular meetings (Thomas 1975:15). Four major groups emerged that eventually played a significant role in shaping resistance to the Germans: (1) the Elders' Council, which consisted of people whose roots were in the Folk High Schools and the Grundtvig circles (Rørdam 1980:96); (2) the Danish Youth Association, a coalition of national youth groups, financed and guided by the Elders' Council (Thomas 1975:15); (3) the underground press; and (4) the loosely formed study circles.

The Elders' Council was composed of prominent members of the clergy, well-known teachers and theologians as well as members of the civil service. The Danish minister of education was a guiding member of the council. The Danish Youth Association eventually became the umbrella organization for grassroots groups of all ages. "The movement generally assumed the form of cultural activity for its own sake and without undertones, and aimed to strengthen the national consciousness by study of the country's nature, people, and history" (Yahil 1969: 37–38).

The regular press entered into a "voluntary" censorship agreement and the news they reported was less reliable than the news in the underground press. Eventually, the underground press had a higher circulation and was more influential than the German-controlled regular press. The growth and influence of the underground press was also due, in part, to the: "well-organized Danish social structure . . . [which] . . . made it easy to find people who could write, print, distribute . . . and finance the whole operation" (Thomas 1975:17). In addition to publishing newspapers, they mimeographed and distributed books, ranging from John Steinbeck's *The Moon is Down*, a fictional account of the Norwegian invasion, to Wendell Willkie's *One World*. Underground newspapers vigorously protested the actions of the German authorities and the government's policy of accommodation (Petrow 1973:176–177). By October 1943 the press had grown from two illegal newspapers created in 1940 with a circulation of 1,200 copies to 166 newspapers with a circulation of 2,600,000 (Thomas 1975:81–91). The underground press played a crucial role by keeping the issue of German actions against the Jews in the forefront (Thomas 1975:85–86).

The most influential groups in the developing resistance to the German occupation and the eventual rescue of the Jews were the study circles, which came to typify Danish collective activity. These were small, loosely-formed groups reminiscent of the "Grundtvig circles" that were crucial in shaping the participatory democracy characterizing the social movements of late nineteenth-century Denmark. Local groups were started, often by a single "activist." Co-workers gathered together and each group eventually branched out into an extensive network (Thyssen 1983: 391–392).

The primary purpose of the study circles was to encourage support for national and cultural unity and to stimulate passive resistance against the Nazi influence (Rørdam 1980:97). Study circles were founded and organized along occupational lines, and consisted of architects, engineers, doctors, teachers, clergymen, civil servants, and trade unionists. "The object was to activate as large a part of the Danish people as possible and not to create a clearly defined organization" (Yahil 1969:226). A group that eventually played a significant role in the rescue operation was composed of the physicians and staff of the largest hospital in Copenhagen. In 1942, after learning of German atrocities against the Jews in Europe,[15] sixty-four of them signed a petition pledging continued support of the government only so long as it did not allow persecution of the Danish Jews. This played a pivotal role during the first week in October. They assisted 2,000 Jews (Abrahamsen 1987:5) and had connections to several of the rescue groups that emerged. In addition to providing shelter to Jews and arranging for their transportation to Sweden, Bispebjerg hospital became the financial clearing house for the large sums of money that were used to pay for passage across the sound (Haestrup 1993).

No statement about Danish attitudes toward the Jews would be complete without explaining the important role King Christian X played in fostering and encouraging support for them. During the occupation, the pronouncements and opinions of the King were a political and moral barometer for Danish citizens. A profusion of "stories" circulated about the King of Denmark's support for the Jews during the occupation. Many of them are apocryphal. But at the time, people believed they were true. While stories emphasized the King's opposition to Nazism and sharply reiterated the traditional Danish antipathy toward Germany and things German, they also placed authority for support of the Jews with the King. According to one of these legends, the King, responding to the German Ambassador's use of the phrase "Jewish question," was supposed to have replied: "There is no Jewish question in this country. There is only my people" (Flender 1963:22) . The stories heavily reinforced Danish solidarity with the Jews in Denmark.[16]

Following the resignation of the Danish government, Werner Best, the German Plenipotentiary in Denmark, instituted plans for the deportation of the Danish Jews. His motives were twofold: to consolidate his power and to satisfy the demands of his superiors in Germany (Hilberg 1967:359). As a preliminary step in the deportation process, the Germans confiscated the records containing the names and addresses of Jewish Danes from the offices of the Jewish community on August 31, 1943 (ibid.). Until that point there was no systematic accounting of Jews in Denmark.

In early September, Best returned to Germany and after consultation with high-ranking German officials, arranged for the deportation to begin on the night of October 1, 1943 (ibid.:341) The rescue operation was set in motion when a sympathetic German official, George Duckwitz, an attaché with the German economic legation, informed a close Danish friend, who passed the word to the Jewish community.

The rescue would have been impossible without the Swedish government's agreement to grant asylum. Escape across the sea to Sweden was considered perilous, however, and it was unclear what the Swedish attitude would be. After intensive lobbying by the influential politicians and other Danes, including Nobel-Prize-winning physicist Niels Bohr, who had already fled to Sweden because he was a half-Jew, Swedish authorities extended an offer of refuge (Flender 1963:74–77).

The warning spread quickly. A teenager at the time, Eric Grün answered the telephone the night before the action. The voice at the other end asked to speak with his father. When Eric asked who was calling, he was told that it was best that he did not know. After the call, he was instructed by his father to spend the following evening with a Gentile friend and wait for further instructions. A few days later Eric, his sister, and his parents left on a fishing transport from Copenhagen harbor. They arrived safely in Malmö, Sweden and spent nineteen months in Sweden (Grün 1993).

By Sunday October 3, 1943, Danes knew that the Germans had failed to deport the vast majority of Jews and that they had gone into hiding. There was no confusion about the moral imperatives they were expected to follow or what their course of action should be. The following statement, written jointly by all the Lutheran bishops and signed by the Bishop of Copenhagen, was read from the pulpit of every Lutheran church in Denmark on the Sunday following the deportation attempt:

> Wherever Jews are persecuted because of their religion or race it is the duty of the Christian Church to protest against such persecution, because it is in conflict with the sense of justice inherent in the Danish people and inseparable from our Danish Christian culture through centuries. True to this spirit and according to the text of the Act of the Constitution all Danish citizens enjoy equal rights and responsibilities before the Law and full religious freedom. We understand religious freedom as the right to exercise our worship of God as our vocation and conscience bid us and in such a manner that race and religion per se can never justify that a person be deprived of his rights, freedom or property. Our different religious views notwithstanding, we shall fight for the cause that our Jewish brothers and sisters may preserve the same freedom which we ourselves evaluate more highly than life itself. With the leaders of the Danish Church there is a clear understanding of our duty to be law abiding citizens who will not groundlessly rebel against the authorities, but at the same time our conscience bids us to assert the Law and protest against any violation of the Law. We shall therefore in any given event unequivocally adhere to the concept that we must obey God before we obey man. (Goldberger 1987:6–7)

The logistics involved in hiding and transporting several thousand men, women and children to Sweden were complex; the Danes needed boats and fishermen willing to make the journey, as well as the money to pay them. Danish Jews who had the resources paid their own way, but there were some who did not have enough money. Raising money did not seem to pose a serious problem. Philip Friedman (1957:171) quotes a pastor and a rescuer of the Jews: "when you needed money you simply went to a bank and asked the teller for 5,000 to 10,000 kroner, stating your purpose, and the money was promptly handed to you."

The issue of payments to fishermen is a sensitive one. In some cases the skippers of fishing boats extorted exorbitant prices for the relatively short trip across the Øresund [the Sound] (Paulsson 1995). The rationale for paying them was to compensate them for putting themselves and their boats at risk. This was a pragmatic and effective way to assure a consistent supply of boats. In most accounts of the financial aspects of the rescue, payment to the skippers appears as a normal and justifiable part of the rescue process. It should be noted that "there were no instances of Jews being left behind because they could not pay" (Kirchhoff 1995:475) and that skippers continued to be paid for transporting people to safety and moving weapons across the Øresund (Haestrup 1993).

Few, if any, records were kept during the rescue operation, so it is difficult to reconstruct the specific organizational contributions and accurately count the number of people who participated in the rescue but never publicly acknowledged their participation (Haestrup 1983:205). In general, the rescue was accomplished by small groups of rescuers working in concert with individuals and other small groups. Using the testimony of 550 agricultural trainees and the Alijah children, Haestrup (1983:50–51) concludes that thousands of Danes participated in the rescue. Thousands of Danes also contributed money for the operation. Contributors ranged from wealthy businessmen and their organizations (Haestrup 1993), to groups of schoolchildren who took up collections (Ulf 1994).

When the rescue operation was completed at the end of October, 5,919 full Jews, 1,310 part Jews, and 686 non-Jews married to Jews had been taken to safety in Sweden (Hilberg 1967:363). Danes continued their support with maintenance payments for those in Sweden and gift parcels for the Jews deported to Theresienstadt. Unlike the vast majority of European Jews, almost all Jewish Danes returned home and found their homes and belongings intact.

Conclusion

The Danish experience is unique to the Holocaust. Although few European countries actively supported the Nazis' attack on the Jews, most were willing to sacrifice some of the Jews within their borders to them, no matter what the level of German domination. After the Nazi defeat of France, the French withdrew their protection of German and Polish Jews who initially found refuge in France and were not French citizens. The Vichy government adopted and administered its own anti-Jewish laws and cooperated in the deportation of Jewish French citizens.

The Jews of "Old" Bulgaria escaped deportation, but the Bulgarian government cooperated in the deportation of 10,000 Thracian and

Macedonian Jews to Auschwitz from territory they acquired as a result of their political alliance with the Germans. The government implemented the first steps necessary to deport all the Bulgarian Jews. Chary (1972:169, 199) notes that officials halted the process in 1943 when the changing fortunes of war made it clear that Germany had diminished power to reward or threaten Bulgaria.

Although the government of Italy passed anti-Jewish legislation, the vast majority of the population never supported the government's anti-Jewish policies (Marrus and Paxton 1989:191–192). Italians actively assisted Jews in evading deportation, but unlike the Danish Jews, the majority of Italian Jews who escaped deportation survived on their own "wits and resources, found their own rescuers, and dealt with individuals rather than organizations" (Zuccotti 1987:276).

The rescue of the Danish Jews was distinctive, primarily because the political climate and Danish solidarity produced a normative atmosphere which encouraged support for them. The cultural traditions and practices embedded in the economic cooperative system fostered the mutual trust necessary to insure the successful rescue. Danes were predisposed to the close social ties that were essential to success. At every step of the way, the Danish position was clear. We shall never know whether, faced with different conditions, they too would have acted differently. The definition of the situation (Thomas 1927) was very different in occupied Warsaw and Amsterdam than in occupied Copenhagen. The decision to assist Jews in other European countries was usually performed in isolation and without the social sanctions that made assisting the Danish Jews a positive social act.

The Danes considered the Jews members of a common community; and the highly assimilated Jewish Danes were fully integrated into Danish society. Working collectively to insure their safety was an ingrained, culturally important value in Danish society. The German occupation heightened the historical tendency on the part of the Danes to view themselves as different from the Germans and political circumstances prevented the erosion of Danish cultural, social and political institutions.

The Danish experience shows that distinct cultural styles and the ideologies that inform them can persist under moderated conditions of political domination. Under the conditions of the German occupation, the Danes could continue to act in a customary manner precisely because their traditional cultural processes never became disengaged from their institutional basis (Yengoyan 1989:10–11).

Only a society with an embedded tradition (Granovetter 1985) of cooperation and pre-existing networks of trust could have facilitated the coordination necessary for the success of the rescue operation. The close physical proximity, pre-existing organizational networks and shared values that were crucial to the establishment and maintenance of rescue networks during the Holocaust (Huenke 1981) were embedded in the normal day-to-day functions of Danish society. The Jews in Denmark were sent to safety because their Danish compatriots could act collectively on their behalf with the relative assurance of support from others and a deep conviction that the task at hand was collectively sanctioned.

Notes

1. See, for example, Fogelman 1994; Philip Friedman 1978; Huneke 1981; Oliner and Oliner 1988; Robinson 1965; Staub 1989.
2. Jews represented the same proportion of the total Danish population as of the total German population – 0.3 percent. However, only 5 percent of the German Jews survived the wars (Fein 1979:52–53). Obviously, the proportion of Jews in a country had little to do with the development of support for them.
3. One need only point to neutral Switzerland, which consistently turned Jews away, to recognize that geographical proximity did not guarantee safe refuge for Jews. The Danish historian Hans Kirchhoff (1995:466), also points out that although Norway has a 1,000-kilometer border with Sweden, 40 percent of the 1,800 Norwegian Jews died.
4. Paulsson (1995:436) proposes an alternative explanation for the successful evacuation of the Danish Jews to Sweden: "The Danish Jews got away because they were allowed, indeed, encouraged, to get away." Paulsson's thesis is that allowing the Jews of Denmark to "escape" was part of a clever German strategy for making Denmark "*Judenrein*" without incurring any substantial costs, among other reasons (Paulsson 1995:440–441).
5. See for example, Arendt 1965; Fein 1979; Flendere 2063; Goldberger 1987; Jegstrup 1986; Robinson 1965; Yahil 1969.
6. As of August 1955 Yad Vashem had granted "Righteous among the Nations" to only nine Danes (Paldiel 1995). The Danish nation has been honored in its entirety, however.
7. "The terms 'collaboration,' 'accommodation' and 'policy of negation' have been debated by Danish occupation historians. When the official

Danish policy is judged on its effects, it can quite reasonably be called "collaborationist,' for it did Germany's bidding. If judged upon motive, the policy was definitely not ideological collaboration" (Hong 1996:65 n23).

8. An exception to this general attitude was the concern and desperation among the agricultural trainees, refugees from Germany, Czechoslovakia and Austria, whose migration to Palestine had been thwarted when they were trapped in Denmark by the occupation. Because of prior experience in their native countries, they had less reason to place faith in Danish assurances. Many of them were eager to escape to Sweden where they hoped they could arrange passage to Palestine (Haestrup 1983).

9. The order to deport the Danish Jews is one of the rare instances than can directly link Hitler to the implementation of the Final Solution (Yahill 1990:734:n3).

10. Hilberg (1967:362) reports the number of Jews deported at 477.

11. Kirchhoff (1995:475) reports that the head of the Danish Red Cross made a proposal to Werner Best that the Danish Jews be shipped to Germany in reprisal for the increasing acts of sabotage. Not all Danish officials were interested in protecting the Jews.

12. Although I stylistically interchange the terms "Danish Jews" and "Jewish Danes," it has been suggested that "Jewish Danes" more clearly describes how Jews and Danes perceived the position of Jews in Danish society (Goldberger 1987) It is a subtle but important difference.

13. As such,they had fewer contacts in the larger society and represented a higher proportion of the Jews who were deported (Bludnikov 1993).

14. Baron (1992:308) estimates the number of Jewish refugees in Holland from Austria, Poland, and Germany in 1939 as 25,000.

15. Mimi Milstein reported that her mother had heard about "bad things" happening to the German Jews, but she only learned of the Final Solution after the war. People presumed the "bad things" were economic crimes.

16. Several times during my research trips to Denmark I was asked whether I knew about "Our King and the yellow star." These references to the completely false story that Christian X wore a yellow Star of David in support of the Danish Jews were meant, I believe, to test how well informed I was about the rescue. Danes find the persistence of this story particularly vexing.

References

Abrahamsen, Samuel (1987) "The Rescue of Denmark's Jews," in Leo Goldberger (ed.) *The Rescue of the Danish Jews: Moral Courage under Stress*. New York: New York University Press: 3–11.

Anderson, Robert T. (1975) *Denmark: Success of a Developing Nation*. Cambridge: Schenkman Publishing Co.

Arendt, Hannah (1965) *Eichmann in Jerusalem*. Revised and enlarged. New York: Viking Press.

Axelrod, Robert (1984) *The Evolution of Cooperation*. New York: Basic Books, Inc.

Bamberger, I. Nathan (1983) *The Viking Jews: A History of the Jews of Denmark*. New York: Shengold Publishers, Inc.

Baron, Lawrence (1992) "The Dutchness of Dutch Rescuers: The National Dimension of Altruism," in Pearl Oliner et al. (eds) *Embracing the Other: Philosophical, Psychological and Historical Perspectives on Altruism*. New York: New York University Press: 306–327

Bludnikov, Bent (1993) Personal Interview. Copenhagen, Denmark.

Chary, Frederick Barry (1972) *The Bulgarian Jews and the Final Solution*, 1940–1944. Pittsburgh: University of Pittsburgh Press.

Davidowicz, Lucy S. (1975) *The War Against the Jews 1933–1945*. New York: Bantam Books.

Fein, Helen (1979) *Accounting for Genocide: National Responses and Jewish Victimization during the Holocaust*. New York: The Free Press (special issue, entirely on genocide).

Fitzmaurice, John (1981) *Politics in Denmark*. London: C. Hurst & Co.

Flender, Harold (1963) *Rescue in Denmark*. New York: Simon and Schuster.

Friedman, Harriet (1978) "World Market, State and Family Farm: Social Bases of Household Production in the Era of Wage Labor," *Comparative Studies of Society & History*, V20:545–586.

Friedman, Philip (1978) *Their Brother's Keepers*. New York: Holocaust Library.

Goldberger, Leo (1987) *The Rescue of the Danish Jews: Moral Courage under Stress*. New York: New York University Press.

Granovetter, Mark (1985) "Economic Action and Social Structure: The Problem of Embeddedness," *American Journal of Sociology*, 91: 481–510.

Gross, Jan Tomasz (1979) *Polish Society under German Occupation: The Generalgovernment*, 1939–1944. Princeton, New Jersey: Princeton University Press.

Grun, Eric (1993) Personal Interview. Copenhagen, Denmark. October..

Gudme, Sten (1942) *Denmark: Hitler's Model Protectorate*. London: Victor Gollancz Ltd.

Haestrup, Jorgen (1983) *Passage to Palestine: Young Jews in Denmark 1932–1945*. Odense: Odense University Press.

—— (1993) Personal Interview. Odense, Denmark. October, 1993.

Hilberg, Raul (1967) *The Destruction of the European Jews*. Chicago: Quadrangle Books.

Hohne, Heinz (1970) *The Order of the Death's Head: The Story of Hitler's SS*. Trans. Richard Berry. New York: Coward-McCann.

Holbeck, Eric (1996) Personal Interview. March, 1996.

Hong, Nathaniel (1996) *Sparks of Resistance: The Illegal Press in German-Occupied Denmark, April 1940–August 1943*. Odense: Odense University Press.

Howe, Frederic (1936) *Denmark: The Cooperative Way*. New York: Coward-McCann.

Huneke, Douglas K. (1981) "A Study of Christians Who Rescued Jews during the Nazi Era," *Humboldt Journal of Social Relations*, 9: 144–150.

Jergstrup, Elsebet (1986) "Spontaneous Action: The Rescue of the Danish Jews from Hannah Arendt's Perspective," *Humboldt Journal of Social Relations,* 13:260–284.

Jones, W. Glyn (1970) *Denmark*. London: Ernest Benn Limited.

Kirchhoff, Hans (1995) "A Light in the Darkness of the Holocaust? A Reply to Gunnar S. Paulsson," *Journal of Contemporary History,* 30:465–479

Lampe, David (1957) *The Savage Canary: The Story of Resistance in Denmark*. London: Cassell.

Levin, Nora (1968) *The Holocaust*. New York: Schocken Books.

Lindstrom, Ulf (1985) *Fascism in Scandinavia 1920–1940*. Stockholm: Almquist & Wiksell International.

MacDonald, Stephen C. (1986) "Lutheran Conscience and the Holocaust: The German and Norwegian Cases," in Jack Fischel and Sanford Pinsker (eds) *The Churches' Response to the Holocaust*. Greenwood, Fla.: Penkevill Publishing Co: 45–54.

Manniche, Peter (1939) *Denmark: A Social Laboratory*. New York: Oxford University Press.

—— (1970) *Living Democracy in Denmark*. Westport, CT.: Greenwood Press.

Marrus, Michael R. and Paxton, Robert O. (1989) "The Nazis and the Jews in Occupied Western Europe, 1943–1944," in François Furet (ed.) *Unanswered Questions: Nazi Germany and the Genocide of the Jews*. New York: Schocken: 172–198.

Miller, Kenneth (1968) *Government and Politics in Denmark*. Boston: Houghton Mifflin.

Milstein, Mimi.(1995) Personal Correspondence. 21 July.

Oliner, Samuel P. and Oliner, Pearl M. (1988) *The Altruistic Personality: Rescuers of Jews in Nazi Europe*. New York: The Free Press.

Oliver, Pamela E. (1984) "'If You Don't Do It, Nobody Else Will': Active and Token Contributors to Local Collective Action," *American Sociological Review* 49:604–610.

Ostergard, Uffe (1992) "Peasants and Danes: The Danish National Identity and Political. Culture," *Comparative Studies in Society and History* 34(1): 1–27.

Outze, Borge (1946) *Denmark during the German Occupation*. Copenhagen: Scandinavia Publishing Co.

Paldiel, Mordecai (1995) Personal Correspondence. August 22.

Petrow, Richard (1974) *The Bitter Years: The Invasion and Occupation of Denmark and Norway 1940–1945*. New York: William Morrow & Co. Inc.

Paulssen, Gunnar S. (1995) "The Bridge over the Oresund: The Historiography on the Expulsion of the Jews from Nazi-Occupied Denmark," *Journal of Contemporary History*. V 30:431–464.

Robinson, Jacob (1965) *And the Crooked Shall Be Made Straight*. New York: Macmillan.

Rørdam, Thomas (1985) *The Danish Folk High Schools*. Copenhagen: Det Daske Selskab.

Staub, Ervin (1989) *The Roots of Evil: The Origins of Genocide and Other Group Violence*.

Tec, Nechama (1986) *When Light Pierced the Darkness: Christian Rescue of Jews in Nazi-Occupied Poland*. New York: Oxford University Press.

Thaning, Kaj. (1972) *N.F.S. Grundtvig*. Trans. David Hohnen. Copenhagen: Det Danske Selskab.

Thomas, John Oram (1975) *The Giant-Killers: The Story of the Danish Resistance Movement 1940–1945*. London: Michael Joseph Ltd.

Thomas, W.I. (1927) "The Behavior Patterns and the Situation," *Publications of the American Sociological Society, papers and proceedings*, 22nd Annual Meeting, 22:1–13

Thyssen, Anders Pontoppidan (1983). "Grundtvigianism as a Movement until around 1900," in Christian Thodberg and Anders Pontoppidan Thyssen (eds) *N. S. F. Grundtvig: Tradition and Renewal*. Copenhagen: Det Danske Selskab: 371–394.

Ulff, Inge (1994) Personal Interview. Lyngby, Denmark.

Walton, John (1992) *Western Times and Water Wars: State, Culture and Rebellion in California.* Berkeley: University of California Press.

Wolfe, Alan (1989) *Whose Keeper?: Social Science and Moral Obligation.* Berkeley: University of California Press.

Wuthnow, Robert (1987) *Meaning and Moral Order: Explorations in Cultural Analysis.* Berkeley: University of California Press.

Yahil, Leni (1969) *The Rescue of Danish Jewry: Test of a Democracy.* Trans. Morris Gradel. Philadelphia: Jewish Publication Society of America.

Yengoyan, Aram A. (1989) "Culture and Ideology in Contemporary Southeast Asian Societies: The Development of Traditions." University of Hawaii, Environment and Policy Institute, East-West Center.

Zuccotti, Susan (1987) *The Italians and the Holocaust: Persecution, Rescue, Survival.* New York: Basic Books.

—— (1993) *The Holocaust, The French, and the Jews.* New York: Basic Books.

German Treatment of Jewish Children during the Holocaust: A Case Study in the Barriers to Resistance
James M. Glass

Many Jews did resist the German Holocaust; the Warsaw uprising is the most dramatic example. Small resistance bands within and without the ghettoes generated some opposition, and many in those groups, particularly in the forests, survived. Yet the ability of Jewish resistance to save many Jews from the crematoria and gas chambers was minimal. Very few Jewish children survived the Holocaust; out of the approximately 3,200,000 Jews in Poland before the Holocaust, only 30,000 survived. The work of resistance and partisan groups, righteous Gentiles like Oscar Schindler and Raul Wallenberg, managed to save at the most a few thousand.

Part of the answer to the question of lack of *mass* or group resistance is to be found in the German assault on Jewish children and infants; the structure and values of Jewish ghetto leadership (the *Judenräte*); and the role of religious belief and orthodox rabbis in the environment of the mass murder of Jews. Of the 3,200,000 Polish Jews who perished in the Holocaust, at least 3,000,000 were orthodox. Where were the rabbis; what was their position; how did they act? Analyzing these questions, however, belongs to another study; the object of this study is the relationship between the annihilation of Jewish children and the lack of a broad-based, mass Jewish resistance.

Children as Racial Threat

The annihilation of Jewish children was central in the genocidal planning and policies of the Third Reich; Himmler, in a speech to the SS, stated that it was the Reich's moral duty to kill every Jewish child and infant to preclude forever genetic or blood poisoning of German citizens.

Institutional reformation, built around the biological values of race exclusion, concentrated and segregated Jewish adults, and legitimized and encouraged the destruction of Jewish children and infants.

"Resettlement" of Jewish populations required new and innovative institutional forms; probably the most strategic of those institutions for the Nazis was the ghetto – not the old established ghettos, home for centuries to Jewish populations throughout Europe, but administrative arrangements that placed Jewish populations in rundown or slumlike areas of large and small cities, with public services all but eliminated. By the time of the transport of hundreds of thousands of Jews from the Warsaw ghetto in spring and summer 1942, it was all but impossible to find running water in the ghetto area, much less adequate plumbing and sewage disposal. The Germans in most ghettos established kindergartens or children's homes, not out of concern for the children but because it was easier and quicker to collect children for transport to the death camps or to surrounding forests for mass execution. The effect of ghetto resettlement and its institutions on Jewish children demonstrate how insistent the Germans were in placing a biological value at the very foundation of all institutional arrangements in the Third Reich.

While one can admire the courage of the children in the face of horrifying adversity, it is a mistake to see children's play as demonstrative of the victory of the human spirit. If anything, the response of children to the horror of the ghettos suggests the victory of the German oppressors and their institutional forms, in annihilating the will to survive and in achieving genocide's stated aim: the death of all children. Over a million and a half children perished in the Holocaust. Fewer than a hundred infants survived the ghettos and the camps. Children were reduced to animal-like conditions, unrecognizable, moaning, begging, will-less, and left to die in ghetto streets and death camp barracks.

What did children do in the ghetto; how did they think, perceive and act? George Eisen's *Children and Play in the Holocaust* (1988) sees the action of play in the institution of the ghetto as an activity with the same meaning play had in less stressful environments: escape, imaginative adaptation and interaction. Play, he argues, was "turned into an enterprise of survival, a defense for sanity, and a demonstration of psychological defiance" (Eisen 1988:8). Eisen (1988:9) continues: "The belief that life must go on, in spite of its wretchedness, held as much power as the fear of extermination. And some ghettos, depending on the various degrees of extremity, constructed and administered play activities for children: makeshift play groups, chess tournaments, play days, sports contests, and so on."

Early in the ghettos' experience, play and performances possessed a distracting quality: in Warsaw and Theresienstadt, before the massive starvation, selections, and extermination, play activities served a critical function in distracting children's minds. In the family camp set up in Auschwitz, with 4,000 Czech Jews from Theresienstadt, the Germans sought to allay panic by encouraging children's activities. Unsure of what to do with Theresienstadt's Jews, Nazi guards for several months kept them in special enclosures. The children performed skits, created games; the camp was treated considerably better than other barracks in Auschwitz. SS officers visited the children's barrack and admired the work of the organizer, Freddy Hirsch. One Auschwitz survivor recalls: "I watched in wonder across the wire as they organized their new and temporary lives . . . I saw them set aside a barrack for the children, a nursery, no less, in the shadow of the crematorium. I saw a blond, athletic man of about thirty (Freddy Hirsch) organizing games, then lessons" (Eisen 1988:47). Six months later, in one evening, the Germans gassed the entire family camp, including all the children.

During the Holocaust, play changed its form and meaning; ghettos became holding pens for the death camps. The children's camp in Auschwitz survived for a few months only because of the perverse interest of the German guards and officers; much more common than children playing was the sight of children dying. Play took on a different meaning for children caught in the midst of continuing death; it was a register into their unconscious phantasies and terrors, graphically illustrating the consequences of being suddenly orphaned and abandoned. Homelessness destroyed the will of children to survive; the sudden disappearance of mothers and fathers appears in many surviving diaries as an equally sudden loss of the will to live. The following is from the diary of a thirteen-year-old girl:

> What a burden it is to be solitary among aliens, fatherless and motherless. There is no one to whom you can run for solace, to embrace, to kiss. Around me are apathetic faces of people. How long can this continue? How can one stand up under it and endure? I want to die so that my suffering will end. Not to live any longer, not to feel the oppression, the hate. What have I done to deserve all this? . . . When will it all end? When will the tears cease flowing? When will the sun rise? Never! (Holliday 1995:134)

Starvation, disease, the sight of people being murdered, dying and suffering in the ghettos, assault consciousness with a ferocious intensity. Nothing brings solace. One young girl sees her family shoved into carts, "eighty people into each wagon . . . one pail of water . . . not even the children cried; all of them were like zombies, like robots. They walked into the wagon so mechanically, without making a sound" (ibid., 124).

Play as a Defense against the Reality of Death

In Theresienstadt, morning exercises, daily play session and competitive games were tolerated by the German authorities. But what do games signify in terms of the child's internal life? What is the relationship between games and emotions the child experiences day in and day out? Is it correct to assume, because children engage in morning exercises or competition sports in a ghetto environment like Theresienstadt, that these games act as a counter to radical dehumanization? Games may not be sufficient to eradicate an unconscious "giving up," an emotional paralysis in the face of fear. Alternately, games may provide children with an opportunity to construct alter-personalities defending against the hopelessness and terror of ghetto life.

> The commandant of the Riga ghetto, Karl Wilhelm Krause, who was known to personally shoot inmates, held strikingly generous views about child care. His was one of the schizophrenic minds so characteristic of the SS hierarchy. An example of his perversity can be seen in his permitting the construction of a rudimentary playground in close proximity of the gallows. After executions, the commandant was often seen to go to the sandbox and give chocolates and candy to the playing children; he liked to be called "Uncle Krause." (Eisen 1988:45)

Periodically, Uncle Krause ordered sweeps of the ghetto and sent the children to the death camps. Games reflect this environment of death and testify to the victory of oppression and the ease with which psychological resistance was swept away.

> They played "Lageraeltester" (camp leader) and "Blockaeltester," (block leader) "Roll Call," shouting "Caps off!" They took on the roles of the sick who fainted during roll call and were beaten for it, or they played "Doctor" – a doctor who would take away food rations from the sick and refuse them all help if they had anything to bribe him with . . . Once they even played "Gas Chamber." They made a hole in the ground and threw in stones one after the other. Those were supposed to be people put in the crematoria, and they imitated their screams. They wanted me to show them how to set up the chimney. (ibid., 81)

Identification, simultaneously, with victim and aggressor suggests a psychological deterioration far more serious than what Eisen calls "moral deterioration," a "fraying of the moral fiber of society" (ibid., 81). Eisen sees the acting out of brutal games as normal for this kind of environment; but his interpretation of games stretches the concept of normal. When the psychotic becomes normal, conventional notions of morality *and* normality have no place. "Normally" children do not identify play and death; "normally" they do not find themselves in contexts where the sight of death becomes more common than the sight of life; "normally" children do not step over corpses on the street, or come face-to-face with other children their age who are so covered with lice that their eyes are not visible.

Eisen argues that it is impossible to judge these games, to take a moral position on whether they are "right" or not. Nor, he adds, is it correct to see them as evidence of a total obliteration of society's moral codes, as a commentary on the absence of civilization. Yet that is precisely what ghetto games reflect: the disappearance of conventional moral codes.

According to Eisen, games like poking corpses were "as normal as the German environment decreed it to be" (ibid.). The fact that children were even able to play, he adds, comments on their strength in the face of adversity. Game playing, however, may not suggest psychological resilience *or* resistance but a desperate response to a transvalued universe brought on by extreme brutalization, the role in the "game" taken on as an alter-personality in the midst of endless violence. The child-self may be zombie-like or roboticized or terrorized on the inside, yet still be quite involved in these so-called games. To see children playing these games as resilience, in the midst of adversity, attributes to games a transcendent property they did not possess. It also minimizes the psychically brutalizing and annihilating properties of the environment surrounding the children. It is to see psychotic-like games as somehow being "normal," instead of what they are: last-ditch efforts to ward off psychological death.

In Theresienstadt two toilets existed for every hundred children; rooms, bunks, hallways, courtyards were fouled during diarrhea epidemics; rats, bedbugs, fleas and lice lived in clothes, shoes and mattresses. A child's perception of "living" in these filthy conditions moves, presumably, to block out pain, hopelessness, the uncertainty regarding life. Children beg their parents to give them "potassium cyanide . . . I begin to understand why my fellow victims go to their deaths without resistance. I have lost the desire to exist and feel a deep disgust for living" (Holliday 1995:71). Bodies become commonplace and literally not noticed. "So many dead were lying about that no one even bothered with them" (ibid., 63). Play in this universe becomes as perverse as the ghetto world itself.

Children "playing" at setting up gas chamber chimneys and then evaporating into smoke are not playing in any sense of what that word means in a normal, expectable environment. These games suggest the action of identification, which means the psychological percept at work here rather than giving or bringing relief enacts what has been seen and what the children know will happen to them. Games reenact the death environment. "Play" moves the self toward the nightmare. Games of death, torture, and brutality suggest responses to horror: consciousness identifies with horror so as not to be blown apart, psychically, by the realization that horror lies at the foundation of everything. Horror is reality, and games defend against psychological death. This is not play at all – certainly not in the sense that it is used to describe what children do at recess, in the school playground, at friends' houses. Play is something else, far more ominous, a reflection of the insanity of the surrounding environment, and not a commentary on normal responses to stressful environments.

Eisen calls ghetto and death camp games "playing out" reality, doing in games what reality does in life. But that is not quite right. Yes, children identify with reality, comply with reality's demands, but such compliance may keep the self from completely collapsing at the sight of imminent and overwhelming horror. This kind of play is a dissociative response, because if the self were *emotionally* to identify fully with ghetto and camp action, consciousness would literally implode. It would cease to be. "Play" maneuvers the self into action, since psychologically the major danger entails will-lessness. Play in the ghetto and camps preserved whatever relational connections existed with reality: it kept the self engaged with an existing, surrounding, reality, where connection allowed the self to *move* in some purposive direction. Children, in their "play," defended themselves from becoming totally mute, disengaged, and therefore psychically dead. Also, by the summer of 1942, ghetto reality was scarcely distinguishable from camp reality.

> In our barracks, forty to sixty women die every day. Near the door, stiff and blue bodies are piling up. A cart to which some prisoners are harnessed arrives. Two of them take the dried up and frozen bodies by the arms and feet, swing them and throw them on the heap of naked bodies. The crematory is working day and night. Next to it heaps of bodies are piling up. And nearly every day, thousands of Jews died in the ghettoes. Every day nearly a thousand people die in the camp. (ibid., 196)

> We are like animals surrounded by the hunter. (ibid., 151)

Psychological Emptiness as the End of Life

A February 12, 1943 entry in a sixteen-year-old Belgian boy's diary reads: "During recent days an emptiness has formed inside me. Nothing motivates me to do anything or write anything, and no new idea enters my mind; everything is as if asleep. Although I do not know from where this emptiness has come, I can feel it with my whole body." March 9, 1943: "The emptiness has spread within me and now fills me completely . . . I am completely in the grip of this nothingness, this lack of will and thought . . . [I am] barren" (Eisen 1988:265).

In the ghettos battles break out between children's gangs; children smuggle food from the Aryan sides for their families, for black-marketeers. When selection for the death camps begins, children hide in cupboards, cellars, under floors, in latrines; play of any kind withers under the onslaught that takes parents from children, isolates children in strange places, and sets up the ghetto as the culture's defining institution. In one ghetto "game," the child who gained the most distinction acted out the role of the head of the Gestapo.

In Emanuel Ringelblum's description of life in the Warsaw ghetto, he describes children playing "a game tickling a corpse" (Eisen 1988:79). But by 1941 corpses littered ghetto streets. It is hard to imagine what a child experienced leaving a room in an apartment shared with five or six other families and stepping over a corpse on the doorstep. Such sights transformed the concept of life and living. By the time the child entered a concentration or death camp, consciousness had been conditioned to expect the worst. In Ravensbrück, one observer describes the children looking like "skeletons wearing rugs. Some had no hair on their heads . . . They even played games. A popular one was '*Appel*,' modeled on the camp's daily roll calls." In Auschwitz-Birkenau, Greek boys were observed to be playing a game "where you slapped, as hard as you could, your playmate's face" (ibid., 79–80).

Is it correct to call adaptive mechanisms in the face of such horror "play"; or is it more accurate to describe such behavior as fragmented and terrorized selves desperately identifying with actions that provide a barrier between an insane reality and its incessant pull, and the self's fragile mechanisms of psychological cohesion, a last grasp at sanity? If, for example, the Lodz Chronicles' (Adelson and Lapides 1989) description of the fate of the Hamburg Jews is any identification – upper-middle-class Jews from Hamburg were in a matter of months reduced to a Hobbesian condition – if such destruction of self could happen to adults with all their experience within six months, why should it not happen to children, sooner and with even more horrifying effects? It appears to me a weak argument to suggest that children are somehow more "resilient" than adults. Children's adaptive mechanisms, in many diary entries, appear to be psychotic, maneuvers to ward off the complete implosion of self, the psychically brutalizing effects of ghetto life.

Dutch children at the holding camp, Westerbork, played in the traditional sense of the word; they had yet to be subjected to places like Warsaw, Lodz or Auschwitz. The breakdown of civil, moral and psychological life eventually consuming millions of Jews herded together in ghettos was infinitely worse than in transit camps like Westerbork and even the so-called "model" ghetto Theresienstadt. How long can a child sustain the following sentiments before she forgets she even has dolls with her?

> I sit with my dolls by the stove and dream.
> I dream that my father came back,
> I dream that my father is still alive.
> How good it is to have a father.
> I do not know where my father is.

> (Eisen 1988:74–75)

Play shielded the child from the imminence of psychological death, muteness, "musselman"- like ["musselmen" was the camp name for the inmates who were most apathetic] apathy (Bettelheim 1967), from the reality of what existed on ghetto streets. In Warsaw, children have "terribly swollen limbs and faces – the swelling of starvation. The bodies of children [lying in the streets] are an everyday sight. . . . The death toll rises higher and higher. The monthly totals [between January and August, 1941] are 450, 800, 1,200, 2,000, 2,500, 4,000, 5,600. Their faces get more and more sunken, their complexions paler and paler" (from a diary written in the Warsaw ghetto (Scharf 1991:51). As long as children could "play" – no matter how bizarre the game – they remained alive psychically. Games allowed children to live from one moment to the next, to build bulwarks between the muteness of spiritual death and the reality of physical death. The institution of the ghetto and the camps became places where people, including children, knew they were going to die. Play kept this enormous brutalizing power from thoroughly fragmenting their already fragile selves. For a child to play meant that, at least for that instant, self or psyche had not been reduced to a will-less bundle of broken psychic pieces.

Children who survived, those who managed to escape detection in sewers, cellars, cupboards and holes in the ground, were forever scarred. A child survivor of Auschwitz moved in and out of uncontrollable rage and mute introversion. An observer, several years after liberation, recounts of this child: "Suddenly in the middle of the best game, she jumped at other children, beat them, yelled, and then again she was quiet and shy" (Eisen 1988:120). Jerzy Kosinski's (1976) description of life in an orphanage at the end of the war reveals a universe where children sought out "games" of crime, violence, and prostitution.

The pitiful few children who survived brought with them the knowledge that survival depended on luck and being invisible to the oppressor. Neither of these two conditions of survival left the human spirit with anything approaching dignity, faith, or heroism. Normal reality had been turned upside-down. "When a concerned adult explained in the Bergal-Elster concentration camp the essence of 'Cowboys and Indians' to ten-year-olds, the children weren't impressed by the game, which they term 'silly' or 'disgusting.' Their game was 'watching the SS-man'" (Eisen 1988:121). The game "Cowboys and Indians" requires a measure of imagination. But in the ghetto the span between reality and fantasy had completely shrunk. Children watched Germans "beat people, kick people, torture people, kill people. Indeed, [children] needed no aggressive play. Reality mirrored their fantasy life. What other children in normal society act out through play, these children *witnessed in reality*" (ibid., 121).

Ghettoization: Children as Disposable Mass

The numbers describe how isolated most children were in the ghetto, and how subject they were to gangs, starvation, and lack of space that might be called "home." In November 1941, two years after the German occupation, 10,000 deserted and orphaned children lived in the Warsaw ghetto. Orphanages set up by social service organizations held perhaps 2,000. That left 8,000 children on the street; in the orphanages 25 percent of the children died; the rate was higher for those living on the street. By the summer of 1942 in Warsaw, about 100 institutions had been established in the ghetto providing support to 25,000 children, one-quarter of all children in the ghetto. Of the remaining 75,000 children, by mid-1942 over half, at least, lived in gangs, alone, on the street and spending most of their day begging.

What happens to the self in these conditions? When starvation and terror become the two defining elements in a child's life, how does the child-self react?

The earliest victims of the Warsaw roundups in July 1942 were children; thousands were taken off the street and then to the *Umschlagplatz* (the square where the Jews were concentrated before deportation to the death camps), where after days of waiting they were forced into freight cars and transported to Treblinka and Sobibor. Beginning on July 30, orphanages were broken down and their children sent to the death camps. Children on many occasions were abandoned in the *Umschlagplatz*; screaming for their mothers, these children were taken for transport. Of the 400,000 inhabitants of the Warsaw ghetto, 100,000 were under fifteen. In 1940, over one-third of Jewish children suffered from some disease or illness; by 1942, the figure had jumped to 95 percent. If children were not executed on the spot, German guards would amuse themselves by physically abusing them. Polish police, German officers, and blackmailers forced children caught smuggling food to crawl back and forth through barbed wire, tearing their flesh, or insisted the children go back into sewers reeking with raw sewage. Many children, because of starvation, were described as "apathetic"; some 2,000 begged on the streets of Aryan Warsaw outside the ghetto walls. In the winter, children froze to death on the steps of destroyed buildings.

Early in the ghettos' existence, a playground from time to time would be set up; long lines of Jewish children waited their turn. The presence of playgrounds drew the children, perhaps reminding them of what had been; perhaps as a momentary relief from the carnage and presence of death. In Lodz children stood at the barbed wire fence looking at Polish children play on the other side.

> The following comment is typical of children who survived: Everybody I was with died in 1941. I travel around, occasionally pinching something. I manage somehow. The day before yesterday some kids set on me so I punched one on the nose till he cried and then I tripped the other one and he ran. The third begged me not to beat him up, so I punched him too and he went away. No one jokes with me, boasted Zbyszek, a cigarette seller. (Ziemian 1975:87)

Janusz Korczak, the famous Warsaw pediatrician who established an orphanage after the Nazi occupation, understood the terror, the way brutalization worked on the child's consciousness of the present. "The city is casting children my way, like little seashells . . . I ask neither where they come from nor for how long or where they are going, for good or evil" (Korczak 1978:138). And "What ghastly dreams! . . . On a train I am moved, a meter at a time, to a compartment where there are already several Jews. Again some had died tonight. Bodies of dead children. One dead child in a bucket. Another skinned, lying on the boards in the mortuary, clearly still breathing" (ibid., 171). He speaks of children with fevers, sores, rheumatism, amputations; he is so overwhelmed by starvation and illness that he refuses to believe his "weighing machine and the thermometer . . . they too tell lies" (ibid., 171). He sees humanity slipping away, and the dreadful, weakened bodies of his orphaned children lack any connection with their past lives; everything in his life battles against starvation and disease. Children are treated like "cattle," "dung."

His spirit weakens: "I feel all smeared, blood-stained, stinking" (ibid., 173). Korczak fears apathy and indifference; "Reading as relaxation begins to fail. A dangerous symptom. I am distracted and that itself worries me. I don't want to sink into idiocy" (ibid., 174). The entire orphanage in the summer of 1942 senses the imminent presence of death: "Only the outer appearances are normal. Underneath lurks weariness, discouragement, anger, mutiny, mistrust, resentment, longing." But the children are too weak and discouraged to act; "they wait, listlessly fighting hunger and illness" (ibid., 189). In July of 1942, food poisoning causes a massive bout of diarrhea and vomiting; "during the night, the boys lost 89 kg among them—on the average a kilogram per head. The girls – 60 kg" (ibid., 190).

Life for children in the ghetto was quite haphazard; forced to hide in cellars, privies, spaces between walls, children witnessed entire families being violently broken up – children literally snatched from their mothers' arms. Husbands or wives would suddenly disappear. Children aged considerably, becoming wise before their time; one eight-year-old girl who had been living with a Polish family was spotted, arrested and taken to the Plaszow, the notorious labor camp outside of Krakow. One of the camp guards knew her mother was in the camp; but when the girl was confronted with her mother, she repeatedly denied knowing her. Eventually forced to acknowledge her mother, both daughter and mother were shot.

Children constantly witnessed actions where informants betrayed their hiding places: "There was a Mrs. Chilowicz, an informer, whose task it was to find out where there were children hidden in the camp and to report their whereabouts to the Germans. Very often, as a result of this treachery, not only were the children shot, but also their parents" (Pankiewicz 1987:74). Hallways, courtyards, streets, alleyways: dead bodies lay everywhere. Children constantly experienced these scenes in the ghettos. Spiritual death occurred long before they reached concentration camps.

In Krakow during one of the roundups:

> In the square, the SS officers and the Gestapo of various ranks were milling around. Almost everyone had some sort of truncheon or a club in his hand, and there was no lack of those armed with pokers which blended wonderfully with the skull and crossbones insignia on their hats. All of these clubs and canes were frequently used on the standees. Age or sex made no difference. They were especially brutal to the elderly, particularly the women. The sight of a beaten and bloodied Jew evoked laughter among the Germans. (ibid., 75)

"God is on Vacation, but He Will be Back"

For the child, the world outside held absolutely no comfort. Dissociation in such circumstances, either through dulled affect or by identifying with an alter-personality constructed for the purpose of play, makes sense in order to survive emotionally, to hold the fragile strands of the self together, to avoid the despair and hopelessness visible in the pictures of abandoned, orphaned children sitting in stairwells with vacant, empty stares on their face, without will or emotion, demonstrating the impact of unremitting fear. Spiritually these children had already been murdered.[1] Not even the alter-self of a brutal game makes its appearance. The child sinks into a listlessness that signifies spiritual death.

Suicides are an index of ghetto despair: in the death camps suicide was rare; if any purpose defined camp life, it was the avoidance of selections. Psychological suicide, however, was very common – Bettelheim's "musselmen" – the loss of the will to survive; massive, often fatal, dissociative responses to the environment. "Musselmen" died quickly, or were selected for death in the crematoria. In the ghettos, physical suicide amongst adults occurred daily; children witnessed adults taking poison, leaping from buildings, throwing themselves on electrified fences, pleading with guards to shoot them. "Playing" in the street, living in crowded rooms, invariably involved watching death by suicide: the elderly, before selections or roundups, were given pills, injections or poisons by their next of kin. Children could not avoid these scenes. "A natural death was not common in the Ghetto" (Pankiewicz 1987:80). The Lodz Chronicles are filled with daily entries listing the names of those who had killed themselves.

What does children's play signify in the midst of these daily occurrences? Piles of corpses, the sudden disappearance of close relatives, constant "crying and lamentations": how does this collective despair register on the child's psyche? One contemporary observer writes: "Some became psychotic, others were constantly tormented with anxieties, still others suffered from deep depression, incapable of thinking about their immediate future" (ibid., 88). Hallways, courtyards, any available space, since the ghetto constantly was being replenished with transports, were filled with possessions, furniture, human waste. Arguments, bickering and fights were rampant over the distribution of living space; if coal was to be used to heat the apartments; whose trunk or bundle had been lost; who had rights to which rooms. Entire families suffered from periodic bouts of insomnia. German patrols ordered Jews to kill other Jews in plain sight of children. Nighttime arrests and selections were common. Germans publicly murdered children and infants at the slightest provocation. And then there was the infamous kindergarten or children's homes:

> In the ghetto, a *Kinderheim* – children's home – was opened by order of the Germans . . . New lies, new swindles, again designed to discourage vigilance. Parents going to work could bring their children there to the age of 14. Cared for by experienced [Jewish] personnel, the children would be busy with all kinds of tasks, such as sealing envelopes and weaving baskets . . . The *Kinderheim* was filled every day with scores of children who entered willingly and with joy, without even the slightest hint in their innocence of the immense danger and tragedy that was imminent. Just imagine that all this was done just for the few weeks before the pre-set date for the murder of all the children who attended the *Kinderheim*. (ibid., 103)

When the Krakow ghetto was emptied and its inhabitants sent to the labor camp at Plaszow, the children were not allowed to go with the parents. Instead, they were collected in the ghetto's *Kinderheim*.

> Children, wandering about, were seized and led to the overcrowded *Kinderheim* . . . People, petrified with fear and agony, broke down completely. . . This was a thousand times more horrible than the physical torture and murder of the defenseless. . . Children who were detected were brutally torn away from their parents. . . Children at the wire looked long and tearfully after the departing parents . . . parents were mercilessly beaten, and the children, in mortal fear, in the cacophony of the unbelievable screams of the mad Germans, would run away in panic, hiding in the doorways of near buildings. . . The poor little ones clutched the wire with their tiny hands, and with tearful eyes, fear and indescribable sorrow, whispered, Mommy, Daddy, don't go away, don't leave me along here, take me with you. Time and again, a new group of Germans led children to the courtyard of a building which was not far from the pharmacy. . . A series of shots left no doubt about what happened there. (ibid., 119)

Small children, while awaiting their turn at execution, "played on the asphalt wet with blood." For reasons of economy, "several children were shot with one bullet by lining them up in a row. Several babies were placed in a carriage and killed with one shot" (ibid., 120).

Apathy, indifference, will-lessness: is it so difficult to imagine children sinking into these states after being subjected to this universe of death? Games of death and brutality might be the only way a child, unconsciously, could cling to some kind of life or will to allow the self to navigate one moment to the next. A twelve-year-old girl writes in her diary: "I am so deeply depressed and almost lifeless. I am not affected anymore by the panic and fright about me. I begin to understand why my fellow victims go to their deaths without resistance. I have lost the desire to exist and feel a deep disgust for living." (ibid., 97–98) "Play" helps to guard against these kinds of feelings, this sinking into abjection where spirit no longer wills any kind of life. In younger children unable to articulate despair, the sense of the world imploding and the psychological position of lifelessness must have been overwhelming (Eisenberg 1982: 97–98). A young boy speaks of "dying passively like sheep . . . our helplessness . . . into what kind of helpless, broken creature can man be transformed?" (ibid., 82).

The omnipresent fear that the child faces, the radical shift in what punishment means and what kind of actions warrant punishment, the horrifying knowledge of absolute consequences transform daily routines into a Hobbesian torment of unexpected outcomes and brutalities. In one ghetto camp,

> [E]verything is forbidden, but the most awful thing of all is that the punishment for everything is death. There is no difference between things; no standing in the corner, no spankings, no taking away food, no writing down the declension of irregular verbs one hundred times the way it used to be in school. Not at all: the lightest and heaviest punishment – death. It doesn't actually say that this punishment also applies to children, but I think it does apply to us, too. (ibid., 91)

One child speaks of herself as "withered grass in the parched fields of life" (ibid., 94).

Conclusion

In Auschwitz alone over 228,000 Jewish children were murdered (Gutman and Berenbaum 1994:417). I would like to conclude this inquiry into institutions and their dependence on values, by quoting from the diary of

a Lithuanian Jew, Eliezer Yerushalmi of Shavli:

The life of this child was short – only three years, five months, and five days. But this brief span was filled with suffering and agony.

When he was a year and a half his father, together with hundreds of other Jews, was thrown into prison, and never came home again. In the ghetto his mother left him by himself, because every morning, before sunrise, she had to hurry to work in the factory. He remained alone in the house, watched over by a bedridden neighbor who could not give him any help. From the first day, he had to stand on his own feet and learn to take care of himself. He adapted himself very easily to this existence. He quickly learned to wash and dress himself and keep his scanty possessions in order. He knew how to take the few morsels his mother left for him, and learned how to get food when she had nothing to leave him.

He knew the exact hour of the neighbors' mealtimes, and when hunger tormented him, he appeared at their tables and stood watching. He did not ask for food, he said very little; he did not stretch out his skinny arms for bread – but his huge, hungry eyes gazed at their plates and followed every spoonful they raised to their mouths. Naturally, the people took pity on him and shared with him their meager rations.

He performed tricks with knives and forks. He knew that everyone at the table smiled when they watched him, and used this to get another morsel. He did his tricks with a serious face, and did not allow the laughter of his hosts to alter his expression.

When he wanted fresh vegetables, he simply went into the vegetable garden and took a radish from here, a carrot from there, or broke off a piece of cauliflower and ate it raw. But when the sun began to sink in the west and the hour approached when the Forced Labor Brigade returned to the ghetto, he went with the grownups to the ghetto gate to wait for his mother. She was a small, thin woman, and next to her Meier felt masculine and protective. Proudly he put his small arm in hers and led her home. His entire being, and all his actions, radiated serenity. He talked very little. Many people in the ghetto had never even heard his voice; in fact there were some who thought he was a mute. Only his closest neighbors sometimes heard him speak and admired the clear, short, but logical sentences with which he came to an understanding with his environment.

On the day of the "Children's Action" he hid himself even more carefully than usual. He climbed into his sick neighbor's bed and kept quiet as a mouse, without moving a muscle. He did not even lose his control when the Ukrainians, assisting the SS, made a house search.

The Ukrainians found him, but the sick old woman ransomed him with a gold watch. As soon as the hoodlums were outside, they sent in a second group, who knew about Meier. But she did not have another watch, so the boy was seized and taken to the children's collection point.

I saw him during these final moments. He skipped between the two soldiers, trying to keep up with their stride. From time to time he raised his large, questioning eyes to them, as though asking, "Why all this?" Although the soldiers were drunk, those innocent child's eyes sobered them and slowed their steps. In one of them a human emotion flickered and he said to his companion: "He's a Jew, but still he's a child." He looked at Meier sympathetically, took his hand and lifted him into the wagon among the desperately sobbing sacrifices. Meier seemed calm. He stood quietly among the crying children and looked around with his large, naive eyes, until the cart started to move. (Eisenberg 1982:46–47)

Note

1. The evidence of dissociative disorders in multiple personality cases suggests how consciousness defends itself against intolerable abuse. The existing self unable to acknowledge or tolerate reality hides itself in an array of alter-personalities that literally take the host's place. In the ghettos, however, the process goes even further; whatever alter-personalities are constructed appear in the children's games.

References

Adelson, Alan and Lapides, Robert (eds) (1989) *Lodz Ghetto: Inside a Community under Siege.* New York: Penguin Books.

Bettelheim, Bruno. (1967) *The Empty Fortress: Infantile Autism and the Birth of the Self.* New York: The Free Press.

Eisen, George (1988) *Children and Play in the Holocaust: Games among the Shadows.* Amherst: The University of Massachusetts Press.

Eisenberg, Azriel (1982) *The Lost Generation: Children in the Holocaust.* New York: The Pilgrim Press.

Gutman, Yisrael and Berenbaum, Michael (eds) (1994) *Anatomy of the Auschwitz Death Camp.* Bloomington and Indianapolis: Indiana University Press.

Holliday, Laurel (1995) *Children in the Holocaust and World War II: Their Secret Diaries.* New York: Pocket Books.

Korzeak, Janusz (1978) *The Ghetto Years: 1939–1942.* Trans. Jerzy Bachrach and Barbara Krzywicks (Vedder). New York: Holocaust Library.

Kosinski, Jerzy (1976) *The Painted Bird*. New York: Grove Press.
Pankiewicz, Tadeusz (1987) *The Cracow Ghetto Pharmacy*. Trans. Henry
  Tilles. New York: Holocaust Library.
Scharf, Rafael F. (ed.) (1991) *In the Warsaw Ghetto. Summer, 1941:
  Photographs by Willy Georg*. New York: Aperture Foundation.
Ziemian, Joseph (1975) *The Cigarette Sellers of Three Crosses Square*.
  Trans. Janina David. Minneapolis: Lerner Publications Co.

Notes on Contributors

Professor Judith Tydor Baumel
University of Haifa
Professor Baumel teaches Modern Jewish History and is the author of fifty articles and several books about the Holocaust. Her most recent book, published in 1997, is *Kibbutz Buchenwald.*

Professor Murray Baumgarten
University of California, Santa Cruz
Professor Baumgarten teaches English and Comparative Literature, and Jewish Studies. He is the author of many books and articles, the founding director of the Dickens Project, and the editor of Judaism, a quarterly journal of Jewish life and thought.

Professor Wayne Bowen
Ouachita Baptist University
Professor Bowen is now (May 1998) with the United States Armed Forces in Bosnia. He teaches history, and his publications include "Spanish Nurses in the Blue Division," in Reina Pennington (ed.) *The History of Military Women: A Biographical Dictionary.*

Dr Martin Cohen
Dr Cohen, an anthropologist, developed scales and a codebook for assessing psychosocial conditions and familial relations in the lives of infants, children and adolescents, as a research associate in the Neuropsychiatric Institute, Center for the Health Sciences, University of California, Los Angeles. He is now working on several projects relating to the Holocaust.

Professor James M. Glass
University of Maryland, College Park
Professor Glass teaches government and politics, and is the author of several books on the interplay between politics and psychology. His most recent book, published in 1997, is *Life Unworthy of Life: Racial Phobia and Mass Murder in Hitler's Germany.*

Professor Myrna Goodman
A Doctoral Candidate at the University of California, Davis, Professor Goodman is the director of the Holocaust Study Center at Sonoma State University, where she teaches sociology and women's studies.

Ami Neuberger
University of Florida
Ami Neuberger has just been awarded a Master's Degree in Communications at the University of Florida. Her thesis examines the Nazi use of gender assumptions to torture women in the concentration camps, and how some women were helped to survive by forming and participating in "families."

Ruby Rohrlich
Professor Emerita at the City University of New York, Ruby Rohrlich is now a research professor in the anthropology department, The George Washington University. During World War II she worked as a propaganda analyst for the Office of War Information, then as editor of the Propaganda Analysis Department, which analyzed German propaganda emanating from Nazi-occupied Europe. Professor Rohrlich has edited two anthologies and written a dozen articles on the anthropology of women, including a profile of a Holocaust survivor and Nobel Prize winner, Rita Levi-Montalcini. The present anthology has its source in the book she is writing about two Jewish-Italian survivors of the Holocaust, Rita Levi-Montalcini and Primo Levi.

Professor Eric Sterling
Auburn University of Montgomery
Professor Sterling teaches English. He has published "Fear of Being 'the other': Racial Purity" in Arthur Miller's *Incident at Vichy*, and is writing a book, *Social Responsibility in the Drama of the Holocaust.*

Professor Nathan A. Stoltzfus
Florida State University
Professor Stoltzfus teaches Modern European History, and is the author of the book *Resistance of the Heart: The Rosenstrasse Protest and Intermarriage in Nazi Germany.*

Professor Nechama Tec
University of Connecticut, Stamford
Professor Tec, a Holocaust survivor, teaches sociology. She was awarded

First Prize for Holocaust Literature in 1995 by the World Federation of Fighters, Partisans and Concentration Camp Inmates, Israel, for her book *Defiance: The Bielski Partisans*. She has written numerous books, monographs and articles relating to the Holocaust, and is a Senior Research Fellow at the United States Holocaust Museum in Washington, D.C.

Professor Eli Tzur
University of Haifa
Professor Tzur is the author of the books *The Second World War: The War which Changed the Face of the World* and *The Landscape of Illusion: Mapam 1948–1952*. He is the director of the Institute for the Study of Youth Movements at the University of Haifa.

Professor Margaret Collins Weitz
Suffolk University
Professor Weitz teaches humanities and modern languages, and is the author of *Sisters of the Resistance: How Women Fought to Free France, 1940–1945*, as well as of numerous articles about women in France.

Index

Index

Index

Index